The L

that

Refused

Commemorative plaque in St Leonard's Chapel, near Ribblehead. The Settle & Carlisle was expensive to build in terms of both money and human life. The only casualties of the six-year battle to save the line were political ones.

Introduction

by John Whitelegg

ON JANUARY 6, 1990, the Settle-Carlisle Joint Action Committee met for the last time. The meeting in Settle, accompanied by a class photograph and good Yorkshire beer, ended a remarkable era in the history of public transport activism in Britain. Quite simply, we had achieved everything we set out to do. We had won.

The discussion at that January meeting was a typical JAC mixture. There was no euphoria and no gloating but plenty of introspection about what should happen next. The meat of the agenda was a proposal that the Joint Action Committee should wind up its affairs and go out of business. The arguments that ensued illustrated both the strengths and the weaknesses of the JAC. In campaigning, the committee had maintained its energy and momentum by an uncompromising and aggressive stance on the need to maintain public transport services in rural areas, and to harness the benefits of rail services for improving both the quality of life, and of the environment, in those areas. It worked best when set against a clearly defined "enemy" and British Rail, together with the Department of Transport, had provided more than enough fixed and moving targets. The removal of the closure threat deprived the JAC of interesting targets and, inevitably, its momentum slowed and its vitality decreased.

The JAC was not a monolithic organisation and the aggressive campaigning stance sometimes clashed with the more gentle and trusting approach that was rooted in a love of the line and the countryside it traversed. This paradox came to the fore in the winding-up debate. For the "aggressive campaigners" the battle was over and energies were needed for other battles on bigger fronts. For those whose link with the S & C was a life-long commitment, the loss of a successful organisation devoted to the line was a problem.

But the argument that we should wind up the JAC's affairs prevailed. All parties to the discussion accepted that the inevitable loss of steam, now that the principal battle had been won, would result in a lingering death for the JAC and this, ultimately, would not be in the interests of the line. There was, moreover, a large supporter organisation (The Friends of the Settle-Carlisle Line Association) and this was the natural home for those who wished to continue an active involvement with S & C issues. If anything, FOSCLA would be strengthened by this move and the confusions which had arisen between the respective roles of FOSCLA and the JAC would become a thing of the past.

The energies which made the JAC such a success are still alive now and would surely re-emerge, redoubled in vigour, should BR once again lose a grip of its corporate sanity and impose a vindictive financial logic on communities in the North of England. The JAC was far more than a rail closure campaign group — it showed how local communities, campaigning organisations and sources of expert advice can come together to beat off the predatory acts of large corporations. It is a model of community resistance, and non-party political community resistance, at a time when central government has become more central than ever, and meaner and nastier about local independence and local determination of needs.

Soon after the reprieve of the S & C, British Rail announced how pleased it was now that the threat to the line had been removed. This is a classic piece of hypocrisy: BR was the threat and BR is still the same animal that brought so much anguish and disruption to communities up and down the line. Moreover, BR appears to have learnt nothing from the experience. In the late summer of 1990 anxious groups of residents and campaigners are preparing for trouble on the Newcastle-Carlisle and the Skipton-Carnforth lines. There is a strong late 1970-ish S & C flavour about BR's service reductions and arrogant dealings with local groups.

The central problems of public transport in Britain remain unresolved by the S & C victory. Public transport suffers from low patronage, low investment and, generally speaking, low levels of service quality. There is no universal law which decrees this to be the natural order. On the contrary, throughout Europe impressive progress has been made with public transport provision — something which is not unrelated to high levels of public investment and careful planning to ensure integration and co-ordination.

In France, Denmark, the Netherlands and West Germany the links between high quality public transport, environmental improvement and economic progress have been discovered and put to good use. Rail transport for both freight and passengers conserves energy, reduces pollution and accidents and prevents the loss of millions of acres of land which would have to be swallowed up to provide roads and parking for vehicles.

German research shows the penalty of neglecting rail and favouring road as a solution to society's need for transport. If we look at pollution and accidents for every tonne of freight carried one kilometre by road and by rail we find that road transport produces five times as much carbon dioxide, 14 times as much nitrogen dioxide (which produces ozone pollution), 16 times as much particulate pollution (which produces cancers) and 25 times as many road traffic accidents.

Road transport of freight is not good value for money and nor is the use of ordinary cars. Put very bluntly we can not solve our problems of urban congestion, road traffic accidents, global warming, acid rain, ozone pollution and rural inaccessibility if we put our eggs into the road/internal combustion engine basket. Nor can we create a satisfactory life style which is kind to children and does not threaten the survival of the planet.

On a more optimistic note, transport issues have moved to the top, or very near the top, of most political agendas. A large number of serious rail accidents, protracted arguments over the Channel Tunnel and links from the tunnel to the north and west of Britain, congestion in cities, abandonment of road construction plans in London, and concerns about global warming have ensured that transport is good material for media attention and for political point-scoring. The intellectual bankruptcy of the Conservative administration on transport issues has left a vacuum which has been filled by a high-profile Labour transport strategy. Past experience does indicate, however, that incoming Labour administrations have a habit of losing or diluting the good ideas which were enthusiastically trumpeted in opposition.

In London, the Department of the Environment has lost the battle with the Department of Transport over the need to have public transport and car restraint policies in the White Paper on the environment which was due to be published in autumn 1990. The government is committed to restrain emissions of carbon dioxide at the same time as the DTp plans to spend £13 billion on road construction and is forecasting a 142 per cent increase in road traffic in the next 35 years. These two policies are in direct opposition. The environment lost out in the debate due to the personal intervention of the Prime Minister to thwart public transport support policies.*

In Brussels the same battle rages, this time between DG11 (the Environment Directorate) and DG7 (the Transport Directorate). Here, environment has made some progress with its publication in June 1990 of an urban environmental strategy document. This states clearly that environment and quality of life in cities can only be achieved by public transport support.

Cities in Europe have made huge gains in air quality and public transport use by heavy investment in trams, pedestrian areas, new buses and integrated transport. Fares have been brought down in Bremen and Berlin on the evidence of the real financial contribution which public transport makes to reducing the costs of accidents, pollution and congestion. In Zurich, public transport use is now the highest in Western Europe as a result of new investment and the co-ordination of bus, tram and suburban train services. In Britain, political and economic dogma are fast driving us in the opposite direction — South Yorkshire's cheap fares policy was outlawed and the pioneering integration of bus routes with the Tyne and Wear Metro system was sacrificed on the altar of bus deregulation. Financial constraints at both national and local level are driving up fares, holding down investment and squeezing quality to impair the attractiveness of public transport when compared with the car.

In case this argument seems a million miles away from the S & C we should remind ourselves that the reason for the closure proposal was financial and that the circumstances which brought about that proposal are now more, not less, likely to occur. BR now has even tougher targets to meet in terms of the government money it can draw on and is faced with the inevitable consequences of poor levels of finance in the past.

---

* *New Scientist, August 25, 1990*

Modern public transport developments, like the Tyne and Wear Metro, above, have been depresingly few and far between in Britain.

The dramatic recent deterioration in rail safety in Britain is the result of cost-cutting and inadequate levels of checking and supervision.

In the meantime, road schemes which are discredited by research programmes around the world go ahead and swallow resources which would easily refurbish the total rail system and allow it to deliver the goods in every sense of the word. Existing methods of investment appraisal are crudely biased against rail where they expect a given rate of return on the investment. For road projects, but not for rail, "user benefits" are taken into account so that 10,000 journeys per day, each "saving" half an hour by using a new road, produce a notional gross time-saving of 5,000 hours at, say, £6 pounds per hour which equals 6 x 5,000 x 365 (equals £10.95m) of "benefit" per annum to set against costs of the road project. The result is more roads and less rail. No calculations are carried out to determine the bottom line of the balance sheet.

In Germany, the bottom line is that cars receive in state support about four times what they pay in taxes. Rail, which is well-supported in Germany, is still not as well supported as road alternatives. Britain's

Train à Grande Vitesse — symbol of France's pride in its railways.

support of its rail system is the lowest of any country in Europe when measured in terms of what proportion of expenditure is met by revenue.

The S & C campaign was a victory, but was a mere skirmish by comparison with what comes next. Britain's transport system is in need of a complete overhaul. The current mix of road and rail is not sustainable on energy or pollution grounds and is exorbitant in its use of valuable land. Unless rail is given a much bigger slice of the action and/or the absolute amount of movement of freight and people goes down, then both cities and rural areas will cease to function. Cities will succumb to "grid-lock" (the graphic American term for absolute congestion) and rural areas will succumb to a combination of zero public transport, engulfment in car-borne tourist traffic and wealthy "ghettoisation" as the only people who can live there will be those who can afford two or three cars per household.

Tourist traffic will rise faster than the 142 per cent average for all types of traffic. In the Lake District and parts of Devon and Cornwall it is already at a level that destroys much of what the tourist seeks. If tourism is not to be regarded as a destroyer and a polluter then its emphasis must shift to public transport. Rail is an ideal vehicle for tourists in rural areas and the S & C story contains much of relevance for recreation and tourism.

S & C campaigners understood the social, community and tourism arguments and led the way which is now being followed by campaigners and politicians around the world. A newly established European Federation for Transport and the Environment has repeated the JAC trick of bringing together interested groups, but this time at the international level, and it has learnt from the JAC experience. It now has a secretariat in Brussels and is lobbying hard for public transport support and rail investment at the European Commission. The JAC did not invent this way of working but it applied it and took it further than any other European group.

For all environmentalists, public transport watchers and rail supporters the message is simple. The S & C story shows that it is possible to win. The aftermath of the S & C also shows that there is much more to do. If local groups bind together, take on the opposition with enthusiasm and take the campaign into all the dark recesses of Whitehall and Brussels they will win friends and supporters and will deflect those miserable and narrow minded bigots who proclaim the freedom of roads and motorised transport and denounce the inefficiencies and subsidies of public transport. More than at any time in the post-war era these purveyors of social disadvantage and environmental blight are in retreat. Let's keep it that way.

John Whitelegg, Lancaster, August 1990

Dr John Whitelegg was the founding Chairman of the JAC and resigned in December 1987 to take up a post with the Ministry of Transport of the German state of North Rhine Westphalia. Based in Düsseldorf, he was engaged in the type of research work which is sadly neglected in the UK. While in Germany, he retained his membership of the JAC committee and returned to England in July 1990 to take up the post of Head of the Geography Department of Lancaster University. He is increasingly recognised worldwide as a leading advisor on public transport policy. He is Chairman of Transport 2000 International which brings together the transport campaigning organisations of 15 countries and is active in the European Federation for Transport and the Environment.

Steam specials became established on the Settle-Carlisle ahead of the rest of the BR network. Ex-LMS Jubilee No. 5690, lovingly restored to its original colours, is having an easy time with little exhaust showing and the safety valves lifting.

1.
Born of conflict: rescued from turmoil

THE six-year battle to save the Settle and Carlisle Railway is, in a curious way, a fitting prelude to a promised new beginning — not just for the S&C but, hopefully, for Britain's rail network in general.

Fitting, because this line perhaps more than any other great British railway, was born out of conflict. Indeed, the political manoeuvrings which characterised the failed closure process bear more than a little comparison with the wheelings and dealings that led to the line's inception.

And, while — unlike the grisly toll exerted during the six years it took to build what British Rail was to dub "England's greatest historic scenic route" — no actual deaths could be laid at the door of the closure battle, the battlefield does remain littered with the odd political corpse.

The epitaph to the real casualties of the Settle-Carlisle lies deep in a lonely dale between the twin bulks of Ingleborough and Whernside. Here stands a tiny church sheltered, or rather hidden, by tall beech trees. The dale was once called Waesdale, after the Anglo-Saxon word for pasture, but became Chapel-le-Dale after St Leonard's chapel of ease was built early in the 17th century. The relatively lush shelter of the valley bottom which once inspired Turner and today provides a living for 200-odd people, is in marked contrast to the wild ruggedness of the fells.

St Leonard's is a focal point for the nearest the dale comes to a centre of population. Inside, on its west wall, is fixed a tablet which reads:

> *"To the memory of those who through accidents lost their lives in constructing the railway works between Settle and Dent Head. This tablet was erected at the joint expense of their fellow workmen and the Midland Railway Company, 1869 to 1876."*

In the little churchyard a grassy bank beneath the trees gives no clue to the fact that more than 100 years ago it was hurriedly consecrated to provide a shallow mass grave for as many victims of a smallpox epidemic. For the windswept, rain-lashed landscape of heather, peat bog and bare limestone pavement which begins at Ribblehead just two miles up the dale — in such contrast to Turner's idyllic Weathercote Cave — was then a centre of considerably greater population.

The plague victims came from a hutted shanty town of wood and felt which housed 2,000 or more navvies and their families. Known originally and intriguingly as Batty Wife Hole or Batty Wife after a feature in the rock, the town became later Batty Green. Its people were engaged to build the two greatest structures on the Settle and Carlisle railway line, Ribblehead viaduct and Blea Moor tunnel. Today, but the faintest signs remain of this or of any other of the wild shanties — Jericho, Salt Lake City, Battle-barrow-bank, and Sebastopol — that sprang up along the 72-mile route.

But if this pinnacle of Victorian engineering achievement was expensive of human life, it was too of time and money. The building of the line was plagued by even wetter, colder weather than usual, adding to the turnover of labour which remained high despite the prospect of then good money at up to ten shillings for a 12-hour shift. The expenditure on candles alone for lighting the work in Blea Moor tunnel rose to £50 a month and as the original four years estimated for building the line stretched to nearer seven, so too did the cost: from £2.2m to almost £3.5m.

In his excellent account of the railway navvies, Terry Coleman describes how at one location high in the Pennines, tipping went on for more than a year without the embankment advancing so much as a yard: "The tip-head stayed where it was, while the masses of slurry rolled over one another in mighty convolutions, spreading uselessly out, and going anywhere but the place they were wanted." The men were drawn from all quarters of the country and one contemporary account tells of the impressive sight they made, toiling almost as one body: "Finer men I never saw, and never hope to see. Man for man, they would fling our guardsmen over their shoulders; they have all the height and breadth of the best picked men in a Prussian Grenadier regiment of the Guards Corps, without their clumsiness. For there is no heaviness in the muscular strength of these navvies. The stiff, greasy, blue-black clay melts away bit by bit from before their indomitalbe, energetic onslaught, each man working as if he wrought for his life."

When the formal closure procedure for this expensively conceived railway was begun late in 1983, some members of the British Rail hierarchy were almost gleefully describing the Settle and Carlisle as "the line which should never have been built", born out of a "fit of pique" on the part of the Midland's general manager, James Allport, who was frustrated at the problems which faced his company in trying to secure adequate routeing for its Anglo-Scottish traffic over other companies' metals. It can be argued that the scheme was indeed conceived as an enormous bluff by the Midland to try and achieve that aim by forcing the hand of its great rival, the London and North Western Railway.

The Settle and Carlisle was a product of what might be called the second period of railway mania in Britain, a mania fuelled in part at least by Parliamentary fear in the mid-19th century that any amalgamation between rival companies would lead inevitably to a much dreaded monopoly. Talks of amalgamation between the Midland, the London and North Western and the Great Northern railways in 1853 so alarmed Parliament that the prospect of approval for that or any future merger became very slim indeed. So the Derby-based Midland, sandwiched between rival routes north from London, was forced to expand to survive. With the completion of its extension to its own London terminal at St Pancras, the company began to look towards increasing its share of Scottish traffic.

The Midland was able to run its trains as far north as the village of Ingleton (at the western end of Chapel-le-Dale), via the Leeds and Bradford railway to Skipton, and from there via the "little" North Western Railway which it also controlled. At Ingleton there was an end-on junction with a branch of the Lancaster and Carlisle section of the London North Western route: and therein lay the problem. The company's passengers were given such low priority by the LNWR that sometimes they even had to walk between the rival stations at Ingleton even though they were connected by a viaduct. The reward for such exercise would often be the sight of the rear of the departing "connection". Nor would the LNWR allow the through conveyance of Midland carriages for Edinburgh; nor stop its expresses at Tebay to connect with the trains from Ingleton. Mr Allport himself complained of having been unceremoniously conveyed by the LNWR in a carriage attached to a train of coal trucks.

The deadlock was such that Mr Allport and the company's chief engineer, John Crossley, decided to look again for their own route to Carlisle through territory which had previously been thought impossible by at least one railway engineer. An enabling Bill for a North of

... then just as the first one
puts a foot on the platform —
— you pull out!
GUARD

England Union Railway linking Hawes with Settle and Clapham on the little North-Western had already been passed by the Commons but before it reached the Lords the Midland intervened and the Bill was withdrawn to be reintroduced by the Midland in modified form. The original proposal envisaged a line down Wensleydale from Hawes, to connect with the main network in the east, and a branch from Hawes to the Lancaster and Carlisle branch at Sedbergh. The Midland plan still linked Settle and Hawes, but also provided a route north to Carlisle. It gained Parliamentary approval in 1866.

But the Midland's problems were not over: merger talk in Scotland between the Caledonian and the Glasgow and South Western railways threatened a bias in favour of the LNWR for traffic south of the border. So the Midland made its own approach to the G & SW with the result that the LNWR offered to reopen the question of Midland rights over its tracks — if the Midland would abandon the Settle and Carlisle plan. Although the Midland at first declined, the building of the St Pancras link and the Peak Forest line to Manchester had stretched its resources and, deciding on a policy of co-operation with the LNWR, the company sought permission to abandon the Settle-Carlisle plan. But by this time the Scottish companies and the Lancashire and Yorkshire Railway (which linked towns like Clitheroe and Blackburn with the NWR, now Midland, at Hellifield, south of Settle) had become enthusiastic supporters of the new line and Parliament threw out the abandonment Bill.

If the whole process had indeed been merely a bluff, Mr Allport soon found out it was a far from inexpensive one, for the Midland — which had been staking out the proposed route somewhat half-heartedly — found itself obliged to build a very costly railway it no longer wanted. The old North of England Union plan had envisaged following the convenient lie of the various dales and the Midland could no doubt at this point have satisfied Parliament by opting for a similar route along more modest lines than the proposed direct Settle-Carlisle route. The fact that Midland did not take this "easy way out" explains why the line is reckoned unique in the world as a high speed railway through "mountainous" terrain.

The company's aim remained to get its traffic to and from Scotland via the shortest and quickest route possible. The new railway was destined to be two miles longer than Settle Junction to Carlisle via Ingleton and Tebay, so the Midland engineers sought to overcome that disadvantage by building a line with no speed restrictions because of bends and with less severe gradients than the one-in-75 of the LNWR route over Shap Fell. The Settle-Carlisle is sometimes described as a "railway over the Pennines" — this is not strictly correct as it both begins and ends west of the main watershed of the Backbone of England. Only at Garsdale Head, near its summit at Aisgill, does the line nudge the "spine" of the range at one of its lowest east-west crossings. On a train journey from Leeds to Carlisle the Pennines are actually crossed just east of Hellifield, less than 500ft above sea level, by means of the Aire gap.

So the Settle-Carlisle is not a trans-Pennine line but a railway driven through the hills. In his book *Rails in the Fells*, the geographer David Jenkinson describes how the Midland's engineers chose "the best and, in fact, the only practicable way through these hills" consistent with providing a straight route with a maximum, or ruling, gradient of one-in-100. "It is doubtful if, even were the line being built today, the chosen route would be very different, fulfilling as it does all the functions one could reasonably expect of a modern rail line," he argues. That route involved a steady climb up the two north-south valleys of the Ribble and the Eden, with a ten-mile "mountain" section to be crossed between the valley heads. Here, remarkably, the line stayed almost level at 1,150ft above sea level, clinging to the valley sides, soaring on lofty viaducts over tributary becks and plunging through the fells in deep tunnels. In all the line has 325 bridges, 21 viaducts and 14 tunnels: the workforce

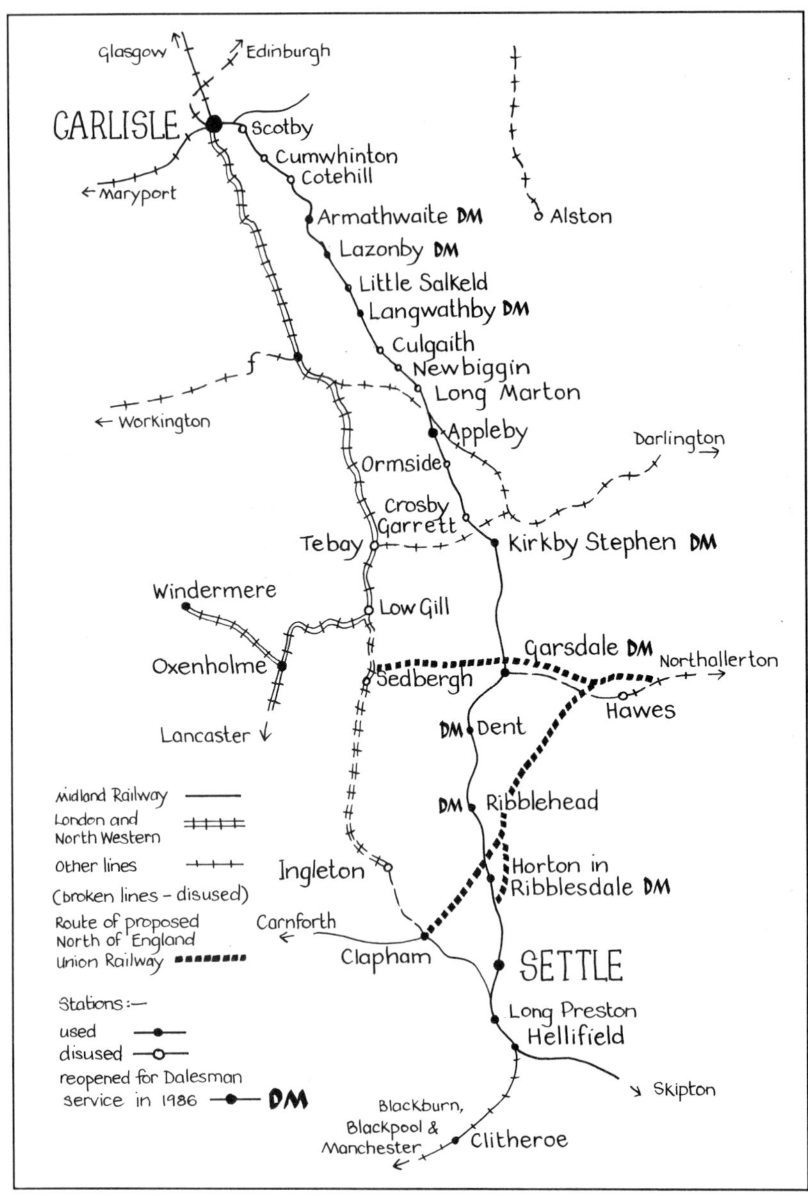

Map showing the S & C in relation to other lines and proposed railways in the late 19th century

which built it peaked at 6,000 and made use of the latest technology, including vertical steam engines, steam lifts, drills and concrete.

The S & C was the last great navvy-built line — indeed, the age of the navvy endured far longer in Britain than in North America, where labour was less abundant and mechanical diggers were widely used. By the time the Great Central was built at the tail end of the 19th century, mechanisation was the norm, although even on this line, the navvy workforce peaked at 9,000.

Although built as a high speed trunk route, it would be wrong to suggest that the Settle-Carlisle made no concessions at all to meet potential local traffic demands: indeed the start of the ascent from the Eden valley to Aisgill is delayed so the railway can properly serve the villages in the valley bottom and Appleby-in-Westmorland, with around 2,500 people the largest intermediate settlement on the line today. The 40 miles between there and Settle is and was some of the most sparsely populated country in England, with only the market towns of Kirkby Stephen and Hawes boasting populations of more than 1,000 now.

The fact that the Midland's Kirkby Stephen station was built more than a mile from and some 350ft above the town is usually cited as the most glaring example of how the line bypassed settlements in its quest for gentle curves and the easiest gradient. But even this needs to be put into context, as there are examples elsewhere of lines which went no nearer than a mile from the towns they were supposed to serve — the similarly sized market town of Kirkby Lonsdale just off the route of the Lancaster and Carlisle's Ingleton branch is an example. And, for that matter, the location of the NER station at Kirkby was not particularly central either. But to have served Hawes other than by the branch line which was built would have meant a major detour which would have slowed the route considerably.

Although there were few settlements of any consequence outside Ribblesdale and the Eden Valley, the Midland nonetheless built 19 stations at fairly regular intervals along the line, some — like Dent which is four miles from and more than 600ft above the township of 600 people from which it takes its name — being no mean distance from any significant settlement. Despite this, detailed analysis of the available information, as carried out by Mr Jenkinson, shows that, once the railway had arrived, it did indeed make "a substantial and valid contribution to local activity in the area", certainly until the advent of motor transport between the wars. So, despite its primary purpose as a trunk route, the line nonetheless generated local traffic by opening up new markets for agricultural produce because it offered a speedy north-south link in an area where communications traditionally ran east-west along the dales.

When it opened, the line carried three through trains daily each way from St Pancras to Edinburgh and Glasgow, with the fastest timing being ten and a half hours to Edinburgh, compared with ten hours ten minutes by the more direct LNWR route, or nine and a half hours by the Great Northern. Mr Allport introduced the Pullman to Britain on the line and later, to the indignation of his competitors, abolished Second Class travel in favour of an upgraded Third Class. Four years after his retirement in 1880 he was knighted "for services to the poor traveller"* — a recognition which preceded by more than a decade the erection of the Chapel-le-Dale memorial to the builders of the Settle and Carlisle!

Through traffic on the line peaked just before the First World War when there were three daytime expresses each way between London and Glasgow and Edinburgh, and one between Liverpool and Manchester and the Scottish cities. One of the London trains conveyed a portion from Bristol and semi-fast services between Leeds and Carlisle carried through coaches from Lancashire and Bradford. Night trains linked London, Liverpool, Manchester and Bristol with Glasgow, Edinburgh and Aberdeen; and London with Stranraer via the direct line through Wigtownshire from Carlisle.

The service cuts caused by the First World War were followed by the 1923 grouping of the railway companies which saw the old rivals of the LNWR and the Midland become part of the London, Midland and Scottish Railway, marking the beginning of the decline of the Settle and Carlisle. Despite the LMS's concentration on the Shap route, there were again by the 1930s three daily return fast trains over the line, including the new Thames-Clyde and Thames-Forth expresses, the latter becoming the Waverley in 1957.

After the war, which had seen very heavy freight use of the Settle and Carlisle, there began the steady process of closures in the area which was to continue unabated until the 70s. The Ingleton branch and the Hawes-Northallerton section of the Wensleydale line closed to passengers in

---

* *In considering the prominent role of Ron Cotton (British Rail's Settle-Carlisle Project Manager) in the eventual salvation of the line, it is interesting to reflect that here, more than 100 years previously, was a man motivated by similar ideals to Cotton's "people's railway".*

1954. The demise of the remainder of the latter, connecting with the Settle-Carlisle at Garsdale, came five years later. The former North Eastern Railway from Kirkby Stephen to Tebay closed in 1960, and trains on the line east from Kirkby Stephen over Stainmore disappeared two years after that, as did passenger services on the Blackburn-Hellifield "feeder" to the Settle-Carlisle. On the Settle-Carlisle itself, the first stations to close were in the Eden valley — Scotby in 1942; Cotehill, Ormside and Crosby Garrett ten years later; and Cumwhinton in 1956. A rare item on the credit side in this period was the use of the line for the new Condor London-Glasgow overnight container service (precursor of the Freightliner). Indeed, the Settle and Carlisle remained an important freight route until the eventual withdrawal of the last unbraked goods trains which could not be accommodated on the Shap route.

Tales of severe weather abound in books about the Settle and Carlisle. They range from the probable, such as one about the icy Helm wind from the Pennines blowing the coal from the fireman's shovel, to the most improbable. The story about a railwayman being blown off a train on Ribblehead viaduct only to be sucked through an arch and back up on to the train at the other side stretches one's credulity. But it is worth mentioning the two harsh winters which succeeded in closing the Settle-Carlisle line: in 1947 it was beneath 12ft of snow and ice for eight weeks from early February. Even a flamethrower failed to open a road, and when eventually it was possible to clear one track, the railway became a vital supply route for the remote dales. In 1962 the line was again blocked, this time for five days in January, an Edinburgh-London express being stranded at Dent until the railway was cleared sufficiently to extract the last three coaches back the way they had come.

The Beeching report brought the first generalised threat to passenger services on the line after the British Railways Board announced its intention to withdraw the local stopping service at 12 stations between Hellifield and Carlisle (*see Chapter 2*). The service's reprieve came in the wake of the election of the Labour Government in 1964, amid the euphoria of victory that can precede the more hard-nosed interpretation of financial figures. Tom Fraser, the new Minister of Transport refused permission for the closure in November 1964 on the grounds that undue hardship would result. The hardship question was — and indeed remains — the yardstick for the assessment of closure proposals by the Transport Users' Consultative Committees which were set up under the 1962 Transport Act.

Freight services had nonetheless been withdrawn from the stations served only by local trains in the course of 1964 and they were then reduced to unstaffed halts in an effort to cut costs. But the reprieve was short-lived as the service fell the wrong side of the line drawn according to the "Cooper Brothers' formula" — the new test introduced at the behest of the Ministry of Transport for assessing the "viability" of rural rail services. In simple terms, the thinking behind this was that services such as the stopping trains on the Settle and Carlisle should bear a proportion of the overheads involved in maintaining the line as a whole.

Now the nonsense of this ostensibly reasonable proposition only becomes evident when you start to talk about actually withdrawing services — because shutting a local service whose contribution to overheads is considered insufficient does precisely nothing to reduce those overheads. The net result is that the overheads fall even more heavily on the remaining services. Nonsense or no, this became the altar on which many lines and services were axed in the late 1960s and early '70s.

In the case of the Settle and Carlisle, the British Railways Board was able to argue that the cost of running the local service was some £102,000 a year, against which fares income from an "official" 43 regular passengers was just £9,000. The figure of £102,00 was so far removed from the actual (marginal) cost of running the diesel multiple units on the line that the passengers could have been given free Champagne breakfasts on every trip within the costs quoted. As Colin Speakman — who was destined later to play a prominent role in the revival of services on the line — observed in a letter to the *Yorkshire Post* in January 1969: "This is a new strategy of rail closure — exaggerate the costs to defeat the protests." Working on figures from the Beeching report, he put the true cost at a maximum of less than half the British Rail figure. This was to prove to be just the first of many occasions on which the Settle-Carlisle balance sheet was "cooked" so as to present the line in the worst possible light. If nothing else, the lengthy Settle-Carlisle proceedings have at least turned the spotlight on the manner in which BR presents financial data on threatened routes. Never again will BR's opponents take BR evidence with anything but a liberal pinch of salt.

The revived closure proposal, as was becoming traditional, came in the run-up to Christmas, at a time calculated to minimise the effectiveness of any opposition. But the news could hardly be described as having come out of the blue. The noises emanating from the BR Board over the past few years had been such that Malcolm Barker, writing in the *Yorkshire Evening Post* in March 1967, had been able to make an authoritative suggestion that "the end is not far away" for the Settle and Carlisle. All that would remain, he said, would be stubs at either end to Horton-in-Ribblesdale and Appleby.

The "regular users" figure was also highly misleading in that it concealed the fact that some stations were well used in summer by visitors to the Dales, many of whom would have travelled on connecting services on other parts of the rail network. It was as if one person making ten journeys on the line in some way counted for more than ten people who each made one journey. Again, this kind of selective presentation of the facts has remained popular in the BR litany of pre-closure tactics. In the summer of 1989, surveys carried out independently by local authorities on the threatened Sheffield to Cleethorpes service revealed substantial passenger loadings which made a nonsense of BR's picture of an aging DMU trundling all but empty past long forgotten halts.

Back in 1968, George Ellison, the chairman of Dent parish council, summed up the dilemma: "We are seeing the Dales die and we want to do all we can to keep them alive. The railway does more than give us a way out — it gives other people a way in." The council noted in a letter to the North West TUCC that there could be 30 or 40 people on trains to and from Dent bound for the youth hostel near the remote station. Ramblers were duly urged to object to the closure plan by Jack Smith, secretary of the West Riding branch of the Railway Travel and Correspondence Society, which in January 1969 ran a special excursion on the Settle and Carlisle which was also the last train to run on the Waverley line from Carlisle to Edinburgh before it was closed in a bizarre quid pro quo to satisfy tacit Department of Transport terms over the electrification of the West Coast Main Line.

In the case of the Waverley it had proved impossible for a powerful lobby of local authorities, industrialists and individuals to prevent the complete loss of a 98-mile trunk route which, while passing through wild and remote country, served sizeable towns whose population totalled about 100,000 — five times that served by the Settle-Carlisle. The chances of success for the 60 individuals, 23 local authorities and other corporate bodies, and 12 youth hostellers who objected to the loss of twice daily Carlisle-Skipton and the daily Garsdale-Skipton and Appleby-Carlisle services were clearly slim.

In April 1969 the TUCC reported that the loss of local services would cause severe hardship to those who relied on them to travel to work, college, hospital, doctors, dentists, chemists and for all the other numerous "social" reasons that people, quite reasonably, use railways. The committee found itself unable to suggest any means of reducing this hardship.

A year after the withdrawal of the local service was proposed, the people of Dent and the other communities served by the Settle-Carlisle line were given another nice Christmas present, when the Transport Minister, Richard Marsh, advised British Rail that — while he appreciated some travellers would face considerable increases in their journey times — their numbers were so small that the retention of the trains could not be justified. The last local trains ran in May 1970 and the stations at Horton, Ribblehead, Dent, Garsdale, Kirkby Stephen, Long Marton, Newbiggin, Culgaith, Langwathby, Little Salkeld, Lazonby and Kirkoswald, and Armathwaite were closed. This left Settle and Appleby the only intermediate stations on the line for all but DalesRail charters, started in 1975. This was how they would remain until the inauguration, in 1986, of the new all-stations Dalesman service.

By August 1970, in response to claims that remaining services on the line were being deliberately slowed down, British Rail stated that 100mph grading was no longer commercially viable. By May 1981, the ruling speed was only 60mph and the idea of closing the line altogether had gained wide currency within BR. Although the official announcement of the intention to close the line was still two years off, a spokesman felt sufficiently bold to tell one journalist: "The eventual aim is that the line will be severed at a point near Horton-in-Ribblesdale and near Kirkby Stephen and will be abandoned between those two points."

In 1977 the loss of the St Pancras to Carlisle and Glasgow services paradoxically brought some improvement as the Nottingham-Glasgow trains which replaced them took the direct electrified route north of Carlisle rather than the detour via Dumfries and Kilmarnock. The six-hour timing for the run was, unusually, half an hour faster than that achieved by the Midland in its heyday. The following year British Rail had a change of heart and added the Settle-Carlisle to lines on which occasional steam-hauled excursions would be permitted. This, then, was roughly the state of play when the two sides began, in the early 1980s, to take up their corners for the great Settle-Carlisle closure battle rematch.

Eventually, even British Rail took steam back to its bosom with the Cumbrian Mountain Pullman series of summer specials over the line. Ex-LMS locomotive No 46229, Duchess of Hamilton, makes light work of its train as it attacks the start of the Long Drag at Settle Junction.

After its systematic downgrading from main line to closure candidate the most important traffic over the line comprised diverted West Coast Main Line expresses. A Class 47 diesel, 47 532, emerges from Blea Moor Tunnel with the diverted morning Liverpool-Edinburgh service in May 1984.

British Rail's initial closure plan would have left two long sidings from Settle and Carlisle, serving the stone quarry at Ribblehead and the Army depot at Warcop, near Appleby. Class 25 locomotive 25 185 is pictured running around its load of ballast from the Ribblehead Quarry at Blea Moor, before the run back to Hellifield and Carnforth. Both locomotive and daily ballast train are now fragments of railway history.

2.
The doctor's bitter pill

THE Settle and Carlisle line was conceived amid a period of railway expansionism. Its proposed demise came towards the end of the most significant period of contraction ever in the history of railways in Britain. The architect of that decline was a man who — until his death in 1985 — was to claim continually that he had been much maligned for his ideas for the "reshaping" of Britain's railways.

The bulk of the railway closures in the so-called "Beeching era" took place during the 1960s. Although there were murmurings about the eventual fate of the S & C back in that period, the line was not formally proposed for closure until 1983, by when the size of the remaining rail network had largely stabilised. However, the rationale of closure as a theoretical solution to problems of declining usage and escalating costs remains firmly rooted in the Beeching approach and has been reflected in subsequent broad-brush attempts to solve what has been perceived to be the problem of British railways: the need for state subsidy to maintain services at competitive prices.

This was how *The Guardian* recorded the death of Dr Richard Beeching on March 25 1985: "He was in the headlines long after ceasing to be British Rail chairman in 1965. His memory reverberates among mourners of quiet country railway stations as well as among students of brisk post-war attempts to modernise Britain."

The demise of the journalist's son from East Grinstead merited some 29 column centimetres, a measure of the notoriety achieved by the man whose name became synonymous with the word "axe". The report continued: "Lord Beeching's attempt, as architect of the 1963 Beeching plan, was one of the first and most drastic [such attempts], and he was always bitter that his 'scientific, free enterprise technique for running a state service' was not allowed to go further."

Richard Beeching's use of the word scientific is telltale. He came from a world where chemical and physical reactions could be observed, measured and reduced to concise written formulae and equations. He sought to impose this neat logic on the imprecise worlds of economics and human behaviour.

Dr Beeching was a brilliant physicist and technical director for ICI who had been brought in by the Tory government to perform drastic surgery on the railway system, for which he was paid what was dubbed the "Himalayan" salary of £24,000. He was to the railways in the 60s what Ian MacGregor became to steel and coal in the '80s. The first phase of his plan demanded the closure of 5,000 out of 17,800 route miles and 2,300 of the 4,709 stations, a process which continued into its second phase until the Labour Government announced a stabilised network of 11,000 miles in 1967.

Although Dr Beeching described his axeman's reputation as "an injustice I shall suffer in history", his was the single most swingeing assault ever on the railways. Yet his report was only one of many learned documents that have helped shape today's residual rail network. The continuing report-chop-report-chop process which created the situation where rail management could glibly propose lopping the 72 miles of the Settle-Carlisle off the national network had its origins half, or even a whole century ago.

If the 20th has become the century of the roads lobby then, equally, the 19th was that of the railways. At a time when Parliament reigned rather more supreme than today, it was estimated that up to 150 MPs represented the "railway interest". Parliament sanctioned the building of all the railways by authorising the acquisition of the necessary land, but there was no attempt by the Government to do so in a way that helped produce an overall efficient national network. Indeed the reverse was true — Parliament's pathological terror of monopoly, which was described in Chapter 1, permitted the proliferation of wasteful duplication. Routes were paralleled: in Nottinghamshire, for example, the Midland, Great Northern and Great Central railways all ran within a few miles of each other north. Cities, towns and even villages where a single station would have sufficed acquired two — often more. Different companies adopted different standards, making any ultimate integration more difficult. Even today the tight tolerances on bridges and other structures on the old Furness Railway render the Cumbrian coast line unsuitable as an alternative diversionary route to the Settle-Carlisle, without major expenditure. Physical links where rival networks crossed were often awkward and clumsy to use, and hence of little practical value. The exceptions were the North-Eastern Railway, which built up a regional monopoly, with consequent savings in efficiency, as did the Great Western in the West Country.

The result — worsened by the problems facing managements in learning to cope with the new phenomena of widely dispersed workforces and assets — was a massive overprovision which turned the railways from a potentially very prosperous industry into one where profit levels were relatively low. Half a century later, the problems of this piecemeal railway development process came home to roost when the government had to deal with the mess. Premier Lloyd George's verdict was that it had been "a gigantic waste".

By the turn of the century, although nearly one in eight of the working population were employed by the railways, the position of many companies was insecure and their numbers declined rapidly as they were absorbed by larger ones. But the imminent threat of war in 1912 prompted the Government to impose on the railways a 20th century national management in the shape of the Railway Executive Committee, whose subsequent operations served to highlight the inefficiencies of the old-style competition. The 1919 establishment of the Ministry of Transport granted wide powers to rationalise, even nationalise, the railways — nationalisation had not then acquired today's party political overtones and was supported by Lloyd George and Winston Churchill. Even earlier — in 1844 — the Gladstone's Railway Regulation Act had given the Government an option on the acquisition, after 1865, of railway companies which had been formed since 1844.

But the railways resisted nationalisation to sink back into their 19th century ways and it was only in the face of looming crisis that the 1921 Railway Act led to the compromise grouping of the railways into four large companies, the London and North-Eastern, the London Midland and Scottish, the Southern and the Great Western. But the Act failed to reform any of the old 19th century powers aimed at regulating inter-company competition and protecting customers from the powers of monopoly transport. So as road haulage began to grow, the railways found themselves obliged by statute (under the "common carrier" principle) to carry small loads of freight at low revenue which the road carriers could refuse to handle. The combined assault of the roads and the deepening depression saw the railways facing falling traffic, to which their response was an attempt to reduce staff numbers and downgrade clerical posts as they became vacant. The collapse of the 1926 General Strike weakened the railway unions and wage cuts and unemployment followed more easily.

Faced with an accelerating loss of trade to the roads, conservative and unimaginative railway managements failed to come up with the sort of aggressive marketing and operating policies which might have helped them retain or expand their traffic. They did not seek to charge higher rates for their captive heavy freight customers like the coal industry, nor did they reduce prices for conveying goods which were most vulnerable to seizure by road competition. The temptation was there, it has been argued, simply to blame the injustice of the common carrier obligation and do nothing. On the plus side, the LMS did take the initiative in introducing the container to rail freight, for which premium rates were charged.

Professor Philip Bagwell, the National Union of Railwaymen's official historian, argues that the railways' meagre financial returns led directly to their failure to invest adequately in modernisation between the wars, at a time when those in other countries were doing so. While gross investment between 1920 and 1938 was £283m, this was only about two thirds of the amount required merely to cover depreciation. The Weir Committee report on electrification in 1931 argued that, to secure the full economic advantage of such a scheme, most of the country's main line system should be converted — possibly with state subsidy — to electric traction, at a total cost including power stations of £341m over 15 to 20 years.

The publication of the report coincided with another severe drop in traffic and all that came of it were token schemes such as the Sheffield-Manchester Woodhead route (now closed). Steam, after all, was a proven technology and Britain still had an abundance of suitable coal. Describing it as "one of the great missed opportunites of the 1930s", Professor Bagwell comments in *The Transport Revolution from 1970*: "In any case, many leading railwaymen were more interested in improving the performance of the steam locomotive than in making exhaustive inquiry into the economics of electric traction." The notable exception was the Southern, whose network was rather more suburban in nature than that of the other railways.

There were areas of business in which, paradoxically, the railways did invest: road and air transport. But rather than using such investment to set up "feeders" to their own services, the companies were more interested simply in "spoiling" the plans of other road and air operators. The Royal Commission on Transport commented in 1931 that the railway companies' principal response to the road threat appeared to be to "get on the road" themselves. "Insofar as this policy makes for the better co-ordination of rail and road services we welcome it. On the general principle of the policy, however, we cannot refrain from expressing a feeling of doubt whether it is wise for the companies to expend large capital sums for the purpose of establishing services which may be in direct competition with their business as railways. We feel that possibly such capital would be better applied to the electrification of their suburban lines."

On the question of air routes, the views of the former LMS Chief Secretary, P E Garbutt, on the company's Railway Air Services venture are quoted in Michael R Bonavia's book, *Railway Policy between the Wars*: "The basic purpose in setting up Railway Air Services and developing internal air services, railway owned, in the United Kingdom was to suppress possible competition... They were mainly concerned with getting in on routes, establishing themselves and then operating a holding exercise, a restraining exercise, to stop anybody else from getting in and building up a substantial air traffic."

The notion that transport operations produced benefits to their users and the areas they served which were not necessarily of direct benefit to the operators themselves began to be appreciated in the '30s. Thus, the seeds of a nationalised transport network were sown by the first minority Labour Government in 1929, and London Transport came into public ownership in 1933.

But it took another strength-sapping war, in which the railways were flogged to the brink of exhaustion, before nationalisation became a reality with the setting-up by Labour in 1945 of the National Transport Board to co-ordinate state-owned rail, road, water and air services. The 1947 Transport Act established the British Transport Commission to which the railways and other transport undertakings were transfered on January 1, 1948. The Act offered the potential of a fully integrated national transport system: unfortunately, the five executives under the commission — rail, London Transport, docks and inland waterways, hotels and road transport — tended to have what Kerry Hamilton and Stephen Potter referred to in their book to accompany the excellent Channel 4 series, *Losing Track*, as "an independence of outlook which positively hindered the transport integration objectives of the Commission".

That wasn't the only problem: the wartime traffic boom had arguably served to inflate the price which the Government had to pay to the operators for the loss of their railways, on which there was a massive legacy of repairs to be carried out. By 1951, when the Tories were returned to power, the only obvious success of the commission in moving towards transport minister Herbert Morrison's dream of an integrated system had been in building up the road haulage side. The Churchill Government's first act was to sell off the road haulage executive with its new lorries at bargain prices, often to the very operators who had received compensation for their battered old fleets only three years previously.

The role of the British Transport Commission as an integrating body was ended by the 1953 Transport Act which denied railways the role of operating the "middle leg" of door-to-door freight services. While the private enterprise road hauliers had been given a spanking new asset to make money with, the railways were still languishing in their pre-war torpor, making do with worn-out, obsolete equipment which was effectively a legacy from the last century. The Government had split them into regions, based largely on the old pre-war companies, which were responsible directly to the British Transport Commission.

But many sectors of private industry were still dependent on an efficient railway and so the new BTC chairman, Sir Brian Robertson, was given a brief to update the system. The commission's plan for the modernisation and re-equipment of the railways was launched with no fewer than three press conferences — one for news reporters, one for leader writers and one for financial editors — on January 21, 1955. It was a bold scheme born out of six months' intensive work. It envisaged spending £1,200m over 15 years to achieve "a transformation of virtually all the forms of service now offered by British Railways". There would be fast, clean, regular, frequent services in urban areas and faster, punctual inter-city trains. Services on other routes would be made "reasonably economic" or transferred to road. Improvements to the freight service would "attract to the railway a due proportion of the full-load merchandise traffic which would otherwise pass by road". The scheme's main elements — which, had they been implemented, would have put Britain at the forefront of European railways — were:

- £210m-worth of track and control improvements, including coloured light signals and removal of bends and other speed restrictions on trunk routes to obtain 100mph working

- A £345m programme to replace steam engines with diesel and electric traction, including the electrification of the main lines from London to Liverpool, Manchester, Leeds and (possibly) York
- Replacement of steam-hauled passenger stock with diesel or electric multiple units at a cost of £285m
- Modernisation of freight-handling services at a cost of £365m.

The Commission envisaged an annual return of at least £85m on this investment, half of which, it pointed out, would be required in any case for normal maintenance work. But by 1959, with many works started, the Government was getting cold feet. The cost of the programme had risen, partly owing to inflation, to £1,500m and the only part which was pursued to completion was the replacement of steam. The reason lay in the advent of mass car ownership which epitomised Harold Macmillan's "you never had it so good" era. The '50s saw the coming of age of the all-powerful roads lobby — whose influence would come to exceed that of the rail lobby 50 to 100 years previously — as the Society of Motor Manufacturers and Traders joined forces with the Road Haulage Association to form the British Road Federation. At the same time, the shift from traditional heavy industry to new industries like car building saw the Transport and General Workers Union in the ascendant at the expense of the railway, mining and other unions.

The rise of the car was reflected and fostered in Government policy until the appointment of Ernest Marples as Minister of Transport in 1959 marked the effective final transformation of the Ministry of Transport into the "Ministry of Roads". Marples owned the major road construction company Marples Ridgeway but sidestepped the problems of having such a clear vested interest by the simple expedient of passing his shareholding to his wife. Thus began a noble Conservative tradition of giving to those with an interest in the roads, positions of power over the railways — a tradition which it seems was still thriving with the appointment of the Serpell committee in 1982.

Even more recently, there was the the resurrection of Beeching's failed bus-substition idea when — as described in Chapter 10 — British Rail was chivvied into a costly and time-wasting review of branch lines to see if any could be closed and replaced by buses. The man largely responsible for this was John Palmer, a senior civil servant at the Department of Transport, who pushed the idea forward within months of his retirement. This poison pill which he slipped BR before his departure has come to be known as the "Palmer legacy". Notwithstanding what many would see as a classic Beeching-style antipathy to the railways, Mr Palmer now has a place on the BR Board to keep him busy in retirement.

The 1955 Robertson Report had made no fundamental criticism of the railways, but Marples was soon able to demote still further their political status when he appointed an advisory group under Sir Ivan Stedeford to examine the running of the BTC. The Stedeford Report called for an end to railway management's "public service" mentality and said the network should be run as a profit-making business. The BTC was duly abolished by the 1962 Transport Act and a member of the Stedeford group, Dr Richard Beeching, was appointed the first chairman of the British Railways Board. Beeching may have disliked the axeman's label, but seen in the context of the politics of the time it becomes clear that if Marples was the contractor who built the gallows for the railways, then Beeching was the executioner.

Trial and sentence were to be by means of a document, euphemistically called *The Reshaping of British Railways*, which appeared in 1963. Beeching may have been a brilliant physicist, but the Beeching Report exposed his shortcomings as a transport econonomist and statistician, certainly by today's academic standards. At best Beeching's assumptions were naïve: at worst they were a crude device to justify railway closures to the ultimate benefit of the roads lobby.

As Hamilton and Potter put it: "The criteria and methods adopted to evaluate the role of the railways meant that major closures were a foregone conclusion.

"For example, the relationship between road and rail was considered only to the extent that Beeching felt free to suggest that unprofitable rail services could be transferred to road. The possible effects on roads and whether it would require more to be spent on roads to accommodate such traffic than would be spent on the railways was not examined. He concentrated attention on the cost of retaining railways and gave no consideration to the costs and consequences associated with developing the road network."

Even in 1990, this narrow measure of the return on railway investment remains the yardstick for assessing the viability or otherwise of developments. In marked contrast is the system for assessing the viability of road improvement schemes. Because, in Britain, drivers do not pay tolls to use roads, there is no measurable financial return which accrues from investment in roads. So road proposals have to be evaluated on the basis of wider social benefits, such as the likely reduction in accidents when a bypass is built and the saving in drivers' time. Provided the benefits that build up over time exceed costs, using a five per cent discount rate, the road is likely to be built. If this is considered a reasonable way in which to assess the viability of road investment policies, why then can it not be applied to investment in railways which — in contrast — was, at the time of writing, required to yield an eight per cent return on capital? In other words, it must either bring an annual increase in revenue equal to or greater than eight per cent of the investment cost, or equivalent savings (for example through lower maintenance costs when lines are electrified).

The argument is that British Rail is only carrying out the sort of financial appraisal that would be undertaken by a private sector company which was evaluating a proposed investment. But private companies need not generally concern themselves with the effect their own investments have on other companies or society at large.

British Rail, on the other hand, is part of the Government-run infrastructure of the UK and the external costs and benefits of schemes are of direct interest to us all as taxpayers, or shareholders in UK plc. Yet, in practice, the cost-benefit technique is generally only used in connection with rail closure proposals and not with investment plans. Even then it is only ancilliary to financial appraisal. Indeed PEIDA, the consultants retained by the local authorities fighting the closure of the Settle-Carlisle line, carried out a cost-benefit analysis on the railway which showed that — even based on the limited service then operated — there was a benefit in the retention of the line.

As far as new railways are concerned, studies have shown* that the financial return of a scheme will rarely exceed the return expressed in cost/benefit terms. Indeed the only occasion when such an outcome is really possible is when there are two directly competing modes of transport over a particular route and investment in one may attract customers from the other without any broader benefits.

It should come as no surprise, then, that there are many ostensibly worthwhile rail schemes which are never enacted because they fail to meet to narrow financial criteria laid down. Where cost/benefit tech-

---

* *British Rail Board/P Mackie, 1973*

niques are applied to rail schemes, the results tend to paint a more favourable picture of investment in the steel wheel. Cost/benefit analysis is widely used to assess investment proposals for railways in other countries. In France, for example, plans to improve the line from Paris to Clermont Ferrand would have yielded a financial return of just 1.5 per cent. The cost/benefit return, by contrast, was some 28 per cent. Even in that bastion of free enterprise and road transport, the United States, a cost/benefit study on the Boston-Washington corridor led to the decision to invest $2,000m in the railroads. In West Germany all rail, road and water proposals are evaluated by means of a cost-effectiveness appraisal which "scores" benefits in points and puts schemes in a priority order to avoid competition and to ensure the three modes complement each other where possible. Thus, if there is a high speed railway alongside the route of a proposed motorway this duplication will reduce the "points value" of the road scheme and make it less likely to show a positive return.

In Britain, by contrast, road and rail schemes are processed through different hierarchies at the Department of Transport and comparable schemes are never looked at side by side. There have been a few cases of cost/benefit analysis on rail investment schemes in Britain, such as those that led to the retention of the Manchester to Hadfield and Glossop lines in 1974. More recently, a study was carried out by the Transport and Road Research Laboratory, Newcastle University, Tyne and Wear County Council and the Tyne and Wear PTE into the effect of the opening of the Metro integrated rapid transit system. The light electric railway was built on Tyneside partly as an alternative to major investment in urban motorways. The *Metro Report* showed the system had yielded an estimated return of eight per cent on net capital cost in its first year. Even given low economic growth the system would give a social return of 73 per cent over 30 years — more or less equivalent to the financial return which would have been obtained by the average private sector investor. Significantly, it led to a major rise in public transport usage among both car and non-car owners and consequently also yielded benefits to motorists through reduced congestion leading to shorter journey times — a success which was only dented by the "deregulation" of bus services in October 1986.

But to go back to Beeching: his analysis was of the crudest "balance sheet" type. This is what he had to say about cost/benefit analysis: "It might pay to run railways at a loss in order to prevent the incidence of an even greater cost which would arise elsewhere if the railways were closed. Such other costs may be deemed to arise from congestion, provision of parking space, injury and death, additional road building, or a number of other causes. It is not **thought** [*authors' emphasis*] that any of the firm proposals put forward in this Report would be altered by the introduction of new factors for the purpose of judging overall social benefit. Only in the case of suburban services around some of the larger cities is there clear likelihood that a purely commerical decision within the existing framework of judgment would conflict with a decision based upon total social benefit. Therefore, in those instances, no firm proposals have been made but attention has been drawn to the necessity for study and decision." We are still, in 1990, awaiting the promised study.

Beeching's idea was that savings achieved through "rationalisation" (closures) might then release funds for investment on the residual network. Any broader analysis of how this rationalisation might affect the country at large was beyond his brief. Similarly, any subsequent investment decisions would be based either on the scope for reducing British Railways' costs or for attracting additional traffic. Dr Beeching's studies led him to conclude that one third of the country's route mileage (5,900 miles) was generating just one per cent of the passenger and freight ton miles. Half the network carried just four per cent of the total passenger mileage and five per cent of the freight mileage, and generated annual revenue of £20m towards costs of £40m. The other half of the network, by contrast, was generating revenue six times its route costs, argued Dr Beeching. These bald figures led him to conclude that the lightly loaded lines should close, and as soon as possible. Ominously, we hear comparable talk today as the better performing lines in the Provincial Sector are sifted out from the rural rump of the network.

Dr Beeching seems to have been particularly deaf to any serious consideration of ways of making lines more economic through investment or improved productivity, and instead offered token consideration to ideas such as fares cuts, reduced services, station closures and rail buses to replace diesel units. This cursory examination led him to assert that the idea that such services could be retained as an economic alternative to buses was "really not so". The Beeching closure yardstick was that any service which did not generate sufficient revenue to cover its "direct costs" should go. In broad terms that has remained the narrow test of "viability" which has applied ever since: all that changes is the accounting trick whereby the Government determines from time to time, through the Public Service Obligation Grant, exactly how far along the scale the stick should be placed.

Beeching made two bold assumptions: firstly, that all former rail passengers would readily transfer to the replacement bus services. In this he chose to ignore all questions of speed, comfort and reliability (particularly in bad weather), and all those marginal sociological and psychological factors which make rail an acceptable form of public transport for many and buses an unacceptable one. Mayer Hillman and Anne Whalley present figures which amply illustrate this point in their study, *The Social Consequences of Rail Closure*. They found that only in socio-economic groups D and E did more than half the former rail passengers transfer to the replacement buses. In other groups the figure was much lower. Among car owners who had formerly used the railways, the transfer to buses after closure was very small indeed. But, of course, nobody really had to worry about the car-owners: they still enjoyed mobility. And so the effects of railway closures became a social problem: the problem of subsidising the lower orders who could not afford their own cars. Again, today, this mentality endures and transport policy, such as it exists at all, is based on the notion that the state should provide roads on which people may drive their cars. The underlying presumption is that individuals, given a choice, would always prefer to travel by their own means. Much is said by politicians under the banner of that most abused of words, "freedom", about the freedom of the car-owner to drive wheresoever he or she wishes: very little about the freedom of the individual to leave the car in the drive, or — heresy of heresies — not to own a car at all.

Soon, then, many of the bus services brought in to replace trains closed under Beeching were losing more money than the trains they replaced — and they did not even have to cover their own "track" costs! Worse news for people in rural areas particularly was that eventually, unlike the rail services, they could be withdrawn without resort to any legal process as had been required when the railways they replaced were closed. This fact was remembered by many when BR detailed its closure proposals for the Settle-Carlisle. The promise of a "protected" replacement bus service that could not be withdrawn without recourse to a full process before the Transport Users' Consultative Committees failed to cut much ice.

Dr Beeching's second bold assumption, made on the basis of just one week's survey work, was that the railways would retain 95 per cent of their traffic after the closures. This assertion was based on ludicrously optimistic proejections about the retention of feeder traffic after the routes on which it was generated had closed. One of the examples he quoted was the direct Hull to York line via Beverley (a line which bears some comparison with the Leeds-Carlisle route, in that it linked two cities via a fairly thinly populated rural area). The service on this line on Beeching's own figures actually more than covered its operating costs, but allowing for terminal and track costs showed an annual shortfall of £60,400. Of the £90,400 direct earnings, Beeching expected to lose £64,790. But out of the £37,680 spent by passengers on the line on tickets for journeys beyond Hull and York (contributory revenue), Beeching expected to retain all but £4,900. Closure, he said would yield a net annual benefit of £81,110.

Experience quickly showed Dr Beeching's assumptions about contributory revenue to be false and by 1969 — with 4,000 route miles axed — passenger journeys on British Railways had slumped from 1,025 million in 1961 to just 805 million. Freight traffic fell by 13 per cent over the same period. There were developments Beeching could not have predicted, such as slower economic growth and the decline of the coal and steel industries: but another factor, the growth of car ownership and use, was in part, at least, a direct consequence of his actions. In simple terms, Beeching had failed — or not wanted — to appreciate that if you cut the roots and branches from a tree the trunk will wither.

The contributory revenue question, of course, is not one that provides easy, cut-and-dried answers. Towards the end of the Settle-Carlisle battle it would become a key issue, with the Joint Action Committee, on the one hand, arguing that BR was not giving due allowance for contributory revenue from tickets bought outside the area for journeys involving an S & C leg. The difference between JAC and BR figures was the difference between the line showing an operating loss or a surplus.

Back in the '60s, the railway unions' attempts to resist Beeching through the TUC appeared thwarted by the increasingly powerful Transport and General Workers Union, with its interests in car manufacturing and road haulage, and alternative plans which would have yielded similar savings through improved efficiency were rejected by the railway management. In all, Beeching's massive closure programme had no appreciable impact on the railways' need for revenue support.

Meanwhile, the annual net subsidy to the roads was running at £600m — four times that given to the railways. The Beeching closures gave an additional fillip to road building by adding to congestion and increasing the clamour for new investment to reduce both delay and the rising toll of accidents. The doctor's reward for this failed social experiment and its catastrophic consequences was elevation to the House of Lords.

As has been seen, Dr Beeching did, almost casually, hint at the need for some broader studies beyond the simple profit and loss account. And, funnily enough, someone else was — on a brief from Mr Marples — doing another study which, had the "Ministry of Roads" chosen to put the two side by side, had important implications for the Beeching Report and vice versa. Colin Buchanan's Traffic in Towns report was already pointing to even greater costs than feared due to congestion, accidents and pollution caused by road traffic.

The Beeching closure programme continued more or less unabated through governments of both main persuasions, certainly as far as concerns the lower density routes with which this book is most concerned (the benefits conferred by the 1968 Transport Act, insofar as they applied to the railways, were important only in the main conurbations).

The test of viability facing branch lines and rural stopping services would go on to see various changes, as already discussed. But now, with the branches well pruned, there arose the possibility of some paring of the trunk itself. The British Railways Board report, *The Development of the Major Railway Trunk Routes,* which appeared in 1965 represented the application of the Beeching branch line philosophy to the main lines. This report sought to present a "critical examination" of the trunk routes "to establish how the through route system can best be developed to match the future pattern of rail traffic demand". Its aim was to rid the railways of the effects of the wasteful duplication caused by the 19th century's competitive building.

It identified major railway traffic centres and the flows between them and then looked at the number of different routes between which that traffic was shared. The report claimed that out of 7,500 miles of trunk route, 3,700 miles were duplicated, 700 were triplicated and 700 quadruplicated. The report suggested that this network was under-utilised to the extent of some 60 per cent. Based on similar assumptions about national economic growth to *The Reshaping of British Railways,* the report predicted a gradual progression over 20 years towards its recommended route pattern. Many of its suggestions have never been imple-

If Dr Beeching had had his way, Dent Station and signal box would never have survived beyond the mid-1960s. Happily, Dent survives as England's highest main line station, though the signal box is now gone. Jack Sedgwick, last signalman at Dent is pictured here.

If BR's own closure plan, published almost exactly 20 years later, had succeeded, this view of Ribblehead Viaduct would also have been lost, with buffer stops at the southern end of the 24 arches.

mented, but the document provides a useful insight into the assumptions which were being made about the railways.

These were typified by the apparent view that trunk routes led from A to Z and the fact that traffic might be generated at intermediate stops from B to Y was given relatively little consideration. There was a further implicit assumption that traffic between A and B could always be retained even if forced to pass via C, where C represented the third corner of a triangle. Thus the report believed that all the Anglo-Scottish traffic could be accommodated on the West Coast route, with the Newcastle to Edinburgh traffic being routed via Carlisle. By and large, the trunk routes have survived the 25 years since the report, with notable exceptions like the Waverley line and the Great Central. Curiously, the Woodhead route from Sheffield to Manchester which was selected as the preferred southern trans-Pennine option became the one which was actually closed (*see Chapter 10*). In some cases the survival of one trunk route rather than another could be seen as the triumph of railway sentimentality over logic. The Great Central is a case in point, with the Midland line being the chosen trunk route to Nottingham and Sheffield, even though the Great Central was built at a later date to a higher standard and to the broader continental, or Berne, loading gauge. Interestingly, at the time of writing, proposals from the Labour Party envisage the resurrection of the southern part of the line as the first leg in a new high speed route linking London with Manchester, Leeds, Newcastle, Edinburgh and Glasgow

If as much energy as has gone into producing reports about how to dismantle the railway system in Britain had been put into making it more efficient, we might today have a viable modern national network. The Serpell Report, commissioned in 1982 at a cost estimated at well over £500,000, is probably the most spectacular example to date and for that reason alone deserves some consideration. Making the same questionable assumptions about bus substitution and the retention of contributory revenue as had been made by Beeching 20 years earlier, Sir David Serpell and his committee set about producing a series of options tailored to varying levels of Government support.

The Serpell Report was born out of the frustrations experienced by the then chairman of British Rail, Sir Peter Parker, as he tried to get the railways' case across to an unreceptive Government and its Minister, David Howell.

Sir Peter told Stan Abbott: "David Serpell was a good and loyal member of the Railways Board but his committee was appointed for him without any consultation with us and he got lumbered with a committee which broke up under him. I wanted a neutral report which could help David Howell see the railway case."

The Serpell committee's conclusions were spectacular in their outrageousness — *Option A* for a "commercially viable railway" envisaged an 84 per cent network cut and no lines in Scotland north of Edinburgh and Glasgow and no East Coast route north of Newcastle. *Option B* reinstated those lines where the "resource cost" of withdrawing the service would be greater than retaining it. The various C options envisaged differing levels of support, while *Option D* reinstated services to towns with a population of 25,000 or more. The high investment *Option H* was so superficial as scarcely to merit mention.

The approach showed conspicuous inconsistencies. On the one hand, the strategically important Newcastle to Carlisle line would be axed under most options. On the other, Serpell saw a future for the northern Scottish routes and for the run-down Settle-Carlisle. The explanation was quite simple — routes like Inverness to Kyle of Lochalsh had had their costs pared to the bone and had been made more efficient through investment. Newcastle-Carlisle had 26 manned signal boxes and so its costs were artificially inflated through lack of investment.

But Serpell's faults ran even deeper. The report's commissioning was a political solution to the differences evident between the British Rail chairman, Sir Peter Parker, and the Tory Government. It was presented by the Government as the review which BR had asked for. But if Sir Peter had agreed to a review, he certainly never wished to see conclusions such as those drawn by the Serpell Committee. The one consolation was that the Serpell report eventually became widely discredited and an embarrassing exercise the Government was glad to forget in the course of the 1983 General Election. It implied that rail safety standards might be lowered towards those pertaining on the roads. There even remains some question as to whether the consultants remembered to include freight revenues in their calculations*.

Now, in 1990, as British Rail acquires an increasingly pre-privatisation look, the question of subverting questions of safety is again arising. In a letter which was subsequently leaked to *The Independent***, Peter

---

* *Hansard, January 20, 1983*

** *The Independent, August 8, 1990*

Rayner, operations manager for London Midland Region, warned that BR's new Organisation for Quality review compromised safety and could jeopardise the implementation of recommendations in the Hidden Report which followed the Clapham rail crash which killed 35 people in 1988. "Only blindly arrogant, politically motivated, personally ambitious people can believe in it," wrote Mr Rayner of the proposed reorganisation.The effects of money-before-safety policies manifested themselves at both Clapham and, arguably, Bellgrove, near Glasgow, where two trains met head-on in a cost-saving single-line section of what had, until very recently, been a full double-line junction. Yet, ironically, as Chapter 9 tells, these accidents and a further one, at Purley, caused by human error, may well have played their part in securing the future of the S & C as Paul Channon, the beleagured Transport Secretary, weighed up the pros and cons of a long drawn out and messy legal end to the closure saga.

The Serpell report can be seen as just another shallow and sorry manifestation of the power of the roads lobby and it is this aspect of it which perhaps deserves more attention than its clear methodological shortcomings. The committee was chaired by Sir David Serpell, a member of the British Railways Board. Its members included Leslie Bond, James Butler and Alfred Goldstein. Mr Goldstein was a senior partner in R Travers Morgan and Partners and Mr Butler a partner in Peat, Marwick, Mitchell and Co, both firms with an obvious interest in road transport. More surprisingly, both firms benefitted directly by being commissioned to carry out work worth several hundred thousand pounds for the Serpell Committee on which their own partners were sitting.

The question was raised as a point of order in the Commons by the then Labour MP for Keighley, Bob Cryer (now Bradford South), who suggested that money had been paid to the firms in contravention of the Government chief accountant's rules*. Mr Cryer's Lewisham West Labour colleague, Christopher Price, called for an adjournment of the House to discuss "the clear breach of the Government chief accountant's guidelines in the appointment of R Travers Morgan and Peat, Marwick, Mitchell & Co as consultants to the Serpell committee". These guidelines stated: "A candidate firm will be ruled out, without detailed consideration, if... there is a clash, or potential clash, of interests that

---

* *Hansard January 20, 1983*

would result from its appointment." Mr Price continued: "Our principal responsibility in the House is to ensure that Government monies are spent properly and without leaving the Minister or his civil servants open to accusations of sharp practice, jobs for the boys, corruption or anything like that." The debate ended with the Speaker ruling that if the question was to be pursued it should be done "in some other way".

On February 16 Mr Cryer asked an oral question of the Transport Secretary David Howell: "Is it not curious that, although the Secretary of State always rabbits on about competition, these consultants were chosen without any competitive tendering whatsoever, contrary to the general rules of conduct applying to such business?" Mr Howell cited the urgency with which the consultants' submissions were required as bringing this unusual practice within the rules: "The consultants were chosen because they could give prompt backing to those selected to help with the review." In answer to a question from Robert Hughes MP, he continued: "The rules for the employment of consultants make it clear that in exceptional circumstances an approach to a single firm may be made." The Tories' landslide election victory which followed the Falklands War removed from the Commons some of those Labour members who had been pursuing the Serpell appointments most vigorously and like so many other issues it is now effectively buried.

The report itself, it has been suggested, was to some extent guided towards its extreme position by Mr Goldstein who subsequently — having made his mark — withdrew from joining in the main report to publish his own minority view in an appendix. Discredited or not, the Serpell report must be considered to have had influence on the course of the railway finances debate if only because any cuts suggested since have seemed preferable to the most extreme suggestions contained in it.

Not only passenger trains were diverted over the Settle-Carlisle. When the West Coast Main Line was out of action, the daily working of empty newspaper vans back to Manchester Red Bank passed over the line. Class 47 locomotive 47 142 (above) is about to plunge into Blea Moor Tunnel with a string of empty vans on a Sunday afternoon in December 1983 while (below), the same train is pictured at Blea Moor in March 1984, with 47 450 in charge. Note the relief locomotive which was always kept on station at Blea Moor during diversions to cover for breakdowns.

3.
If at first you don't succeed...

SO, despite surviving the excesses of the Beeching era, the S & C in 1983 stood condemned. However, the line which had proved so hard to build was clearly going to be no pushover when it came to "unbuilding" it, as British Rail soon began to find out.

December 15, 1983, saw the publication of the Settle-Carlisle closure notice, following the announcement the previous August of BR's intention to withdraw services. By August 9, 1984, the closure express remained firmly stuck in its siding. Indeed, its prospects for imminent departure were, if anything, less than they had been eight months previously, thanks to two false starts.

The first closure notice was withdrawn in April 1984 under the threat of legal action from the Settle-Carlisle Joint Action Committee over the definition of those groups of people entitled to lodge objections to the proposed closure.

The second, revised, closure notice followed in May and — with the simultaneous reissue of closure notices for the Goole to Gilberdyke service on the Doncaster to Hull line — marked the first known occasion on which a closure procedure had had to be restarted.

But August saw the issue of a third closure notice, following the "if at first you don't succeed" philosophy. This notice was remarkable in that it related to just three miles of track with no stations. And because there were no stations, the closure notices had to be posted at the nearest sizeable settlement, the upper Wensleydale town of Hawes, some six miles from the Settle-Carlisle line and last served by its own branch back in 1959!

That the closure process laid down in the 1962 Transport Act should have got off to such a faltering start is perhaps a little surprising, given that British Rail had had quite some months in which to rehearse: it is clear that the closure of the Settle-Carlisle line was firmly on the British Rail agenda by 1981 at the latest.

It was in April 1981 that the magazine *Steam World* published a story under an "exclusive" label suggesting that BR was considering building a new viaduct at Ribblehead at a cost of £4.5m. The new structure was needed because of the condition of the famous 24-arch structure and the article said that refusal of funds for the project could lead to the closure of the line. Another article in the *Yorkshire Post* of May 19 that year, by the *New Civil Engineer*'s northern editor, David Hayward, described the viaduct's condition as terminal. Quoting British Rail's divisional civil engineer, Alan King, Mr Hayward wrote that BR had spent £600,000 on repairs to Ribblehead over the previous ten years but had ended up with a structure in worse condition than when the work had started. A number of cosmetic operations had been carried out on Ribblehead viaduct over the decade and these had included strengthening the pier corners with concrete and replacing the brick lining beneath two of the arches. But the failure of the waterproof membrane on the structure's deck had allowed the piers to fill with water which then washed the mortar out from the inside. This in turn had the effect of leaving the limestone blocks of which the viaduct was built supported upon the different sized grains of mortar which remained, thus subjecting them to uneven loadings. The 290 million-year-old limestone had reached the end of its life and a replacement viaduct was needed, the report concluded bluntly.

We now know, of course, that the viaduct's condition was far from terminal — at the root of the problem lay the condition of the decking. Blame for the failure of this waterproof membrane and the consequent penetration of water into the viaduct itself can now be laid squarely on the shoulders of the original contractors who built the viaduct. All the other structural problems stemmed from this basic failure and — as later chapters will describe — the viaduct would prove capable of being brought back into sound condition for less than half the cost of the replacement viaduct, even after allowing for ten years' inflation.

But, in 1981, the condition of Ribblehead viaduct and BR's estimate for replacing it could be subjected neither to independent scrutiny nor to the kind of "test repair" to an arch which would only be meaningful once repairs were done to the deck. And so it became the cornerstone of the argument for closure.

Of course, British Rail made repeated and strenuous denials at the time that there was any connection between the decision to "go public" on Ribblehead and the various other decisions affecting the fate of the Settle-Carlisle. This posture seemed difficult to swallow at the time and events since then — both on the S & C and elsewhere — have only served to reinforce the view that the viaduct was indeed no more than a scapegoat, an excuse by which to justify closure. Some of those "other decisions" were made quite publicly, such as the announced intention to reroute the Nottingham-Glasgow InterCity service via the West Coast main line and Manchester, thereby avoiding both Leeds and the Settle-Carlisle. It was maintained that this decision — to take effect from May 1982 — was a purely commercial one (unconnected with concern about the condition of Ribblehead viaduct) on the part of InterCity which saw the revised route as likely to generate more intermediate traffic. The Yorkshire Area Transport Users' Consultative Committee was sceptical about BR's assurance that this would not prejudice the future of the Settle-Carlisle "especially as the proposed alternative services for Yorkshire passengers are ill-drafted and inadequate".

The committee noted that these Yorkshire passengers represented more than 50 per cent of those using the existing service — for the first time in more than 100 years there would be no through trains from Leeds to either Glasgow or Nottingham. The subject provoked more complaints to the committee in 1981 than did any other. If the InterCity managers had identified greater potential for a service via Manchester they were also prepared to forego known traffic via Leeds and further worsen an already poor service between Leeds and Sheffield. Typical journey times between Leeds and Nottingham were extended from less than two to almost three hours, leaving the door wide open to coach operators to pick up the already proven traffic. Passengers from Glasgow and Carlisle to Nottingham, meanwhile, faced a longer journey and the withdrawal of the new service via Manchester two years later merely served to confirm suspicions that this, too, was no more than another ploy in the complex game-playing surrounding the run-down of the S & C.

Rather less public than the hard-to-hide removal of a train service were the behind-the-scenes machinations from which it is clear that a decision to close the line had indeed been taken in principle well before the announcement of the Nottingham-Glasgow diversion. A confidential BR document in August 1981 linked the condition of Ribblehead viaduct with the broader issue of whether the line was needed at all and it predicted closure by 1984. The then fairly considerable freight traffic and the Nottingham-Glasgow trains should all be diverted via the West Coast route, it said, and a "residual" Leeds-Carlisle service introduced as a legal stopgap. It was anticipated the transport users' committees' considerations would be concluded by May 1984. Through freight traffic was indeed diverted — often by ridiculously circuitous routes — and local quarry traffic was forced on to narrow Dales roads as BR cited a lack of available locomotives to convey it. The line was reduced to daytime only working.

So clandestine were the discussions leading to this policy, it seems, that even the BR chairman, Sir Peter Parker, was not fully aware of them, for he was able to write to Barbara Castle MEP in July 1981: "Once again let me stress that our recognition of the changing role of the Settle-Carlisle line does not imply that we are anxious to ensure its closure. At present we have no plans in that direction." In October, Sir Peter was again putting pen to paper, this time in a letter to the Leeds Tory MP Sir Donald Kaberry: "I feel it worthwhile to emphasise that while we certainly have no desire, or indeed plans, to close the line at present we do have very real problems with investment." These "problems" included Ribblehead and other viaducts and tunnels which were in imminent need of major remedial work. Sir Peter hedged his bets even less in a letter to Ben Ford, the Labour MP forBradford North. "I would ask you to accept my assurances that we have no desire, or at this time plans, to close the Settle-Carlisle line," he wrote. One must assume that the BR chairman, then, was unaware of the plan contained in the August document, all but the last stage of which had by this time been put into effect. Indeed, in earlier correspondence with the Westmorland MP, Michael Jopling, Sir Peter had been at pains to stress that the issues of Ribblehead and the timetable changes were unconnected.

With BR now saying that no decision would be taken pending the findings of an independent consultant's report on Ribblehead, West Yorkshire County Council voiced concern at the increased burden the diversion of the Nottingham-Glasgow service would place on the Leeds and Bradford to Skipton link.

The damaging uncertainties continued into 1982 and in March, at a private briefing, MPs were told by BR officials at Preston that closure was planned but that this information was not for public release. The Yorkshire TUCC noted in its annual report: "Throughout the year the shadow of impending closure loomed over the Settle and Carlisle route, described by British Rail as 'the most spectacular main line in England'. By the beginning of October informed opinion was of the view that a Section 54 Notice giving prior warning of closure proposals would be

The end of the Nottingham-Glasgow expresses saw a marked change of status for the Settle-Carlisle. From May 1982, only two daily Leeds-Carlisle "local" trains ran, even though only two local stations along the route — Settle and Appleby — were open at the time. A Class 47 diesel, No. 47 433, looks almost lost in the Dentdale landscape with its five-coach train, crossing Arten Gill viaduct in October 1983, two months after BR's closure proposal was officially revealed.

published by January 1983; something which the London Midland region did not seek to deny to the committee at the time."

But in November 1982, the Tory MP for Skipton and Ripon, John Watson, claimed the British Railways Board had over-ruled the London Midland Region plans for imminent closure, possibly because of the likely political row. The London Midland general manager wrote in reply to letters from the TUCC: "There is no change in the situation regarding this line — we are still collating information." The TUCC noted that the line had probably been granted a stay of execution rather than a reprieve and commented that if BR wished to seek closure it "should have initiated closure proceedings prior to the re-routeing of the Nottingham-Glasgow service away from the line, thus absolving themselves of any charge of 'closure by stealth'".

Against a background of refusal to make simple improvements to the Leeds-Carlisle service — typified by the arrival in Leeds of the train from Carlisle two minutes after the departure of the King's Cross train with which it had connected comfortably in the previous year's timetable — BR maintained this "no decision" stance until August 1983 when the intention to publish a closure notice was announced.

This news did, if nothing else, mean that BR's cards were at last on the table and everyone knew what they were up against. BR's past insistence that re-routeing the Nottingham-Glasgow trains would not prejudice the future of the Settle-Carlisle line for which it said it had no closure plans, were described charitably by the Yorkshire TUCC as exhibiting a "lack of candour". Bob Cryer, ousted as Labour MP for Keighley in the 1983 "Falklands" General Election landslide, was rather blunter and blamed a Government-inspired "hush" policy which had kept BR's true intentions secret until after the election and the subsequent by-election in William Whitelaw's Penrith and Borders seat.

It is worth noting that, in the meantime, the old excuse of left and right hand synchronisation difficulties was still trotted out regularly by BR. When Mr Cryer described the missed connection at Leeds to Stan Abbott as "a deliberate attempt at sabotage", Peter Maynard at the London Midland's St Pancras press office replied: "If the Eastern Region have recast their InterCity 125 services I can't explain that from a London Midland point of view, because I don't write their timetables." He added: "We are not deliberately setting out to prevent people from making connections."

Between August and the commencement in November and Decem-

Putting the line up for closure did not prevent British Rail from continuing to use it for diversions, publicity stunts and steam specials. The official line was that BR was making the most of it while it was still there. Duchess of Hamilton makes the most of a Cumbrian Mountain Pullman working near Armathwaite in the Eden Valley.

ber of the closure procedure in accordance with the 1962 Transport Act, the financial basis of BR's case began to emerge. It was claimed closure would save an annual operating loss of £600,000 and £9.75m in maintenance over the next five years. Alan Whitehouse, writing for the *Yorkshire Post,* delved a little deeper into the figures. BR's projected 1983 running costs of £722,000 compared with an actual cost in 1982 of just £304,000. That staggering 137.5 per cent increase was made up as follows:

- Diesel fuel — up from £59,000 to £147,000 at a time when the true increase was under 12 per cent
- Short-term maintenance of locos — up from £37,000 to an astonishing £158,000
- Train crew costs — up from £11,000 to £27,000, whereas the national pay award was equivalent to just 4.5 per cent
- Maintenance — up from £48,000 to £153,000
- Depreciation — now £11,000 instead of £3,000, whereas the only actual change was the addition of two coaches to trains.

The cause of these inflated figures appeared to be the sudden allocation to the line's accounts of 2.5 locos and 14 coaches compared with 0.6 locos and 4.4 coaches in 1982. It seems that with the re-routeing of the Nottingham-Glasgow trains which only travelled over the line for a fairly small proportion of their total journey, BR was now able to attribute all the costs of the two loco-hauled daily trains to the Settle-Carlisle alone. It was also suggested that some maintenance work, such as the relining of Blea Moor tunnel, had been accelerated so as artificially to load maintenance costs on the line. Questioned as to the confusing nature of these figures, BR told Alan Whitehouse: "To discuss individual sets of figures would serve only to confuse the issue." The authors dismiss subsequent BR attempts to explain the sudden massive increase in costs by claiming one set of figures related to a half and the other to a full year.

Meanwhile the disincentives to travel continued: Paul Holden, then station master at Appleby and, since summer 1990, the Settle-Carlisle Line Manager, had to run his own campaign to extend the Super Saver fares available at stations on the West Coast route to those on the Settle-Carlisle. Who was going to travel from Appleby to London for £52 when they could go from Penrith, a few miles away on the main line, for just

£17? Receipts at the station, it need hardly be said, had already slumped alarmingly from the last week of the Nottingham-Glasgow through train compared with the first week of the new service.

So the steady process of attrition was now well under way — but in the meantime, the opposition had also been marshalling its resources. In June 1981, prompted by the uncertainty fuelled by the Nottingham-Glasgow diversion plans, the Friends of the Settle-Carlisle Line Association held its inaugural meeting at Settle town hall at the instigation of

Graham Nuttall and his dog Ruswarp at Garsdale Station in 1985

DalesRail enthusiast Graham Nuttall from Burnley. David Burton, a Rolls Royce aero-engine worker from Colne, was elected chairman. Mr Nuttall would later acquire some fame as the owner of the only dog to lodge an objection to the closure of the S & C. That privilege belonged to Ruswarp, a border collie cross named after a station on the line from Middlesbrough to Whitby. As there was nothing in the legislation to suggest that dogs were not allowed to object to the closure and, as Ruswarp was certainly a user of the threatened services, his objection was allowed to stand and he appeared in 1986 at the TUCC closure hearings when Mr Nuttall presented evidence on his behalf. Ruswarp would go on to acquire fame in more tragic circumstances in 1990 when he was found, weak with starvation, near the body of his master who had died on a winter walk in Wales. Ruswarp had apparently stayed by Mr Nuttall for nearly three months until he was found, too weak even to walk. His bravery and devotion were subsequently recognised by a Superdog award from the National Canine Defence League.

Although the Friends quickly built a substantial membership, there were grave doubts among more seasoned lobbyists as to the association's ability to mount the sort of informed political campaign necessary to counter British Rail's advantage. Images of a meeting of the Bradford Railway Circle early in 1983 spring vividly to mind for Stan Abbott who had gone there to interview Mr Burton for the *New Statesman*. A group of wide-eyed railway buffs sat huddled in a draughty church hall and gazed lovingly at a nostalgic slide show of mighty steam engines plying the Settle and Carlisle. At the back of the hall Mr Burton set up a trestle table from which he sold items of railway memorabilia: the message that seemed to come across was "let's hope they don't close the line or we won't be able to take pictures of steam-hauled excursions at Ribblehead".

A few months and one closure announcement later, the Friends, with about £1,000 in the bank, were thrust to the forefront of the fight to save the line — could they handle it? In March that year the Railway Development Society — the national rail pressure group — had launched its own campaign at a meeting in Leeds. The society's North West chairman, Richard Watts, had been in close touch with the Friends but was concerned that the association was ill-prepared for the imminent announcement of closure proceedings.

"I had tried several times to gear up the Friends as an effective body," said Mr Watts, a history teacher from Preston. "It was pretty obvious we had to get them into a campaigning frame of mind — to make them a little more politically aware." To that end he had produced for the Friends a leaflet setting out the events which suggested BR was engaged in "closure by stealth", and this had become the association's principal campaign document. But the leaflet failed to catalyse any independent action by the Friends — attempts to politicise the association seemed doomed.

At the same time, Richard Watts was in contact with John Whitelegg and Peter Horton at Lancaster, who ran Cumbria and North Lancashire Transport 2000 as a vigorous campaigning group. An exploratory meeting of representatives of all three bodies revealed a wide divergence between the way the RDS and Transport 2000 saw the Settle-Carlisle campaign developing and what the Friends were prepared to do. "It was obvious it was necessary to have a new body that had the appearance of uniformity," said Richard. And so out of that was born the tri-partite Settle-Carlisle Joint Action Committee, an at times uneasy alliance between the Friends, who had strength in numbers, and the RDS and Transport 2000 who had campaigning and political experience.

With Dr Whitelegg in the chair, the new alliance quickly adopted a high profile campaign. It accused Transport Secretary Nicholas Ridley of misleading the Commons over the Settle-Carlisle closure plans so as to protect the Under-Secretary David Mitchell and avoid further embarrassment over the discredited Serpell report; it called for a full Public Inquiry into the closure rather than the limited format of TUCC hearings; it prodded and probed at the BR hierarchy teasing out the odd leak here, the odd half-truth there. Trains and homes throughout the North were subjected to a leaflet blitz. It all added up to a style which did not come naturally to the then Friends' leadership — but if the new alliance needed them, then equally the Friends needed that alliance too, or face eclipse in the public eye.

At first the members of the Joint Action Committee met only briefly at the various public meetings held along the length of the line. "That was obviously very unsatisfactory," said Richard. "It was obvious that more and more of the work was apparently being done by John and Peter and we began to wonder what the Friends were up to." The salvation of the alliance proved to be the formation of a limited company, master-minded by Peter Horton, which formalised the relationship between the three independent groups in August 1984. John Whitelegg became company chairman, the tireless Peter Horton its secretary. The other board members were Richard Watts and — from the Friends — Philippa Simpson and Brian Sutcliffe, their new chairman. The committee opened an office in Lancaster and set out on a major fund-raising initiative, primed by a £2,500 grant from the Rail Union Federation. At the suggestion of Des Wilson — the Freedom of Information campaigner who addressed a meeting at Settle town hall — the campaign base was widened to include all the other interest groups involved in the Settle-Carlisle fight. This broad base was formalised at the committee's December 1985 annual meeting when some 18 groups, ranging from chambers of trade to the Youth Hostels Association acquired the right to board membership.

Peter Horton went on, through the board of Transport 2000, to establish the national Standing Conference on Rail Closures — the first body with the aim of co-ordinating opposition to rail closure plans nationwide.

The anti-closure bandwagon was attracting support from an increasingly wide range of people from landed gentry to Labour — the Shadow Transport Secretary, Gwynneth Dunwoody, presented a lengthy protest petition to the Government and the party's deputy leader, Roy Hattersley, pinned Labour's colours to the campaign mast when he travelled on the National Union of Railwaymen's "special" over the line in February 1984. The action committee claimed to be able to reach the parts their peers couldn't, with senior civil servants telephoning the committee to check discrepancies between its claims and those of BR. "They are coming to us because we have demonstrated there is more to this closure proposal than the Minister is aware of," said Dr Whitelegg in the summer of 1984, adding: "It's very rare that a dialogue has opened up between central Government and a group of 'unwashed scruffy campaigners'."

But for all the self-denigration, Dr Whitelegg was able to draw upon a not inconsiderable professional and academic experience in transport and the workings of Government which enabled him to represent the Settle-Carlisle case on an equal footing with BR and the Department of Transport. Graduating from the University of Wales at Aberystwyth in 1970, he completed a research project on industry in the Potteries to gain his PhD. From 1973-76 he directed a Department of Transport-funded project at Cardiff into the movement of heavy freight, thereby gaining an insight into the workings of the department on his weekly visits to the Marsham Street headquarters. The purpose of the research was to predict demand for the transport by road and rail of iron, steel and coal. One of the principal findings was that political decisions on the location of industries had exacerbated transport problems. "It was typical Government-funded research," said Dr Whitelegg. "We made all sorts of recommendations and nothing was done with the information."

He then worked for 18 months as Transport and Development Officer for the Western Isles Council on Benbecula in the Outer Hebrides,

CAMPAIGNERS: On board the NUR train over the S & C are, from left, Peter Horton, John Whitelegg, Roy Hattersley and Jimmy Knapp.

before taking a lectureship in Lancaster University's geography department. Dr Whitelegg saw the action committee's independence as vital in enabling it to present a "more aggressive" case against closure at the TUCC hearings than, say, local authorities which might find themselves constrained by political protocol.

He was to leave his prominent role in the S & C campaign, more than a year before its successful outcome, to work in West Germany on the kind of transport planning programme which remains an almost wholly alien concept in a Britain governed by "short-termism" and the whims of the market. He was succeeded in the Joint Action Committee chair by Peter Horton, having played a key role throughout the early campaign posturing and the lengthy programme of TUCC hearings.

Returning to 1983: the local authorities were also far from idle. Once a closure proposal appeared to be on the cards, a joint steering committee of officers and members of West Yorkshire, Cumbria and Lancashire county councils was established. This led, upon British Rail's formal announcement, to the commissioning of the £34,000 PEIDA report which was to become the first substantial independent assessment of the line's structures and potential and, as such, a cornerstone of the case against closure in the first round of the battle that culminated with the TUCC hearings and the ensuing months of "phoney war". The commissioning of the PEIDA report typified a remarkable degree of co-operation between authorities of differing sizes, interests and political complexions. While the Steering Committee comprised two members each from West Yorkshire, Cumbria and Lancashire, financial contributions also came from Bradford, Calderdale, Carlisle, Craven, Eden, Leeds, Pendle, and Richmondshire districts; Settle town council; the Countryside Commission, the English Tourist Board, the Yorkshire Dales National Park Authority and British Rail. The last named may sound curious, but those who rode on the *Cumbrian Mountain Express* Press special (which ran on December 17, 1983, to mark the commissioning of the PEIDA Report) will remember the apparent confidence of BR's man Ron Cotton (whose astonishing part in the S & C affair is described in detail later) that the report would substantiate its claims about the line's financial position. "We are convinced of the facts of the case from a business point of view," he said.

The only significant absentee from that local authority line-up was North Yorkshire County Council which was afflicted by an apparently historic antipathy towards rail, as opposed to road, transport and which seemed at times to regard the Craven district traversed by the S&C as some sort of Siberian fastness beyond the Pennines and, therefore, light years away from the county's main north-south axis in the Vale of York.

Back on the Cumbrian Mountain Express in December 1983, the British Rail line for the Press was pretty unambiguous. This is how BR's Manchester-based PR man, John Searson, put it in an interview with Stan Abbott: "The huge disparity between revenue, no matter how well extended to cover all the markets we think might exist, and the very high outlay to maintain the bridges and tunnels is so great that whilst the study may shorten the gap a bit, it will never shorten it to such an extent that the viability of the line can measurably improve." He went on: "As we see it, the line has not got a cat in hell's chance of ever achieving viability." So how did BR intend to cope when engineering requirements, or unavoidable accidents such as fallen power lines, forced the diversion of traffic away from the West Coast Main Line. The only logical alternative route between Preston and Carlisle was via Blackburn, Hellifield and the Settle-Carlisle, as the only (partial) alternative

Pictured in front of the Cumbrian Mountain Express at Garsdale in December 1983 are, from left: West Yorkshire Council leader, John Gunnell, the enigmatic Ron Cotton of BR, Eric Martlew, chairman of Cumbria County Council, and Donald MacKay, of PEIDA.

— the Cumbrian coast line — would need massive investment to enable the passage of InterCity trains through stations and bridges which had been built to a narrower loading gauge. "Better management of mishaps" was the curious solution offered by Mr Searson. In time it was to emerge that this would mean disembarking large numbers of passengers at Preston or Carlisle and transferring them to fleets of waiting buses.

Indeed, the wisdom of Mr Searson's remark was soon called into question by a succession of diversions over the line, most notably in June 1984 when it was used on at least four separate occasions because of track and overhead wire failures on the West Coast route. Since then, the line has seen regular use as a diversionary route and on more than one occasion this was for the so-called "last time".

Meanwhile, Ron Cotton was about to get his teeth into a job which combined a misleading title with a very wide-ranging — and pioneering — brief. As Project Manager for the Settle-Carlisle Line, Mr Cotton was to be in charge of shutting it down. But he would also be responsible, in the meantime, for marketing the doomed route in such a way as to maximise BR's revenue from its vanishing asset (or liability). This aspect of the brief, it was to emerge very much later, was incorporated at Ron Cotton's own insistence and it was to prove the key to unlocking the rich, untapped potential of the Settle-Carlisle.

In his first few weeks in the job, Mr Cotton embarked on the marketing side with some enthusiasm and the summer of 1984 would see the scheduling of an additional train on the line to cope with increased demand. But, as suggested at the opening of the chapter, the closure side of his brief was running into trouble almost from the outset. In January 1984 a letter from Roger Smith, vice-chairman of the Greater Manchester Transport Action Group, prompted the Yorkshire TUCC to look closely at the detail of Section 56 of the Transport Act under which the closure procedure was being carried out. What it found was to have wide repercussions not only for British Rail plans to close the Settle-Carlisle but for other closure proceedings in hand. The TUCC found a major discrepancy between the British Rail notice of closure published under Clause Seven of Section 56 of the Act and the grounds for objection as set out in Clause Eight. Although the format of the closure notice was the same as that which had been in use for 20 years, it seems nobody had noticed that, whereas the BR notice stated that "any users of the rail service it is proposed to discontinue" could lodge an objection, the text in the Act actually said "any user of any service affected" was entitled to do so. The committee immediately drew BR's attention to the discrepancy — the initial response was an insistence from BR that the only valid objectors to closure were those who travelled over the section of line it was proposed to close. Under the possible threat of legal action from the Joint Action Committee, BR gave way and in April announced that the Settle-Carlisle closure notices would be reissued, along with those relating to a simultaneous proposed closure on Humberside — the line from Goole to Gilberdyke. As BR stated, indeed understated, this was to "broaden the scope for making objections".

The effects of this climb-down by BR were twofold: in the first instance it settled the row which had been brewing over the question of people who, as users of DalesRail charter services, had lodged their objections to the Settle-Carlisle closure even though the BR notice limited the scope for objection to those who travelled on regular BR services to and from Settle and Appleby. Secondly, it cleared the way for a whole new field of objections from DalesRail passengers using the reopened stations on both the Settle-Carlisle and the Blackburn-Hellifield link. On May 17 the notices were reissued and the closure procedure was started again from scratch, with the result that — during the six weeks allowed for objections — the number received by the Yorkshire TUCC alone rose by 5,931 to 7,467.

To paraphrase Oscar Wilde, to mess up one set of closure notices might be regarded as unfortunate, but to do it twice surely smacked of carelessness... or intent. One Sunday early in August 1984, Stan Abbott received a tip-off that BR, fearing a red light further down the legal track, was about to reissue its Section 56 notices yet again. This if-at-first-you-don't-succeed approach to railway closure seemed hard to believe and demanded disturbing Ron Cotton at home: the tip-off proved well founded. BR had overlooked the fact that the line strayed briefly, near its summit at Aisgill, into the Richmondshire district of North Yorkshire which fell within the area of the North-East TUCC rather than that of the Yorkshire TUCC. Mr Cotton said: "We decided to readvertise in the North-East to make sure there is absolutely no cause for criticism and to block all possible loopholes. And, putting a brave face on things, he added: "I don't think it puts us back at all — the only fact as I see it is it gives six more weeks for people to get objections in."

The new setback attracted inevitable ridicule and disbelief. When Stan Abbott told James Briggs, the North-East Area TUCC chairman, about this new development, he refused to believe it until he had phoned Ron Cotton for himself. Mr Briggs said the question had already been discussed and the need for reference to his committee had been discounted because there were no stations on the stretch of line in question. On having the truth confirmed, he said: "It's amazing to me if BR have given way on this as they have already given way on one issue." His opposite number in Yorkshire, James Towler, was less incredulous: "It's really quite extraordinary and bizarre, but I have been about sufficiently long not to be surprised or astonished at anything involving BR." The Joint Action Committee immediately planned to make the most of the extension by means of a leaflet blitz throughout the North-East and Dr Whitelegg said: "It's absolutely astounding — it proves the whole thing has been messed up from the word go." And he observed: "I think BR are basically incompetent and I think with more time and resources they could have been tripped up on practically any railway closure."

Although the BR notice, published in Darlington newspapers, invited objections to be sent only to the North-East TUCC, some 7,430 were sent to the Yorkshire TUCC over the next six weeks, compared with just 69 to the North-East TUCC. The Yorkshire committee found itself obliged to remind BR that objections could, under the Act, be lodged with any of the three TUCCs and advised BR that its view on the validity or otherwise of objections was irrelevant and "could be mistaken as an attempt to interfere" in the committee's business.

This most high profile of proposed railway closures had the effect of exposing the application of the 1962 Act to a degree of legal and other scrutiny hitherto unknown and there emerged other apparent discrepancies between BR practice and the requirements of the Act. One of these concerned West Coast main line trains which had been timetabled to use the Settle-Carlisle when engineering work was taking place and for which BR was accustomed to publish special timetables. BR had failed, as the Act the required, to advertise the alternative service for passengers whose trains would hitherto have been diverted for this reason over the Settle-Carlisle. Indeed BR had already ceased to use the Settle-Carlisle for diverted services except in "emergencies" earlier in 1984, prompting the Yorkshire TUCC to note that it was "most irregular" to withdraw a service in this way in the course of closure proceedings. The "alternative service" which BR should, arguably, have advertised was a bus link between Preston and Lancaster, for example, or — in the case of Anglo-Scottish traffic — rail diversion via the East Coast route on the other side of the country.

But the legal diversions certainly helped push the Settle-Carlisle issue further into the public eye, and among national lobbies to join the protest were Friends of the Earth, who made Appleby station a call on their cycle ride from Land's End to John O'Groats, and the Ramblers Association which held a rally at Settle, led by its president at the time, the singer-comedian and Dales resident, Mike Harding.

Another legal question concerned the more general point that, in three attempts, BR had failed to publish one comprehensive closure notice which complied in all respects with the requirements of the 1962 Act. Such arguments would, no doubt, have been aired had the whole conduct of the closure proceedings been sent for judicial review — as would surely have been the case had the decision on the line's fate gone the other way. But by the time the TUCCs had deliberated not once, but twice, on the closure question and months had passed in the pursuit of multi-partite rescue packages, such preliminary squabbles had begun to lose their significance. They were just additional symptoms of the inappropriateness of the legislation, now in its third decade, to deal adequately with the proposed closure of a major trunk railway in the 1980s.

4.

Wanton neglect: the Ribblehead bogey laid bare

IN OCTOBER 1989, the truth was finally out after a decade during which the great viaduct at Ribblehead had enjoyed an undeserved role as the anti-hero in the unfolding Settle-Carlisle saga. Ribblehead Viaduct: the doctors had pronounced a terminal condition on the basis of superficial examination. Now, at last, exploratory surgery had given the lie to this sloppy diagnosis.

It was during an earlier trial repair to one of the viaduct's 24 arches — scheduled as part of the Government's fan dance to attract a private buyer for the line — that it had been declared that the viaduct's condition was not so awful after all. Contractors had discovered mysterious square holes in the original bitumen waterproof decking of the structure which had for years being allowing water to cascade into the great limestone piers, leaching out the mortar and adding to the viaduct's waterlogged condition, in which the play of frost could take its toll. Blocking the holes would end this cascade at a stroke.

Now, in the spring of 1989, with the S & C finally plucked from the jaws of closure, Ribblehead viaduct again had a long-term role to play and must be given a clean bill of health. At last it was time to follow up the the exploratory surgery with a full diagnosis and remedial action. And so, October of that year saw British Rail engineers granted the kind of extended period of track possession which had for so long been denied them during the S & C's twilight years as a freight route: years during which engineers had attempted to tackle Ribblehead's malaise with a sticking-plaster approach to its undersides, while what was really needed was tourniquet to staunch the flow through great holes in its superstructure.

The two-week possession saw the first concerted onslaught on the line's shameful backlog of maintenance: the "wanton neglect" uncovered by the consultants, PEIDA, appointed by the local authorities in 1983 to carry out an independent assessment of the line's condition and prospects.

The remaining single track over the viaduct (the singling operation had been carried out in 1985 to reduce the outward forces on the viaduct's spandrel walls) was lifted and the ancient compacted ballast removed for the first time in more than a century. Revealed in all their glory were six-inch square holes in the decking at regular intervals along the viaduct's length. Comparison with plans and early photographs of the viaduct under construction led to the inevitable conclusion: Ribblehead's decline had been largely thanks to shoddy working practices by the self-same contractors who helped make the S & C the archetypal built-to-last Midland Railway. For it seems the contractors, perhaps pressed for time, had laid the bitumen decking around the wooden scaffold poles and then sawn off the protruding stumps. In time, the wood had rotted, leaving free access for water into the viaduct itself. With the emergence of this, the most likely, explanation for the holes, another more fanciful theory was laid to rest — that the holes had been cut during the last war to make the viaduct more easy to demolish in the event of a German invasion. The theory was that landmines could have been inserted in the holes and detonated from a safe distance.

The shoddy worksmanship hypothesis was put forward by BR engineers when they opened the doors to the Press as the £600,000 two-week October repair programme swung into action on the line.

Their main task was £400,000 worth of work to renew the waterproof membrane and decking on the viaduct after more than a century of being subjected to the elements at perhaps the wettest and windiest gap in all the Pennines. The re-decking operation began with the lifting of the track by permanent way staff ready for the two-day ballast-shifting operation to start on Sunday, October 15. Sub-contractors used six excavators to dig out the old clogged ballast and tip it over the side of the viaduct more than 80ft above ground. With that operation well underway and exposing more of the pierheads, resident engineer Tony Freschini explained how the percolating water washed the mortar from between the viaduct's huge limestone blocks, leaving them prone to cracking because of the uneven stresses upon them.

The S & C is generally dubbed the last great navvy-built line, although those who originally worked on the construction of Ribblehead viaduct did have the use of some machinery, including steam cranes and hoists. One thing that hasn't changed, however, is the Pennine weather which helped push the original cost of building the line up from £2.2m to £3.5m.

Work begins on repairing Ribblehead Viaduct after the reprieve. Thousands of tonnes of old ballast were removed by mechanical digger and thrown over the parapet wall. Inset — the viaduct's decking exposed. In the foreground are Stan Abbott and daughter, Hannah.

RIBBLEHEAD BY NIGHT: Almost as soon as the line was reprieved, serious remedial work began on Ribblehead Viaduct, with a two-week closure to give the engineers a free run. This dramatic picture shows work going on round the clock.

4. WANTON NEGLECT: THE RIBBLEHEAD BOGEY LAID BARE

The relatively balmy conditions prevailing during the Press visit were replaced on the first night by driving wind and rain. Yet it was a remarkable credit to the round-the-clock operation that by Thursday October 26 only half a day's work had been lost to the weather and the operation remained on schedule for the line's reöpening the following Monday.

With the ballast removed, the works team — under BR's Manchester Construction Manager, and drawing on labour from throughout the north-west of England — set about strengthening the walls of the viaduct in three-arch sections by pouring concrete into wooden shuttering at the foot of the parapets.

The new waterproof membrane was constructed on the ground beneath the viaduct in 15-metre lengths, protected above and below by synthetic Terrafix matting, and lifted on to the deck using a 120ft tall

For all the world like carpet underlay, the Terrafix matting awaits installation

crane on permanent standby throughout the operation. Some 2,500 tonnes of new ballast provided the bed for the relaid track.

Mr Freschini likened the whole operation to the re-roofing of a house — there's not much point in replastering the bedroom walls while water is pouring in through the roof. Now, with Ribblehead's "roof" repaired, the way was at last clear for other work to begin in 1990, including repairs to the brick-lined arches and the pressure grouting of the piers. That was expected to cost close to £2m, of which English Heritage had pledged £1m and local authorities £500,000.

The total sum remains well short of the £4.5m price for a replacement viaduct in 1981, or the near £7m, cited by BR in 1983, since when inflation would have pushed the price up to beyond £12m.

So, the wheel had turned full circle for Ribblehead Viaduct: at the time of writing, there were even suggestions that it might be restored to double-track working. But the condition of the viaduct has played such a central role in the whole Settle-Carlisle saga that it is worth looking in more detail at how it came to be in the condition it did — a condition symptomatic of that of the line in general — and how the greatly exaggerated rumours of its death came to gain currency.

The true scale of the S & C's engineering problems was spelt out on July 26, 1984, when Professor Donald MacKay told a press conference at County Hall, Kendal, the findings of his Edinburgh-based firm's six-month survey of the route. Prof MacKay was the leading light in the Edinburgh consultancy, PEIDA. The consultants' "track record" included an assessment for the Highlands and Islands Development Board of the remote Inverness to Kyle of Lochalsh line which was threatened with closure in the 1970s.

"At that time the Kyle line was in the same situation that this line is in now," Prof MacKay had told Stan Abbott seven months previously. "Our study suggested that the economics were a good deal more favourable and the usage much higher than BR's figures." PEIDA found the figures had omitted key elements such as journeys by people on "Rover-style" and other special tickets. The line was subsequently reprieved and investment made in it, including the provision of radio signalling.

But anyone who thought PEIDA would simply pour a bucket of liberal economic whitewash over the Settle-Carlisle to come up with the answers the counties wanted to hear would have realised with only a little research that this was unlikely to prove to be the case. Donald MacKay — professorial fellow at Heriot-Watt University — was well known to readers of the quality daily, *The Scotsman*, for his regular column on economics. You don't need to know your Keynes from your Friedman to recognise the writings of a committed monetarist. Prof MacKay defined his personal views on the subject thus: "I believe in an efficient, cost-effective method of public transport." And John Gunnell, the leader of West Yorkshire County Council, summarised exactly what his own authority and Cumbria were after: "We want a decision to be taken on the basis of fact rather than sentiment."

County Councillor Gunnell got the facts he wanted that day — but Prof MacKay's words at the Kendal press conference laid bare British Rail's culpability in acquiescing in the decline of the S & C to the point where major investment was needed on a number of different fronts. PEIDA agreed with BR that retention of the Settle-Carlisle would involve continued operating losses and substantial capital expenditure. But the fact that the required expenditure was as high as it was, was due in considerable part to British Rail's own policy: BR was guilty of "wanton neglect" of the Settle-Carlisle line, PEIDA charged.

"British Rail has simply not carried out the level of work necessary to keep the capital structure in good order and that imposes substantial future costs that would have been avoided if BR had acted sensibly," said Prof MacKay. Indeed, maintenance on the line since 1980 had been minimal and BR had allowed repairs to mount so that about £17.5m. would have to be spent simply to retain a single-track railway, said the professor. "The major contributory factor to the deficit has been the financial policy followed by British Rail itself — in effect, BR determined to close this line some years ago and has proceeded on the basis that it would close. And so BR's policy has been to carry out on the line only the most minimum work necessary for safety purposes — it has not carried out good husbandry."

British Rail's Settle-Carlisle Project Manager Ron Cotton rejected the "wanton neglect" allegation, but said: "Like any other business organisation we have not been investing in an area where there is some indecision as to the future." To have acted otherwise would have been "reprehensible" in the circumstances, he said.

The wanton neglect of the S & C 's structures, uncovered by PEIDA, was paralleled in observation by others of the rolling stock allocated to the line after BR downgraded it to a secondary route. Then, it quickly became apparent that the two sets of four coaches assigned to the line represented probably the worst that BR could find. Springs poked through dusty, unwashed upholstery. The toilets were almost always filthy and rarely seemed to work and the carriage windows were habitually covered by that adhesive brown-grey dust that railways are able to produce in large quantities — and this for a ride over the country's most scenic route!

The locomotives, too, gave the impression that they had been hand picked for their run-down condition and the line in 1982 and 1983 saw many superannuated types normally confined almost entirely to freight working. Enthusiasts may have warmed to such as classes 24 and 25, but they were grossly underpowered for a line like the S & C.

The line hit rock bottom, however, one December morning in 1983,

More diversions: A Class 47, No. 47 552 (above) runs into Dent Station with the diverted Liverpool-Edinburgh working in March 1984, while a Class 37 makes a rare appearance over the line with a train of empty coaches. These trains of plush, air conditioned Mark III coaches contrasted sharply with the run-down sets of dirty, uncared for Mk I coaches being used on the Leeds-Carlisle local trains at the time.

with the closure notice issued and an air of resignation hanging over BR employees. At Leeds, staff were attempting to couple two sets of two coaches, but the Mk I coaches were so worn out that the couplers could not be made to work. Eventually, they simply gave up and the Leeds-Carlisle and return ran as a paltry two-coach train.

While the PEIDA report clearly did not show BR in a particularly good light, it did in many ways support the general BR thesis, namely that the line was unlikely to generate an operating profit. In doing so it took as read the BR case that the Settle-Carlisle was surplus to main line network requirements and rejected any case for upgrading it to take High Speed Trains. It conceded that a "tourist operated" line might make a profit "but this must be subject to some doubt and any profit would be very small relative to the capital and maintenance costs of the central section".

But leaving aside the question of the backlog of maintenance, PEIDA found that — even back in those days before the advent of the Dalesman service — the Settle-Carlisle's performance was not substantially different to that of other lines in the Provincial Sector. By eliminating waste as exemplified by the train costs quoted in Chapter Three (PEIDA found productive train time at 18 per cent was only half the normal level) it was reckoned the annual operating deficit could be brought down to about £205,000.

So Prof MacKay was able to say: "The problems are not different in principle or practice from the problems affecting other lines in the UK. The line — properly maintained and marketed — is no better or worse than other provincial lines." Logically then, he continued: "If Settle-Carlisle goes it certainly follows on our analysis that other provincial lines will follow — and quite a number of them." This would run against the practice of successive governments which had been to retain such lines because of the wider benefits they brought which were not apparent in the simple financial returns. There could be no justification, he said, for "picking off lines piecemeal".

The extent of the line's engineering problems was considered in a survey for PEIDA by the Leeds-based civil engineers, W A Fairhurst and Partners. Their report commented: "The structures on the railway line, having been completed in 1875, should by modern standards be nearing the end of their designed life of 120 years. Despite the remoteness of the route, its altitude and exposure to the ravages of winter weather, the structures have stood the test of time remarkably well and remain in fairly good condition throughout."

But, the report continued: "Inspection demonstrates that many of the structures, particularly the viaducts, are now showing the effects of inadequate maintenance and the failure to carry out timely repairs as a result of insufficient investment funds being made available. Deterioration is much more severe where limestone has been used as the predominant construction material than where sandstone or millstone grit has been used."

The most serious cause of deterioration found by Fairhurst's was water, particularly where it had gained access to viaducts through failure of the waterproof membranes below deck level, as exemplified in 1989 when the ballast was eventually lifted at Ribblehead. Yet, astonishingly, the engineers added: "The problem has been recognised by BR since the late 1940s but finance has not been provided to replace the waterproofing."

Deterioration had accelerated and, with a parallel further slowing of maintenance through insufficient funding, a point had been reached where the report predicted "failure to keep pace with maintenance could well result in some structures having to be replaced".

In all, of the estimated £9,928,000 needed to give the line another 20 years' life, some £5,390,000 would go on repairs to viaducts excluding Ribblehead, repairs to which were costed at £2.1m — a figure remarkably close to the sum eventually spent.

If Ribblehead Viaduct were to be replaced the bill would rise to £12,278,000. The major problem on the track itself was the condition of many of the wooden sleepers — on one stretch rotting sleepers had allowed the track gauge to widen by $^{3}/_{16}$". But singling the track would allow maximum use to be made of the best remaining stretches while avoiding some of the worst parts. Including the installation of radio signalling, this singling scheme would cost £5,474,000.

The figures showed that Ribblehead Viaduct was only one, admittedly significant, element in a large repair bill. It must also be remembered that Ribblehead was in many ways unique, combining limestone construction with exposure to one of the harshest climates in England at a point where winds are funnelled at great speed through the Pennines and the effect of freeze-thaw action on the masonry is considerable.

W A Fairhurst and Partners compiled their report on the basis of physical inspections of the viaduct after which they then checked their own observations against BR records which gave the exact dates on which particular defects were seen to appear. The company summarised its main findings as follows. The technical terms used are explained in the diagram.

- Disintegration of the limestone blocks, this being worst at the pier corners.
- Separation of the spandrel walls from the arch rings which also allows water to penetrate the piers and arches.
- Cracking of the arch rings beneath the internal dwarf walls which carry the track ballast (most of the outer arch rings had already been relined at the time of inspection).
- Leaning and misalignment of the parapet walls.

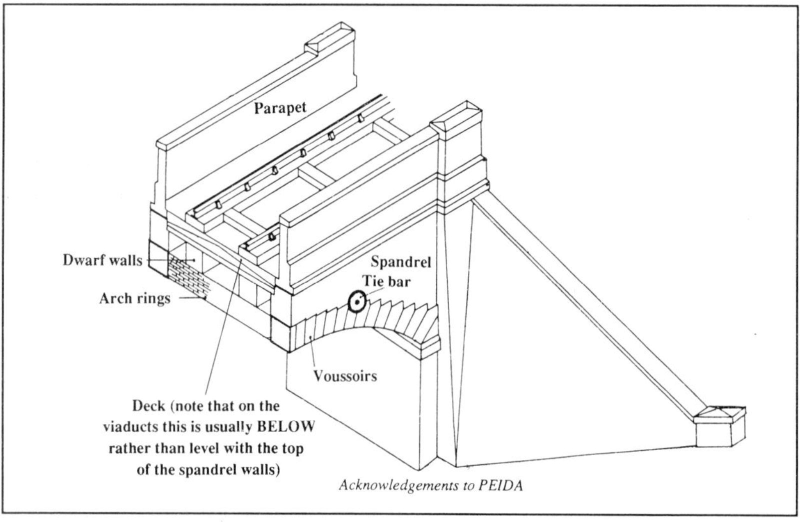

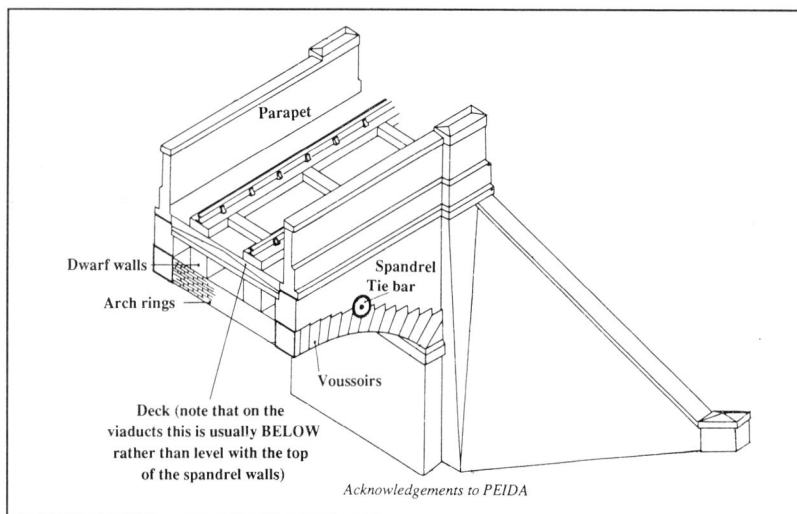

Acknowledgements to PEIDA

The Fairhurst survey suggested the viaduct's deterioration was accelerating to such an extent that in five years' time repair might no longer be a viable option. The company suggested that to secure the life of the viaduct for 15 years would demand an immediate £2.1m. two-year programme followed by another £0.44m. worth of work over the next 13 years. At that point, it predicted, repairs would again begin to mount significantly — in years 16 to 20 they could be expected to total about the same as for the previous 15 years (all 1984 prices). That the viaduct did not, apparently, see further significant deterioration in the ensuing five and a half years before its re-decking can be attributed in part to a string of relatively mild winters. The feeling now is that Ribblehead Viaduct can look forward to decades more useful life.

But how had the viaduct actually reached that sorry state? The following account is compiled from internal British Rail sources (some of whom can not be named) and interviews with former BR employees.

Although Mike Carruthers of Fairhurst's suggested the problem of water penetration had been identified as early as 1934, Ribblehead did not start causing BR major problems until the 1950s and '60s when it was noticed several pier ends were cracking. At that stage the problems were still manageable if increasingly expensive. But then BR succeeded in complicating the issue by making a somewhat open-ended promise to the Department of Transport that once the West Coast Main Line was electrified the Settle-Carlisle could probably close. This was far from the case: if anything traffic over the route increased after electrification as — because there were no catch points on the main line — all the old-style, non-continuously braked freight traffic had to travel via the Settle-Carlisle.

But maintenance had already been cut back because of what had been said to the Department of Transport and when it was proposed in the late '60s the viaduct should be re-waterproofed the scheme was dropped because of lack of finance and paranoia lest the DTp's "spies" should find out. But major repairs were becoming increasingly urgent and, as bricks began falling from beneath the arches, it was decided to reline some of them. This necessitated single line working and because there were no cross-over points between Horton and Blea Moor it meant single-line working for some six miles. To have installed a new set of points at Ribblehead would have meant resignalling Blea Moor. The budget resources were not available to do this without the BR Board being made aware, a prospect which was considered undesirable as the work would be construed by the DTp as "investment".

But the traffic was simply too great to contemplate doing the work in summer. And so repairs were carried out in winter when the extreme weather — which can be evil at Ribblehead even in summer — cut productivity by something like 50 per cent. BR's spending of £100,000 a year on Ribblehead maintenance between 1974 and 1984 should be seen in this context. After about £250,000 had been spent relining arches it began to be appreciated the extent to which this was really only attacking an effect rather than the cause of Ribblehead's problems. It was rather like painting an old car without first removing the rust. And so the London-Midland's bridges and structures engineer, Frank Leeming, concluded that the solution lay in building a new viaduct to replace an unknown quantity of annual repairs with a known quantity of interest (notional) on the capital cost. That was not a decision taken lightly: it should be seen first of all in the context of an engineering climate in which repairing structures was becoming more expensive due to higher labour costs, while the price of new structures was falling due to lower manufacturing costs. Building bridges was something engineers knew all about, but repairing them often involved dealing with unknowns. Ribblehead epitomised the problem.

Meanwhile, it must be remembered that no-one was proposing the closure of the Settle-Carlisle at this time — as far as Mr Leeming was concerned he was recommending action to ensure the continued running of a railway with an indefinite life to take 25-ton axle-load freight trains at 70 mph and passenger trains at 90 mph. A variety of options for Ribblehead were considered and approaches were made to a number of major contractors for their ideas for repairing the viaduct. It became clear that none of them were keen to tackle the work as specified because they submitted high estimates with no guarantees as to the effectiveness or otherwise of the remedial work. At the root of the problem was the fact that no-one knew for certain the exact mechanism of failure of the viaduct beyond the obvious fact that water penetration was playing a major role. Other options were considered — casing the entire structure in concrete was dismissed as unsightly and too costly, while BR's Derby research laboratories concluded that replacing the viaduct with an embankment could result in trains blowing off the track (a conclusion the Midland Railway engineers had come to more than 100 years previously). In short, everything pointed towards Mr Leeming's rebuild option at a cost of £4.5m.

Mr Leeming himself (by this time retired, in line with BR policy to do away with specialist bridge engineers) recalled in 1985: "We were looking towards a continuing railway — my job was to inform my management what the situation was for a continuing railway and we decided reconstruction was the most economic in the long term. We tried all sorts of schemes but the soundest was to replace it — when you start tarting up old structures you don't know what you are getting.

"We knew what the problem was but nobody will ever believe the professional," said Mr Leeming. "It was age — I am still of the opinion that if you want the line there for another hundred years the scheme put

"When you start tarting up old structures you don't know what you are getting..."

forward by the railways originally is the one to follow. I don't believe there are any techniques for repair work for that particular structure which are valid. It's an open-ended contract as to the amount of money you will pour into that viaduct because you don't know what you are tackling."

Now, with the viaduct given what is reckoned to be a more or less indefinite new lease of life, time will be the ultimate judge of the wisdom of Mr Leeming's claims — and of the Fairhurst prediction that repair costs would begin again to mount after 15 years.

But, at the time, building a new viaduct had other attractions: "One of the main considerations is to interrupt traffic as little as possible — we could simply build a new viaduct alongside the old one and the original structure could stay if it wants." Of course, quite what the Yorkshire Dales National Park Authority would have had to say about a — presumably — pre-stressed concrete viaduct across Ribblehead is another question.

This internal London Midland debate was going on at a time when the Government was just beginning to turn the screw on BR spending. But what really threw the cat among the pigeons, as Mr Leeming put it, was the public revelation of it all in an exclusive in the magazine, *Steam World*, in April 1981. The subject was the question as to whether BR should undertake a major investment in building a new viaduct, a decision which could only be taken at British Railways Board level. It was a subject the Board was presumably not even aware of — until members read about it in *Steam World*. But the article not only set out exactly the options drawn up by the then Divisional Civil Engineer, Alan King — it also included artist's impressions from Mr Leeming's bridge office at Euston of three alternative designs for a new viaduct. *Steam World* commented: "This is a subject on which BR officials will say nothing at the moment, but it is reasonable to assume that refusal of funds for the new Ribblehead Viaduct will result in the closure of the Settle & Carlisle as a through route."

The *Steam World* scoop appeared to represent a leak of exceptional proportions, yet from the fact that Mr King was later elevated to Assistant Regional Civil Engineer for London Midland Region it can only be assumed that any part he may have played in it was not considered reprehensible. It can be surmised that the immediate effect of the leak, once the shock had worn off, would be to leave the BR Board quite gleeful: here was a ready-made pretext on which to lose 72 remote route-miles at a stroke and nobody would be greatly upset. The latter assumption — and it certainly was a widely held one within BR — was of course to prove very wide of the mark.

The track mileage problem was also very much a London Midland one — while other regions had been carrying out a steady rationalisation programme, the London Midland seemed to be plagued by problems which prevented easy solutions to complex track patterns. At a time when most of its resources were going into the West Coast electrification programme, the region had still not come to grips with its excess track mileage. Closing the Settle-Carlisle could be an easy alternative to a more considered process of rationalisation. By contrast, other regions had gone a long way towards solving their problems — the Eastern, for example, had achieved considerable savings through the fiercely contested closure of the Woodhead freight route between Sheffield and Manchester *(see Chapter 10)*.

Of course once the fuss caused by publication began to subside a

A graphic illustration of what the weather can do to a viaduct if the waterproof decking is allowed to deteriorate. This example is on the NER line at Smardale, not far from where it crossed beneath the S & C. BR was refused permission to demolish the structure after a public inquiry. Note the slender piers of the viaduct compared with the no-nonsense Midland approach.

little, people began to look round for a scapegoat — as usual it was the poor old engineer. Frank Leeming had already been associated with the problems of the Barmouth viaduct which threatened to close the Cambrian Coast line and, as he put it, "my name has been bandied about for various reasons". "People seem to forget that we were professional railway bridge engineers — I had been in that job all my life, unlike a lot of people who come along and they may be civil engineers, but they are not used to maintaining structures." As the Settle-Carlisle Project Manager, Ron Cotton, put it to Stan Abbott: "As far as the engineers are concerned it's very much a subjective judgement and you do get different views from people, equally well qualified, on the same problem. What you have got fundamentally, underneath, is a quite justifiable fear that if anything did happen they carry the can ultimately — you may well say that there is a certain erring on the side of safety."

Railway history is indeed littered with the corpses of good engineers who have often had to carry the can for the mistakes of others (such as Sir Thomas Bouch, designer of the Tay Bridge which collapsed disastrously because the builders — used to dealing with vastly over-engineered structures — cut corners during construction).

That is not to say, however, that the work of the engineer "on the ground" can not be used (misrepresented even) for political ends by others higher up the organisational tree.

It is worth considering how the Ribblehead problems compared with other major engineering bills facing British Rail around that time: these ranged from tens or hundreds of thousands of pounds, as in the case of the Durham viaduct on the East Coast Main Line and the Lune viaduct on West Coast route, to what may be presumed to be the odd million or two for viaducts like Marsh Lane in Leeds or the old Great Northern viaduct in Wakefield, on both of which continual work had been observed for ten years or more. The £1.2m realignment of the East Coast line where it was slipping into the sea at Burnmouth swallowed a large proportion of the Scottish Region's repair budget in 1983, amid very little publicity. Projects in the pipeline included the closure for waterproofing of the East Coast Main Line viaduct at Welwyn, while on the West Coast Main Line, the price of electrification "on the cheap" without the installation of new ballast and sleepers suitable for high speed running had necessitated a massive ongoing replacement programme. Nonetheless, there was some question at the time as to whether BR's annual budget provision for bridge repairs actually ever got spent.

Engineers also took advantage of the extended possession in October 1989 to carry out a number of other repairs on the S & C as BR began to make good the horrendous backlog of maintenance identified in the PEIDA report. At the time of writing, BR was planning to continue spending at the rate of £1.5m a year in addition to further spending on Ribblehead. Station improvements at Settle, Appleby and Kirkby Stephen — including raising and lengthening platforms to accommodate four-car Sprinter trains — were among urgent priorities.

Other work carried out in October 1989 included the strengthening of overbridges, relaying a level crossing at Culgaith in the Eden Valley, replacing a bridge at Langwathby (a job which had been scheduled years previously but shelved during the period of uncertainty) and work in one of the air shafts in the mile-and-a-quarter Blea Moor tunnel to check the uncontrolled flow of water. A farm accommodation bridge in Garsdale was repaired at a cost of £30,000, saving £90,000 on the replacement price, thanks to the pioneering use of a Hungarian technique. The sprayed concrete method was developed for lining coal mines and involves the use of a spray "gun" to apply successive layers of liquid concrete to the underside of bridge arches to give a high-strength finish with low shrinkage qualities.

Interestingly, BR had tested the broader application of technique on the Windermere branch and currently holds the UK marketing rights. When engineers discovered the need to replace a number of overbridges on the Windermere branch — which leaves the West Coast Main Line at Oxenholme, near Kendal — there was real concern for the very future of the line as it was questionable whether traffic levels could justify the spending of several hundred thousand pounds. Area Civil Engineer, Peter Forbes, said that by applying the technique on the Windermere branch, BR had saved around £0.5m.

Ribblehead Viaduct under construction around 1873 — the wooden scaffolding would come to have a lot to answer for a century later

The sun does not always shine for steam specials. Ex-LMS Black Five No. 5407 battles through a snowstorm at Dent Head in February 1981.

5. The unsung hero with the Midas touch

PIN STRIPES in the Pennines — like the unfortunate traveller at the one-platform station at Ribblehead, Ron Cotton would eventually find there was only one direction he could go.

HE CAME to the Settle and Carlisle in 1983, the man everyone loved to hate. By the time Ron Cotton took early retirement from British Rail, a little more than three years later, he had set the line he was supposed to be closing on the road to economic recovery and eventual reprieve. But the true scale of the remarkable Mr Cotton's activities as a fifth columnist at work for those opposing closure have only really emerged in the years since he departed BR, a largely unsung hero, in February 1987.

Unsung, because Ron Cotton never received more than grudging recognition for conceiving the off-peak Saver ticket in response to the threat of competition from the newly deregulated long distance coach operators. Yet it was the advent of a flexible, demand-led fares policy which arguably saved BR from financial disaster in the face of competition from the coaches. Along with his crucial role in saving the S & C, this was Ron Cotton's greatest contribution to rail travel.

That praise, however, should be so scant for the man dubbed "the greatest General Manager the London Midland Region never had" is perhaps not surprising in an organisation which has only recently broadened its horizons beyond the narrowest view of running a railway.

Like so many innovators, Ron Cotton was always something of a square peg in a round British Rail hole. His colourful 39-year career, in which he became the only manager to work in all five BR regions, began in a lowly clerical position when he joined the newly nationalised railway at Marylebone, near his London home, straight from school in 1948.

He rose steadily through the ranks, filling various posts in London, Birmingham and Manchester, where he was appointed Deputy Chief Controller in 1962. By the time he was appointed head of freight movements in the Southern Region in 1964, he was already acquiring a reputation for conjuring up radical solutions to sticky problems.

No great respecter of inter-disciplinary boundaries, it was in this freight role that he helped fashion an unlikely reprieve for the Beeching-threatened Reading-Guildford-Tonbridge passenger line. The line had been earmarked for closure and its future lay in replacing the costly steam locomotives, a task for which no new locomotive or rolling stock provision had been made. "We devised a most extraordinary method of getting steam off the line," he told Stan Abbott. The solution lay in making use of electric trains which had been transferred to the Southern Region when the Tyneside suburban lines were converted from electric to diesel traction.

With help from engineering colleagues, Mr Cotton and others succeeded in grafting the Tyneside trains on to available diesel units to make the celebrated "tadpole" trains — one of their three coaches built to a wider loading gauge than the other two — which ran successfully for another 13 years.

"We had these strange trains which were half diesel and half electric: we saved £224,000 a year and saved the line from closure. Indeed, it's still there today."

Mr Cotton then took what was nominally an operational job in Edinburgh and ended up marketing steam-hauled excursions. It was to be his first dabble into the realms of marketing which was to make his reputation.

Ron Cotton was driven by a vision of a people's railway that was to set him at odds with the ruling traditionalists in the railway hierarchy,

"The public likes the laughing train logo — what more reason do we need to remove it!?"

and on moving to Newcastle in 1968, as passenger manager, he got the chance to try and put his ideas into practice.

"I felt there was a mass market for cheaper fares — the people's railway. I couldn't get over the concept of selling Saver-type fares at that stage, but we did get a special cheap train." That train was called the Highwayman and offered travel between Newcastle and London at rock-bottom prices on a pre-booking basis. Following the stipulations of Ron Cotton's seniors, the Highwayman had to run slower than service trains and so it took a circuitous route via Sunderland and the Durham coast to terminate short of King's Cross, at Finsbury Park. The train was a great success and always ran full, yet, on Ron Cotton's departure for Liverpool in 1971, the Highwayman met summary justice and quietly disappeared from the timetables.

It was as Divisional Passenger Manager at Liverpool that Ron Cotton really began to exercise his marketing flare. "I produced the Merseyrail brand name, gave all the lines names, produced maps London Transport-style and had a cartoon character of a laughing train stencilled on the side of each carriage," he said. "I then had to go on a long course, and while I was away, there was such official disapproval that the cartoons were taken off and withdrawn: senior management didn't like laughing trains."

The idea was to give train services on Merseyside a strong local identity which could then be marketed. Since then, not only has Merseyrail — albeit minus the jocular loco — stuck as a brand logo, but the concept has been copied throughout the country, from Network South East, to Network North West, to ScotRail.

Liverpool became a testing ground for other Cotton initiatives: he pioneered the mass movement of football fans by rail before the subject became a dirty word, and in one military-style operation dubbed "Ron's Red Army" he saw 5,500 Liverpool fans to and from the European Cup Final at Rome. "At one stage in Liverpool we were doing over half the total revenue from football trains in all of Britain — we took over £1 million."

He brought in special student tickets long before the advent of Student Rail Cards and fell foul of sex equality legislation by selling hugely successful Quick Trip ladies' tickets to London which opened the door to a day's shopping in the capital for only about £1.50.

"On one occasion, the booking office rang up and said they suspected three men in drag had just bought tickets," Mr Cotton recalled. Never one to miss a good public relations opportunity, Ron Cotton tipped off the London media and a posse of photographers lay in wait by the barriers at Euston for ladies dressed as men, who then failed to materialise. "They'd obviously changed back into men after their tickets had been checked," said Mr Cotton.

"We were convinced we were making money and then I started getting threats. We had a warning from the Equal Opportunities Commission: by that time other parts of the country were copying us and when the EOC wrote to BR, all the others rapidly dropped out." However, Mr Cotton saw further PR opportunities in extending the argument and the ensuing TV debates and newspaper column inches served only to sell more and more tickets.

But it was in formulating the response to the Government's deregulation of long-distance coach services that Mr Cotton's people's railway really came into its own. He came up with his solution at a time, in 1980, when the coaches were making quite serious inroads into BR traffic. "Against quite considerable scepticism and downright opposition" Ron Cotton slashed fares by up to 72 per cent on certain trains to London — yet still saw a 27 per cent increase in revenue in the first year. National

"Three Ladies' Quickies please, mate!"

Travel's response was to up its schedules to eight coaches a day between London and Liverpool, but "gradually we forced them back to three".

His Big City Savers spread throughout BR, becoming the standard cheap fare and the word "Saver" was even adopted by British Airways.

BR had feared deregulation could spell disaster — instead Ron Cotton's Saver revolution had created extra net revenue of up to £100m by 1987 when it accounted for 57 per cent of all InterCity earnings. And that was just new business: no-one can say how much traffic might have been lost for good to the coaches without such an imaginative response.

"Gradually my critics grudgingly had to admit that they were wrong, but it was a bitter battle against a lot of opposition which came from people whose job it was to dictate national policy."

Ron Cotton was accused by his seniors of "debasing" the railway for wanting to cut fares and of creating operational difficulties because he wanted to run trains to meet demand. He was described by one industry commentator as BR's "UFO" whom senior management pretended did not exist.

And so instead, perhaps, of elevation to the BR Board, Ron Cotton was rewarded in 1983 with the most unpopular job on British Rail:

closing down the Settle-Carlisle. It was a job Ron Cotton said he was "told" or "advised" to take. He had been given a pistol, but chose not to oblige his enemies by shooting himself. Instead, he was again soon donning his salesman's hat, warning his superiors that closure without an honest attempt at marketing an arguably unique line could run into serious opposition.

And so Mr Cotton began his career on Settle-Carlisle doing what he was best at. He marketed the line according to the philosophy he had evolved at Liverpool and elsewhere: simplified fares and reduced fares to match demand and capacity. He was given a virtual free hand to milk the S & C for all it was worth before closure and so the three years of Cotton's reign saw innovations like a £5 maximum fare for Leeds-bound passengers and even a £1 early bird ticket for those enthusiastic enough to take a return trip between any stations from Skipton to Appleby on the early morning northbound Dalesman service. Then there was Ron Cotton's answer to Live Aid: under the Rail Aid scheme, for every £5 taken by BR through the sale of day saver tickets on the S & C in October 1985, £1 would be given to Live Aid's African appeal fund.

But even before all this, Ron Cotton's touch was felt soon after his arrival and the summer of 1984 saw such a boom in passenger numbers — despite the inconvenient timings and antiquity of the rolling stock — that he was forced to schedule an extra daily train after angry would-be travellers were left standing on the platform at Appleby. So hastily had this service been inserted into the timetable that even BR's own Travelcentres were unaware of its existence the day it started running, a deficiency the Joint Action Committee set about remedying by producing its own promotional leaflet in the guise of an official British Rail one. This JAC action was a foretaste of the kind of co-operation that was to develop during Ron Cotton's tenure, once the mutual mistrust began to subside, and it helps explain how the Friends of the Settle-Carlisle Line Association was able easily to undergo the metamorphosis from campaign body to user group once the line's future was secured.

By the end of 1984, revenue on the S & C was 80 per cent up on 1982, the year the Nottingham-Glasgow service was re-routed. In the winter of 1985, Ron Cotton came up with £5 special offer: "If you haven't travelled the Settle-Carlisle in winter — you ain't seen nothing yet!" Overcrowding was so acute that relief trains had to run on five Saturdays in February and March. Even week-day trains were running full with people standing. On one historic Saturday in March, nearly 1,500 people travelled north on the line.

But Ron Cotton was not against more covert action in order to give his marketing initiatives a fair chance of success. Having come to the job with an open mind as to the line's potential, the early successes convinced him more time was needed. At no time was this more crucial than during 1984 and 1985 when he was nurturing the germ of an idea. Ron Cotton's plan was to extend services on the threatened line by the addition of a new local service calling at stations which, for ten years, had only seen the occasional DalesRail weekend charter. But, even at the best of times, it can take months to draft timetables and ensure the availability of rolling stock and — in the case of what would become the Dalesman service — there would be complicated negotiations over local authority support and regarding the status of any service introduced on a line which was scheduled for closure*.

If the mix-up over the Settle-Carlisle closure notices had been a happy accident, it nonetheless brought publicity for the S & C — and it also generated a welter of objections which would greatly delay the convening of the Transport Users' committees' statutory public hearings. Ron Cotton was certainly not averse to further exploiting this delay. With TUCC hearings pencilled in for May 1985, Mr Cotton resurrected an acrimonious exchange with the Yorkshire TUCC which had begun the previous September with a request by BR for copies of each individual objection to closure which had been lodged. The TUCC had argued in September that it was for it to consider the objections, and not the job of British Rail. But Ron Cotton wrote: "We had correspondence some months ago over my request for copies of individual objections to be sent to myself. We have considered the matter again in the light of your reply and feel that it is essential that we have copies of individual objections.

"The summary is insufficient for us to fully understand the detail of objections and to be properly briefed for the Public Hearing.

"In these circumstances I would ask you to please let me have a copy of every individual objection. I am sure you must agree that it is every bit as essential that we understand the full nature of the objectors' case as it is for them to understand ours."

---

* *The service was actually introduced under the terms of the so-called Speller Amendment, after the Devon MP, Tony Speller. This allows the experimental introduction of services without the need for recourse to the full TUCC procedure before their withdrawal.*

This renewed request was like a red rag to a bull for James Towler, the TUCC chairman, who wrote in the following terms in his own book about the S & C saga, *The Battle for the Settle & Carlisle*. "I was very cross indeed. Quite apart from the fact that I thought the matter had been settled last September, I felt Cotton — who in terms of British Rail seniority was several grades higher than John Moorhouse — was trying to 'pull rank' in order to overrule a decision made by the committee and which had been confirmed in correspondence by myself."

John Moorhouse was the Yorkshire TUCC secretary — a position to which BR staff are effectively seconded, notwithstanding the nominal impartiality of the TUCC set-up. Mr Towler's committee's annoyance stemmed not only from the broad question of its own autonomy, but also the issue of civil liberties: some 14,897 people had lodged objections with the Yorkshire TUCC and surely they were entitled to have their submissions treated in confidence? Some objectors might well be British Rail employees who could feel compromised by the scrutiny of their submissions by BR personnel. Moreover, why should BR demand such detailed information when its own Heads of Information document — the basis for the closure proposal — was scant to say the least? The TUCC's case was not helped by the fact that its counterpart for North West England had readily acceded to the BR request for copies of individual objections.

The row had all the ingredients for a classic confrontation and the exchange of letters rumbled on through 1985. By this time other factors had come into play, including the outcome of a judicial review of the London Regional Passengers Committee (the London TUCC) into aspects of the hearings into the closure proposals for Marylebone station. Eventually, the Settle-Carlisle hearings were scheduled for the spring of 1986 and the question of the rights of the individual objectors, it seemed, quietly disappeared. But, by now, Ron Cotton — for all he had lost in short-term popularity — had gained the time he wanted, and the closure hearings were followed after a few weeks by the remarkable announcement of the new all-stations Dalesman service *(see Chapter 7).*

Ron Cotton's extraordinary delaying tactic and the effective duping of the TUCC was something that he would only admit to many months after his departure from BR. Indeed, while others might have replied to the S & C short straw with the proverbial "I quit", Ron Cotton's demeanour throughout was that of an impeccable British Rail employee. There were those who suspected he might have more than a little

Ron Cotton's marketing efforts are shown to best advantage in this picture of a Settle-Carlisle "local" train taken in August 1984. Instead of running from Leeds, one train was extended to and from Hull. The train length has been more than doubled and the collection of antique and underpowered locomotives used immediately after its downgrading from main line status has been replaced by the Class 47 — one of the most powerful on BR at the time — pictured here.

sympathy with the the anti-closure case, but Ron Cotton ensured this remained speculation as he stuck throughout loyally to BR line. Indeed, in answer to suggestions he had been a fifth columnist all along, his reply was uncompromising: "I think I tried to do the other half of the job [the closure brief] and fairly. I attended 42 TUCC sessions of three hours each when no-one else from BR turned up." When asked whether he thought the boom in passenger numbers was a temporary phenomenon brought on by the desire for one last ride before closure, he would always reply that there were two schools of thought, without ever saying to which school of thought he subscribed. Only after leaving BR would he say that he had come with an open mind on the question, but after three years of growth, the idea that all these new passengers were still taking one last ride no longer washed. Ron Cotton had come to believe in the other hypothesis: that the Settle & Carlisle was a line of immense potential which had been sadly undersold for years.

By the time Ron Cotton took early retirement in 1987, revenue on the

S & C had quadrupled, services more than doubled and eight stations had reopened. Mr Cotton had broken new ground by working with his anti-closure opponents on promotional material and was rewarded by them with a retirement present. James Towler commented: "He is a great innovator and a great loss to BR — he's the best London Midland Region General Manager they have never had."

Ross Furby, BR's Director of Passenger Marketing Services, did concede: "Ron Cotton was the pioneer of the London Saver ticket from Liverpool and it was the success of that ticket that paved the way for the national introduction of reduced price rail travel."

But Mr Cotton said then that BR had still not completely grasped the nettle: "My philosophy was the people's railway. What we needed was mass movement. The opposing forces believed in high quality and high prices and now the process has only gone half way."

Today, BR has the highest rail fares in Europe and has abandoned the idea of meeting demand for travel in favour of controlling demand by raising fares as it struggles to meet ever more onerous financial targets.

Now, Ron Cotton supplements his BR pension with consultancy work: he worked on the English Tourist Board's study of the Settle-Carlisle and was involved in work for Lincolnshire County Council when rural lines there came under recent threat *(see Chapter 10)*. He has helped Lancashire County Council on work regarding the reintroduction of regular trains to Clitheroe and Hellifield and his experience organising football specials has also put him in good stead for the advisory role he now enjoys for the Football Trust.

Perhaps the finest accolade is that, now Ron Cotton has left BR, some "Stalinists" in the hierarchy are seeking to rewrite history and to take credit for Cotton innovations ranging from the Highwayman to Saver tickets.

6.
All the fun of the Down Goods Loop

RAILWAY closure hearings are normally sombre affairs: a large panel of committee members and staff gaze down, usually from some form of raised platform, as ordinary passengers struggle and stumble through little speeches describing why they believe their local line should not close.

Levity of any kind usually has no place. There is too much at stake. Anti-closure campaigners are often armed with only the flimsiest statistics about how well or badly their railway is doing in attracting passengers, and British Rail steadfastly refuses to divulge any financial information. The message to the ordinary ticket-holder is a simple one: it must close because it is losing money. It is losing money because we say it is losing money.

But on this bright spring morning in Skipton, the town hall rang with laughter. Just for once, the anti-closure campaigners had British Rail on the ropes. Not surprisingly, their tormentor was James Towler, chairman of the Yorkshire Transport Users' Consultative Committee which had begun the second leg of the Settle-Carlisle closure hearings in Settle a week earlier on April 14, 1986.

The venue switched to Skipton and, almost as an idle afterthought, Mr Towler decided to ask a detailed question about the timetable proposed for British Rail's alternative Leeds-Carlisle service, via Giggleswick, Carnforth and Oxenholme. He had noticed that after the northbound morning service reached Carnforth — where the train had to reverse direction to gain access to the northbound tracks of the West Coast Main Line — an unusually long time was allowed for the 13-mile leg between Carnforth and Oxenholme: 51 minutes to cover just 13 miles.

Why, he asked BR's closure project manager, Ron Cotton, was this portion of the journey going to take so long? It proved to be a conversational hand grenade.

Mr Cotton took a deep breath and admitted that after the locomotive

"Couchette for Oxenholme, please."

had been run from one end of the train to the other it would have to stand for 30 minutes in the Carnforth Down Goods Loop waiting for a path between other services on the main line.

Mr Towler maintained afterwards that he believed at first this was some kind of joke. "You'll have to lay on a floor show or cabaret to keep the passengers amused," he responded. But Mr Cotton made it clear he was not joking. This was BR's serious alternative proposal to the Settle-Carlisle.

"Words almost fail me," replied Mr Towler. With travellers' interests obviously at heart, he asked: "Will passengers be allowed to use the toilets when the train is standing in Carnforth Down Goods Loop?" Ron Cotton could not win and he knew it. A gale of laughter swept around the hall. "We do frown on people using them in stations and sidings," he replied.

In fact, it later emerged that the southbound trains would also suffer a similar delay. British Rail's credibility took a sharp nosedive when someone spotted that one of the southbound trains left Carlisle just ahead of a Carlisle-Lancaster train and was then shunted aside for half-an-hour to allow the following Lancaster train to overtake it. Cotton attempted to persuade the hearings that this timetable was merely an "illustrative" one, and the actual timings of the real post-Settle to

Carlisle closure service would be different. The sceptics remained unconvinced.

James Towler's philosophy was to try and maintain the interest of the proceedings by ensuring that they were punctuated occasionally by lighter episodes, and another quip which he would use to lash Ron Cotton mercilessly concerned British Rail's gaffe on the proposed alternative provision for Settle passengers at Giggleswick station.

But, overall, there were precious few light moments in a marathon series of public hearings which still hold the records for attracting the largest number of objectors and for being the longest running railway closure inquiry in British history. But there was a splendid symbolic start to the whole affair.

The hearings opened in Appleby, under the auspices of the North West Transport Users' Consultative Committee. Monday March 24, 1986, dawned with a blizzard which swept across the Yorkshire Dales and Eden Valley, reducing road transport to chaos. But the packed 09.03 from Leeds got through, albeit an hour late. It would have been difficult to find a more convincing demonstration of the railway's value as a lifeline.

That blizzard was not the first event to suggest that Someone Up There was keeping a benevolent eye on the battle for the S & C — after all, there'd been the small matter of the overhead wires blowing down on the West Coast Main Line the very day British Rail had announced its closure desires, leading to a dramatic demonstration of the line's value to InterCity as a diversionary route. The real question was, however, whether the TUCCs would provide a suitable vehicle to persuade Her Majesty's Government towards more terrestrial acts of good will.

The question of the power, or lack of it, of the two TUCCs involved had been the subject of much debate in the months leading up to the first hearing in Appleby — as had the apparently contrasting style of the committees, epitomised by their respective chairmen. On the one hand was James Towler, the railway traveller's Clark Kent, whose North East TUCC adopted a high profile approach, addressing a range of concerns from poor time-keeping to dirty rolling stock to, of course, service cuts and closure proposals. In one celebrated case, the committee (in its former guise as the Yorkshire TUCC) had concluded that the proposed withdrawal of passenger services from the direct Leeds-Sheffield line would cause hardship to users of trains diverted occasionally over the line and to travellers between Leeds and Sheffield "who would not have the benefits of improved services using all or part of the routes proposed for closure". These improved services were entirely theoretical and assumed investment in the infrastructure of the line as proposed by objectors, and an increase in the number of trains between Leeds and Sheffield.

James Towler's justification for the decision typified his approach:

James Towler — traveller's friend

"Now there's a situation where the committee was very conscious of the fact that the service had been run down and run down until it hardly represented a service at all and the committee felt they had to take cognisance of that."

The North West TUCC under Olive Clarke, on the other hand, had failed (or not chosen) to gain a similar reputation as the champion of the passenger's cause, preferring to pour oil on troubled waters where differences arose between BR and its customers. In the days before the merger of the old North East TUCC with Towler's Yorkshire, the North West TUCC had this response to suggestions that it had failed in its primary duty of sticking up for the passenger: "We are just here as arbitrators — we are not here to stick up for the railway or the public. The Transport Act says we look at it under the hardship it [closure] would cause. It has been broadcast for some while that there is a difference of opinion [between the North West and the Yorkshire committees] — we

A happy eventual outcome for the North West TUCC's Olive Clarke. She is second from the right in this group shot taken at Ribblehead following the redecking of the viaduct.

are sticking to the statute."

Speculation that the Government might see in the inauguration of the new TUCC for North East England the opportunity to ditch the troublesome Mr Towler and perhaps enjoy a more low key, Towler-free Settle-Carlisle hearing had proved ill-founded when the outgoing chairman of the old Yorkshire Area TUCC was appointed by the Secretary of State in April 1985 to head the new body for two years — at the same time, Mrs Clarke was given a new three-year term.

The fact that there were now just two TUCCs deliberating on the future of the S & C was thanks to a decision by the Department of Trade to merge the Yorkshire TUCC with the TUCC for North East England which had had a peripheral role in the S & C case, thanks to three miles of track which strayed into its area near Garsdale, as discussed in Chapter 3. This merger had originally been planned for the autumn of 1984 and also involved the transfer of responsibility for the Craven district of North Yorkshire (including Skipton and Settle) to the North West Area TUCC. In the event, the Yorkshire/North East merger was deferred to April 1985 and the Skipton transfer was put off until after the

Settle-Carlisle hearings, thereby sidestepping an inevitable row, had the the North-West committee been left with sole responsibility for conducting the hearings.

The hearings themselves quickly settled into a pattern of oral and written evidence taken in heavy bursts, punctuated by welcome tea-breaks. British Rail had decided to take as few chances as possible and had hired Mr Michael Harrison QC to field any legal questions from the TUCC members and to respond to similar points made by objectors. These were few and far between and much of the flak was directed at Ron Cotton.

Already seen by many as a sort of hired gun, the axeman brought in by British Rail to supervise the run-down and closure of the line, he was a natural target for the ire of both individuals and organised groups of objectors. In fact, as events were to show, Mr Cotton was prepared to wriggle his toes well across the British Rail party line if he saw any potential benefit for the Settle-Carlisle.

Amid the welter of evidence, it gradually became possible to identify some general trends, to begin to build a picture of precisely what the grievances and fears of the objectors were and where they felt the BR closure case was weakest. One of the earliest of these was the stubborn refusal of BR to release any but the most superficial financial information about the performance of the line and how well or badly it fared in relation to similar rural railways — for, whatever it had now become, the Settle to Carlisle was no longer the main line to Scotland of Midland Railway dreams.

The Joint Action Committee hammered at this point repeatedly, stressing its difficulty in presenting a coherent objection to the BR closure proposal when there were no financial details to contest — and this despite an assurance in the Commons by David Mitchell, the public transport minister, that the figures would be presented.

The precise definition of "hardship" — the main term of reference of a TUCC hearing — was also brought into question. The main function of a TUCC closure hearing is to provide the secretary of state for transport with an accurate picture of the levels of hardship which a community or communities would suffer from the closure of their railway line. While the scope of the TUCC hearings was broadened considerably, with an agreement from the public transport minister, Mr David Mitchell, that he would also consider other evidence collected by the TUCCs, the hardship question remained the core issue.

Critics of this state of affairs lost no time in pointing out that this effectively prevented the TUCCs from questioning BR on almost any meaningful aspect of its closure proposal, or the thinking behind it. Why, for example, was the ticket revenue from Settle station not counted in with the line's earnings? Why was contributory revenue — the money the rest of the BR network earned when someone travelled from, say, Bristol to Carlisle, to ride over the line not given due credit? And what about the revenue from the burgeoning charter train traffic the line was generating, disparagingly described by British Rail as people wanting "a last look" before the Settle-Carlisle closed?

Mr Towler himself addressed these points in a statement which pointed out that using the accounting methods which BR was applying to the Settle to Carlisle line, it would be perfectly possible to demonstrate that the East Coast Main Line between Retford and Newark was a loss-maker which should be closed!

The Joint Action Committee weighed in with more "lost" money, which it claimed would put the line in a far better financial light. The JAC reckoned that the Settle-Carlisle was earning around £250,000 per year by handling traffic diverted from the West Coast Main Line for engineering work or in the event of an accident. BR, predictably, declined to discuss the details.

As the hearings progressed, this attitude began increasingly to count against BR. A consensus began to emerge among objectors that not only did the Settle-Carlisle line pay its basic running costs, but it was probably also one of Provincial Sector's best performing routes. Why else would BR refuse to divulge even the most basic financial information? And if this was the case, surely BR, far from saving money, would actually lose revenue by closing the line.

On the "hardship" question, British Rail took the view that only regular, daily commuters could suffer significantly. The joint county councils and JAC could not agree, pointing out that while people living in the scattered Dales and Eden villages might use the line less frequently than city commuters, when they did use it they were more dependent on it than urban dwellers, because it might be their only means of access to visit friends and relatives.

Then there was the important question of the hardship that closure of the S & C would cause to troubled Halifax Town Football Club. This was raised at the Appleby hearing by Andrew Connell, a teacher at the town's Grammar School, who soon got into the swing of the debate

"'Ere we go! 'ere we go!' shows admirable club loyalty, but we feel it is hardly the basis of a meaningful dialogue with this committee..."

about what might or might not constitute hardship. It was just possible, he said, for him to use the train and catch a bus from Keighley to attend the team's matches. Closure would render the journey impossible. "It's certainly a form of hardship to the club who need every spectator they can get," he said. Cases such as his might well be considered trivial, he admitted, but it was trivia which, taken collectively, made up the pattern of use of a railway.

James Towler, though, had always made it clear what definition of "hardship" he would be working to. Before the hearings began, he told Stan Abbott: "I stick very closely to the Chamber's Dictionary definition which I think mentions the word 'privation'." A quick check under "privation" shows that following Chamber's can broaden the interpretation of the 1962 Act to encompass such loose concepts as "loss or lack of something". And so, Mr Towler's committee would again work to this broad definition to allow it to consider a variety of evidence which did not, on the face of it, fall within the definition of questions of hardship.

Indeed, for all the hype about the differences between the two committees, there was little ostensible divergence between the organisations in the manner in which the two series of hearings (five in all) were conducted. This was due in part to a perceptible narrowing of the gap between committees over their interpretation of the Act, thanks perhaps to efforts at rapprochement with the North West TUCC on the part of the Settle-Carlisle Join Action Committee and — more importantly — to a meeting in London in 1984 when both Mr Towler and Mrs Clarke were summoned by the Department of Trade and Industry (the "parent" department of the TUCCs) to discuss the conduct of the TUCC hearings. These were, at that time, anticipated to take place in early 1985 and the foundations for common action by the two TUCCs had already been laid in an agreement in 1984 that each should hold its own hearings into the S & C closure proposal, to be followed by the submission of a joint report.

To return to the business of the hearings: it was at Appleby, too, that the Joint County Councils began to unveil the considerable firepower in their armoury as the months of behind-the-scenes technical work and research by officers finally saw the light of day. The steering group's chairman, Councillor Bill Cameron, in his inimitable bluff Cumbrian style, set the scene, crisply dismissing BR's case as non-existent. At later hearings, he was followed by officers from the various authorities whose work was ably brought together by Peter Robinson and Alan Thompson, of Cumbria. They showed that if BR would not or, more likely, could not present an accurate picture of the line's usage, potential and finances, then the local authorities certainly would. A picture gradually unfolded of a line at the heart of the communities it served, offering local people essential travel links, but underpinned by the considerable revenue that could be attracted by its remarkable heritage and the superb opportunities for enjoying the Dales and the Eden Valley. By the end of the hearings in Leeds a month later, BR's case was in tatters and few doubted that the objectors had won handsomely in terms of quality of information and argument.

Among questions raised at the hearings was one concerning the fate of regular travellers who would have to transfer to the replacement Leeds-Carnforth-Carlisle service if the line were to close. It quickly emerged that BR had done little homework — quite apart from the ludicrous business of the Carnforth Down Goods Loop. Giggleswick station formed the central core of the objectors' arguments. Skipton's MP, John Watson, set the ball rolling with his amusing and deadly accurate description of Giggleswick's shortcomings.

Apart from being well over a mile from Settle, along a narrow and unlit lane, the station itself was little more than a halt. One of its platforms did not even have a shelter, and the one which did had the building cunningly situated so that its opening faced the direction of the prevailing wind. There was no telephone, a poorly surfaced car park and no means for passengers to find out what had gone wrong if their train did not turn up.

Ron Cotton responded with offers of a shelter on both platforms, a BR phone link with the nearest signal box for passengers to get train information, a public phonebox would be provided — rented by BR itself if necessary — and the car park would be resurfaced.

Alas, this last gesture would quickly have been rendered meaningless. One sharp-eyed objector spotted that the planned A65 by-pass around Settle was intended to drive a course straight through Giggleswick station yard. A disbelieving TUCC called for plans of the road and quickly found that the claim was quite accurate. James Towler referred to Giggleswick as "Giggleswick Parkway" throughout the rest of the hearing in a mocking reference to BR's policy of setting up out-of-town park-and-ride stations.

And what of the people who used the line for recreational purposes? The success of the DalesRail trains was proof that significant numbers wanted a transport link between the city and the country which allowed them to forget about driving for a day or two and enjoy the walking instead. Before the Settle-Carlisle hearings, this concept of recreational deprivation was no more than an abstract, a vague nagging only occasionally articulated by objectors at railway closure hearings.

All these were issues which surfaced again and again, many objectors claiming a pent-up "latent demand" for better public transport which was not being satisfied by the existing indifferent bus services — many of which had recently been withdrawn as a result of the increased competition brought about by bus deregulation which made it difficult, if not impossible, even for bus companies with a social conscience to cross-subsidise loss-making village buses with profitable town routes.

These objectors had the satisfaction of seeing their prophesies come true. If there was a "latent demand", then a new local rail service should be an almost overnight success. The theory was to come to be tested soon after the end of the closure hearings with the launch in July 1986 of the Dalesman service, described in the next chapter. It prospered quickly, attracting a healthy mix of classic commuters, students and shoppers to rub shoulders with fell-walkers and holidaymakers.

In fact, BR had proposed a better deal for some communities near the line with its offer of replacement bus services from Appleby to Penrith, connecting with West Coast Main Line trains, to supplement the two daily re-routed Leeds-Carlisle services. The reaction to this idea was a pure throwback to the Beeching closure hearings of the 1960s.

It quickly became apparent that rail travellers have long memories and a number of objectors voiced the fear that as soon as the line was closed, the replacement buses would be quickly wound down into a skeleton service so unattractive that few would use it, allowing a speedy closure. The fact that the same 1985 Transport Act which de-regulated the buses would also provide statutory protection for the substitute bus — with a new closure hearing required before it could be axed — cut little ice. The more organised objectors preferred to recall 1969, when the Government of the day removed similar statutory protection for the bus services brought in to replace branch lines chopped by Beeching.

In fact, the idea of replacement buses was a non-starter, as the TUCCs themselves were later to prove when requested by the transport minister to investigate journey times and frequencies as part of the second round of closure hearings two years later. The committees found that some bus trips would take well over twice as long as the equivalent rail journey and that any road service would be subject to delay or cancellation in the event of bad weather.

Buses, of course, had also emerged as British Rail's solution to the problem of what to do when the West Coast Main Line was closed for track maintenance or bridge renewals. At one stage Ron Cotton was invited specifically to deny the existence of an internal BR memorandum which explained how the East Coast Main Line would be used for diverting London-Scotland services with buses running along the M6 motorway nearer the blockage itself. Mr Cotton declined to deny the document's existence, adding fuel to the claims of several objectors that closing the Settle-Carlisle line would make rail journeys for thousands of passengers at best inconvenient, at worst a nightmare.

Some of their fears were to emerge in more concrete form later, with the leaking of a proposed timetable which involved routeing a Liverpool-Glasgow Sunday service via Manchester, Leeds, York and Edinburgh.

But these claims from objectors did push BR into setting out what its strategy for diverted services would be if the Settle-Carlisle was allowed to close. In essence, this rested on using the Cumbrian Coast Line for blockages north of Carnforth, and the Blackburn-Hellifield line for blockages south of Carnforth, diverted trains running via Giggleswick and Carnforth to regain the main line.

This was quickly seized on by other objectors who pointed out that the investment needed to bring the Cumbrian Coast Line up the standard needed for running Mk III coaches would be £1.5m — a sum remarkably similar to that needed to patch up Ribblehead Viaduct and give it, according to BR, a few more years of life. BR quickly rallied with a revised figure of £100,000 to cut back platform edges and single some stretches of track where restricted clearances between Mk III rolling stock and bridges would have caused problems. So had the other £1.4m been spent? No, assured Mr Cotton, the £1.5m originally quoted by BR to the North West TUCC was to upgrade the line to full InterCity standards for regular high speed running. That was not now proposed.

So did this diversionary strategy mean that BR was now no longer seeking the closure of the line between Blackburn and Hellifield which had always formed part of the S & C closure proposal? The answer appears to be that, even at this late stage, the situation regarding West Coast Main Line diversions remained fluid. Even BR did not really know what it wanted and hence the "catch-all" closure proposal. There have been precedents for the granting of consent to the withdrawal of services, without BR subsequently withdrawing the services in question.

A final, and bizarre twist was added to the Cumbrian Coast Line argument with an outburst from the joint county councils' steering committee chairman, Councillor Bill Cameron. With the bluntness which was to become his hallmark in the later stages of the closure affair, he told the closure hearing that he had been made an informal offer by BR before the Settle-Carlisle closure ever got off the ground.

The terms were simple, said Councillor Cameron. If Cumbria County Council raised no formal objection to the Settle-Carlisle closure proposal, then BR would begin a £7m investment programme which would both safeguard the future of the Cumbrian Coast Line, by clearing a backlog of maintenance and improving sea defences on the more exposed stretches, and reduce journey times by raising speed limits. It was a claim vigorously denied by BR and was in any event incapable of being proved one way or the other. No official documents, no minutes, no letters setting out the deal existed. It came down to one man's word against another's — as did the councillor's claim that the deal also included a BR promise that the new (and ill-fated) Advanced Passenger

Train would stop at Carlisle on its way to London from Glasgow.

Councillor Cameron was far from the only objector to hint at a "dirty tricks" campaign to undermine the Settle and Carlisle. Many speakers at the public hearings, and others outside them, complained of an apparent unspoken policy on the part of BR to discourage anyone from using the line. In some cases, objectors who had travelled some distance to reach the line complained that local railway staff from booking clerks to train guards appeared to believe the line had been closed.

Scottish guards on southbound West Coast Main Line trains would, it was claimed, never include Leeds in their announcements of available connections at Carlisle. Others would go to almost tortuous lengths to avoid recommending use of the line. However, these allegations are notoriously difficult to pin down because few people ever note the precise day or time when apparently inaccurate or incomplete information has been offered. And anyway, advice on train connections and timetables is often given by phone from train inquiry bureaux, making it even more difficult to find the person who dealt with any particular enquiry. As with Councillor Cameron's experience, it always comes back to one person's word against another's.

It would be surprising if railway workers themselves had been knowingly doling out inaccurate information about the Settle and Carlisle, given the strenuous opposition of the rail unions to closure. The National Union of Railwaymen, in particular, had itself run foul of BR bureaucracy when it was initially refused permission to charter a diesel multiple unit to run a pro-Settle-Carlisle special over the line. The train eventually ran with the NUR general secretary, Jimmy Knapp, on board (*see page 67*).

But the public hearings were by no means completely negative. There was no shortage of advice from professional and amateur alike on how to attract more passengers to the Settle and Carlisle, how to cut costs to make the balance sheet look more encouraging, how to repair the viaducts, bridges and tunnels more cheaply.

Some objectors produced ingenious timetables, designed to make better use of the existing rolling stock. Others suggested extending the service to give a year-round York-Leeds-Carlisle service. At the northern end of the line, trains could run on to Glasgow, widening the range of journey opportunities.

The Joint Action Committee weighed in with a professionally-researched proposal to restore the line to its full main-line status, but in high-tech form which would generate around £1m worth of profit per year — a far cry from the lame duck which BR presented as fit only for closure.

The JAC proposals were researched by TEST (Transport and Environmental Studies), a group of specialist transport consultants, who suggested in their report, *Retraining Settle-Carlisle,* that the line should be reduced to single track, but laid with continuous welded rail to allow high speed running. The worn-out mechanical signalling would be replaced by the emerging radio electronic tokenless block system being pioneered by BR for re-signalling remote branch lines such the Kyle of Lochalsh, West Highland and Far North lines in Scotland.

The system is expensive to instal, but has few running costs and allows long stretches of line to be controlled by one signal box. Trains are given authority to enter single-track sections by means of a radio link, which passes an electronic "token" to each locomotive in turn. Instead of a physical token in his cab, the driver has the reassurance of the radio token displayed on a small screen. Failsafe interlocking prevents the computer which controls the system from issuing two tokens for the same stretch of line at the same time.

This equipment would be fitted to a batch of High Speed Trains, made redundant by the East Coast Main Line electrification scheme. The TEST proposal envisaged running one HST power car with four trailers, one of which would be converted to driving unit so that the train could operate as a push-pull unit. Interestingly, this same configuration was under evaluation for possible application on the North East-South West InterCity route at the time of writing. The TEST report proposed four trains each way per day as a commercially viable timetable, running from Leeds to Carlisle and Glasgow, restoring — and improving — the link between West Yorkshire and Strathclyde lost when the Nottingham-Glasgow service was diverted away from the Settle-Carlisle. The first and last trains of the day would be diverted into Bradford Forster Square station, improving that city's rail links with the outside world, at a time when this was a source of some anxiety as BR was steadily reducing the number of direct trains between Bradford and London as an economy measure.

The report suggested that while £30m would have to be spent on repairing bridges, viaducts and tunnels, laying the single track high speed line and installing radio signalling, it would repay the investment in 13 years and over 30 years would generate about £35m profit. It would also meet the Government demand that all railway investment schemes should demonstrate a seven per cent rate of return — a figure later raised to eight per cent.

John Whitelegg, the JAC's chairman described the report as the centrepiece of the committee's evidence to the public hearings and added: "We have the evidence, we have the information, we have the moral high ground. We are confident we can win."

The report appeared two weeks before the public hearings began, and began to foster the idea that the Settle-Carlisle might not be the hopeless loss-maker British Rail liked to suggest. Around the same time came the JAC's *New Life in the Hills* report, compiled by Transport 2000, the transport pressure group, which laid the foundations for reintroducing a local all-stations stopping service, as described in Chapter 7. Taken together, the reports painted an encouraging picture of a railway capable of sustaining a timetable of six trains per day, serving a mix of business travellers, day trippers and local people who wanted a train to get a better job in Carlisle, have the chance to go on to further education — or simply go shopping in the city. All this, and a profit too. Interestingly, this proposed service mix is not so different from the service actually operating on the rejuvenated line at the time of writing.

The expanded service idea was a strand of argument which was to be increasingly developed by the anti-closure campaigners as we shall see later. Before the affair was finally played out, British Rail's own minimal financial information had been taken by the objectors and reworked to demonstrate either a minimal loss of around £66,000 per year, or even a small profit.

The overall feeling among many objectors was that if the backlog of repair and maintenance work could somehow be overcome, the line need not be a poor financial performer and, with the healthy passenger growth already in evidence, could even make itself financially secure. And here lay another deep well of mistrust in British Rail and its closure plan.

Few, if any, objectors believed British Rail's claims that Ribblehead Viaduct was life-expired and in imminent danger of collapse. Instead, they saw a solid structure of Pennine stone, a little careworn but badly neglected by a careless owner. A high degree of scepticism greeted the official repair estimate of anything from £4.25m upwards.

One speaker at the Skipton session, Christopher Wallis, brought with him detailed drawings based on his own survey of the viaduct, along with a diagnosis of what he saw as a comparatively trivial problem of water penetration which could be put right from just under £1m, supplementing the findings of Fairhurst's and PEIDA, as discussed in Chapter 4. Curiously, British Rail has since spent approximately that amount on preliminary repairs and Ribblehead is regarded as having an indefinite lifespan.

Finally, the public hearings heard fears expressed that the line was a victim of a BR policy of "closure by stealth". This term was first coined in relation to the closure of a short section of line at Dore, on the outskirts of Sheffield. Running from Dore South Junction to Dore West Junction, it forms the third side of a triangular junction between the Midland Main Line and the Hope Valley Sheffield-Manchester route. It allowed Derby-Manchester trains to turn off the Midland Main Line and run direct along the Hope Valley to Manchester, by-passing Sheffield.

All was well until British Rail withdrew the Derby-Manchester service. Outraged passengers learned they could not object and the TUCC was powerless to act because the line still carried a passenger service — a summer Leicester-Blackpool train. Worse, when that was proposed for withdrawal some years later and the line had to be formally proposed for closure, only travellers using the Leicester-Blackpool service were eligible to object to the closure. Although the Derby-Manchester users had seen their service axed, they no longer had any rights of objection or speech. They were effectively disenfranchised.

The term "closure by stealth", where BR runs down a service to silence as many potential objectors as possible before moving in for the actual closure, is usually credited to Dr Hugh Porteous, a tireless worker for the Sheffield Passengers' Association.

The tactic raised not only the question of BR's conduct over closure issues, but also the powers of the TUCCs themselves. The public hearings certainly bolstered the argument that the TUCCs had somehow been left behind by changing events. The rules and guidelines governing how the committees work date back to 1962. But times change and so do the circumstances surrounding railway closures. Had the time come for an overhaul of the rail passenger's only statutory voice?*

The question of hardship, the main plank of all TUCC evidence to Government ministers, is perhaps the best example. In 1962 many, many people had no access to a car. Motorways, dual-carriageways and by-

---

* *See Appendix 3 for a summary of attempts to modernise the workings of the TUCCs.*

passes were few and far between. Motorway coaches had not been thought of and most bus journeys were tiresomely long and subject to severe dislocation in winter weather, snow clearing and road gritting techniques still being in their infancy.

Few, if any, of these considerations apply today, yet they remain the basic guidelines on which TUCCs must base their opposition to any railway closure. The suggestion that a passenger may feel recreational deprivation, through not being able to get into the Yorkshire Dales or Eden Valley so easily, can not, according to a straightforward interpretation of the Act, enter into it. Even wider issues are also excluded from the equation.

In a similar affair to that of the Dore Curve, BR ran down services over the Wortley Curve, a similar piece of track, again forming one side of a triangular junction, this time on the Bradford-Leeds line, about half a mile outside Leeds station. It allowed Bradford-London trains to run direct, without the need to call (and reverse) at Leeds, thereby saving around 20 minutes.

As InterCity began trying to balance its books before becoming ineligible for any Government grant, Bradford-London services were steadily run down. Finally, in 1985, the main business train of the day, the Bradford Executive, was routed via Leeds, for "commercial reasons" according to BR. This left the Wortley Curve used only by summer Saturday holiday trains.

When the last of these was inevitably axed, BR rejected all calls for a TUCC public hearing and a formal closure proposal, simply tearing up one track and dismantling the junction with the Leeds-London main line. Protests from Bradford City Council that its future prosperity might be directly linked to the quality of its railway links with the outside world were brushed aside.

The issue went to law and British Rail lost at the High Court, being ordered to go through the statutory closure procedure. It did so, but by this time the piece of railway under discussion had been derelict for several years and legitimate objectors to the closure were, to say the least, thin on the ground. To no-one's surprise, BR was ultimately given permission to go ahead and formally close the line.

It is an issue which will not go away. More recently, BR has made substantial cuts on local services throughout the North of England. Hull Paragon station saw the last train of the day on each of the three routes into the city axed so that it could be closed overnight to save staff wages.

The Esk Valley, Leeds-Goole and Cleethorpes to Barton-on-Humber lines have all seen their timetables cut by half. Yet no-one has any right of objection, even though these are all loss-making rail services kept alive in the first place by BR's annual grant from the taxpayer.

In its 1990 annual report, the North East TUCC expressed concern at British Rail's attitude towards the Northallerton-Middlesbrough line, where BR had declined to begin a formal closure proposal, suggesting that, although no trains were running over the line (formerly the direct route for London-bound InterCity services from Teesside), they had been "suspended" rather than withdrawn.

It is difficult to escape the conclusion that, had the public transport minister not agreed informally that the legislation did indeed allow the TUCCs to receive evidence on questions other than hardship (although their report had specifically to deal with the hardship that closure might cause), and had the various anti-closure groups not vociferously threatened legal action to secure a judicial review in the event of British Rail being given consent to close the line, then the public hearings, although a valuable sounding-board, might have turned out to be little more than a sideshow. And the destiny of the Settle-Carlisle would have been quietly decided at some other level by unnamed bureaucrats untroubled by the public gaze.

Indeed, as will be described in Chapter 9, it is clear that the Government paid only the most scant regard to the recommendations of the TUCCs whose members and staff had deliberated at such length and expense on the Settle-Carlisle question. It seemed as though the TUCC hearings were no more than another hoop through which the campaigners would have to jump on their way to eventual victory.

And make no mistake, the TUCCs had worked hard — the mammoth task of collating 22,265 human, and one canine, objection, and the 17 days of hearings were only the beginning. At the end of the final hearing in Leeds, the compilation of the joint report remained to be done. The North West TUCC's consideration of objections and public hearings ran to 85 pages, and that of the North East committee to some 350. The finished document, with its 86 appendices, apparently weighed some 22 kilos when its was despatched by Red Star from York. There were some disagreements when it came to finding a consensus. Most concerned mere semantics, but the North West TUCC was anxious not to be associated with the Mr Towler's committee's desire to place on record what was seen as BR's "lack of candour" in not coming clean on

its intention to close the line prior to the formal announcement in 1983. In the end, that section of the report was prefixed by the statement to the effect that the matters contained in it related to events which had previously concerned only the old Yorkshire TUCC and which were therefore outside the province of the North West TUCC.

And so the committees concluded harmoniously: "On the basis of the undoubted hardship that closure of the line would close, together with the strength of the commercial case presented for its retention, the committees strongly and emphatically recommend that consent to British Rail's proposal to close the Settle-Carlisle line be refused."

And that — if the Act was still worth the paper it was written — should surely have been that. But the moment the report landed on the desk of David Mitchell, the public transport minister, at Christmas 1986 marked instead the start of the long and exasperating phoney war with its postponed announcements, false dawns and behind-the-scenes negotiations with all and sundry. The story is told in Chapter 9.

Life for the committees, meanwhile, returned more or less to normal: except for James Towler. In March 1987, Mr Towler paid the price for being the travellers' caped crusader when — in response to a request for advice as to what the future might hold beyond the expiry on March 31 of his term of office — he was again summoned to London.

In his own account, Mr Towler writes of his meeting with Lord Lucas, the consumer affairs minister: "From his attitude and tone it appeared he'd been got at. This did not surprise me as I was aware a number of senior managers within British Rail were already relishing my imminent demise." Mr Towler was not reappointed and his departure from the S & C scene — coming as it did so soon after the loss of Ron Cotton — caused something of a furore, with his committee immediately lobbying to seek a reversal of the decision. John Watson, the Tory MP for Skipton and Ripon, was quoted in the *Yorkshire Post* as saying: "The overtones are that he was not reappointed to the job because he had become a thorn in BR's side. If this was the case, then that was every reason to make sure he was reappointed. It is his job to be a thorn and some TUCC chairmen are not." An attempt by David Mitchell, the public transport minister, to defuse the row backfired when Lord Lucas refused to allow Mr Towler a place as an independent member of the Central Transport Consultative Committee (the TUCCs' parent body). And so the redoubtable Mr Towler left the fray to trumpet the railways' cause from within the ranks of the Railway Development Society.

A diesel-hauled coal train meets the Cumbrian Mountain Pullman, hauled by the Duchess of Hamilton. The Class 45 diesel on the coal train was once the mainstay of express passenger services over the Settle-Carlisle.

A Class 47 locomotive races through Garsdale with a diverted West Coast Main Line express. The sidings in the foreground are now completely disused and the trackbed of the branch line to Hawes can be seen at the bottom of the picture.

7.
New life in the hills

JULY 14 is celebrated by the French as the anniversary of one of the most significant events in the Revolution of 1789. In the history of the Settle & Carlisle, too, July 14 is its Bastille Day — the day in 1986 that the forces of change at last began to roll back the frontiers of the old order. The day a local daily stopping train returned to eight stations in the Eden Valley and the Yorkshire Dales which had last seen a regular service way back in 1970. As the two-car diesel multiple unit loomed out of the early morning hill fog at lofty Garsdale Station, St Swithen's Eve might have seemed a more appropriate analogy. It hardly seemed real: feeder lines to fairly big cities were not immune from the threat of closure through lack of patronage, yet here we were witnessing the birth of a commuter service which left a Yorkshire market town at the crack of dawn to trundle the best part of 90 miles through wild, open (and often wet) countryside to a city whose regional importance really belied its modest size and population.

The train was reasonably full by the time it reached Garsdale, but it was an artificial fullness born of the desire of so many S & C campaigners to rise with the lark to witness this historic moment which, all felt, would make or break the case for the line. Here we were, the TUCC hearings behind us and the joint report of the committees not anticipated until the end of the year, with the calls of campaigners and local authorities answered by British Rail. If the new Dalesman service fulfilled the most optimistic predictions of its fiercest proponents, its success could only strengthen the case for retaining the line — even though that case would rest, theoretically at least, on the recommendations of the TUCCs based on evidence relating mainly to the limited service whose only stop between Settle and Carlisle was at Appleby. If, on the other hand, the Dalesman service proved a flop, then that could only provide proof positive of what BR had been saying all along: that there had been no significant market for local trips in 1970 and nothing much had changed since.

The realisation of the Dalesman dream marked the happy coincidence of a similar train of thought being followed by three principal protagonists in the closure battle: the Joint Action Committee had launched its stations reopening campaign that March as a means primarily of retaining some momentum after the TUCC hearings; Cumbria County Council was looking to build on its commitment to the line and to cement its role to the fore of the joint local authorities' campaign, following the demise of West Yorkshire upon the abolition of metropolitan counties; the still enigmatic Ron Cotton, encouraged by his early successes, wanted to test the potential of wider markets.

But the foundations for the Dalesman experiment had really been laid some years previously with the innovative DalesRail charter service, pioneered by the Yorkshire Dales National Park Authority. The man best equipped to tell the story is Colin Speakman, the prime mover in getting DalesRail on the tracks.

Back in 1970 he was a 29-year-old English teacher in Leeds. Born beneath the red rather than the white rose, like so many others he fell in love with the Yorkshire Dales while at Leeds University and chose to stay east of the Pennines. At that time his organisational bent was satisfied within the West Riding Ramblers Association, for which he became access officer, then transport officer and finally area secretary.

"In those days I was a weekend rambler, with no car," he recalled. In the late '60s it was quite easy to be a weekend rambler without a car as British Rail ran ramblers' specials from Leeds to places like the North York Moors, the Peak District and the Yorkshire Dales. The Dales excursion ran on the Settle and Carlisle line and "there was a great tradition in this region of trains, countryside and walking". "Everybody used to say that the best one of the lot was the Settle-Carlisle excursion."

In addition to the excursions, lobbying by the ramblers had persuaded British Rail to introduce cheap day tickets on stopping trains to intermediate stations on the Settle-Carlisle line. "The crunch came in May 1970 with the end of stopping services — that effectively cut off a third of the Yorkshire Dales National Park for people without cars," said Mr Speakman, whose family found themselves deprived of their principal leisure activity. "I was a militant anti-car person but we gave up and bought our first car — not to get round town but to get round the countryside."

But it was another four years before the germ of the DalesRail idea was sown — in the shelter of a dry stone wall on a rainy Pennine Easter

Monday. Colin and fellow ramblers Jim McDermid, Fred Andrews and Jeff Grange were taking a rest while on a gritstone walk from Rochdale to Marsden. They were indulging in that time-honoured pastime of bemoaning the stupidity of British Rail, when it was suggested that the Ramblers Association should put its money where its mouth was and charter a train over the Settle-Carlisle.

Getting BR permission to stop at the closed stations as a "one-off" proved, contrary to expectations, rather easier than subsequently persuading the West Riding Ramblers Association to risk putting a relatively small amount of money up front to charter a train. "We had a hell of a meeting and it went finally by a very small majority in our favour," said Colin Speakman. "We went ahead and advertised it as well as we could and there was an avalanche — we started off hoping we might get 200 people. We ended up with a ten-coach train loaded to the 'gunwales'." So when the train actually ran in late summer 1974, not only were cost-conscious members of the Ramblers Association silenced, but 500 walkers enjoyed a grand day out and the people of Garsdale station were able to do something they hadn't done for more than four years as they came out of their former railway cottage homes and waved to passengers on a departing train.

Also in 1974, local government in England and Wales was undergoing its biggest shake-up for decades as county boundaries were redrawn, new counties created and old ones abolished or swallowed up by their larger neighbours. As part of this reorganisation, the Yorkshire Dales National Park Authority ceased to be simply a joint planning committee of the North and West Riding county councils and became instead a fully fledged National Park Committee under North Yorkshire County Council. It also included representatives from Cumbria and members appointed by the Secretary of State to represent the special "national" interests of ramblers, conservationists and other amenity groups. Colin Speakman was one of the appointed members.

Around the same time, a threat from British Rail which had been looming in the wings suddenly moved centre stage: it was claimed that if the Settle-Carlisle was to provide a satisfactory diversionary route for the West Coast Main Line, the platform edges of its disused stations would have to be demolished to allow sufficient clearance for the new Mk III coaches. This would obviously have put paid to the idea of ever repeating the successful ramblers' special — and yet BR's claims seemed to be quite inconsistent. It was never satisfactorily explained, for example, just precisely what it was which necessitated a different amount of clearance at a disused station compared with one which remained in use. Was this a cynical attempt to pre-empt any successful ramblers' service on the Settle-Carlisle lest it should eventually prejudice attempts to close the line? BR engineers were told as much by national park committee members at a stormy meeting at Settle in the winter of 1974.

Yet out of that working party meeting, which brought together representatives of the national park authority, British Rail, Cumbria county council, Eden district council and the United and Ribble bus companies, came a decision to restore five stations and operate an experimental charter service with connecting buses from Garsdale station to Hawes and Sedbergh. Colin Speakman proposed to the park authority a fully-fledged rail service for the Dales. The committee backed the idea and Mr Speakman, having resigned his member's seat, was subsequently appointed Field Services Officer with responsibility for its realisation.

"DalesRail could not have happened with the old authority," he said. "The crisis of the stations and the success of the ramblers' train all happened just as the new authority was coming into being." Armed with all the optimism of the park committee, Mr Speakman and the Assistant National Park Officer, George Hallas, went to Leeds to talk to British Rail about the cost of restoring the stations. "They told us 'we in this room represent 140 years of railway experience and we think this is a total waste of time'. But we eventually persuaded BR to restore stations to a standard fit for 'occasional use' for a grand total of £5,000 instead of the £15,000 each which BR had quoted."

Colin Speakman attributes the progress made to David Harrison, the then Passenger Manager at BR's Preston Division, who clearly saw in DalesRail an opportunity to win for British Rail a cash injection, albeit a very small one, from local authorities and thereby set a useful precedent. The next major hurdle was presented by the Railways Inspectorate whose safety requirements for an advertised DalesRail service were somewhat higher than for the odd excursion stopping at the occasional disused station. With the first scheduled train just three weeks away and all the publicity material ready to go out, there was still no approval from the inspectorate. A question in the House from the Keighley MP, Bob Cryer, finally elicited the necessary information and the first DalesRail service ran in May 1975 from Leeds, Bradford, Shipley, Bingley, Keighley

Walkers disembark at Garsdale from a lengthy DalesRail service in October 1983. Holding the door open is Laurie Fallows, a guided walk leader for the Yorkshire Dales National Park Authority.

and Skipton to the stations in the national park, plus Kirkby Stephen and Appleby. There were two trains on the Saturday and one on the Sunday, when the connecting buses were extended to run into Swaledale. Guided walks led by volunteers were arranged from various stations and bus-stops.

The legal niceties included indemnifying British Rail against possible injury to passengers, and providing voluntary wardens to look after passengers at the stations. At Ribblehead — where the private owner had earlier woken one morning to see bulldozers demolishing the down platform and waiting room to make way for new sidings at the British Rail ballast quarry — special arrangements had to be made and new access provided to the remaining platform.

Despite the short period left for publicising the venture, the first DalesRail service was well used and the loss of £127, rather than the £372 which had been budgeted for, was judged by the *Yorkshire Post* to be "beyond the revivalists' wildest expectations". The deficit was due entirely to the cost of running the connecting buses and the offer of concessionary fares which were enjoyed mainly by Dales families using the southbound trains. The national park committee's chairman, Keith Lockyer, declared: "There are 18,000 people living in the park area and they receive seven and a half million visitors every year, most of them in cars. We want to cut down the number of cars coming into the park and give the locals a link with the West Riding shopping centres."

Things went from good to better as the June and July trains ran with standing room only and by the end of the six-day experiment 3,370 people had used the service and there was support for an extended trial, aided by a £4,000 three-year grant from the Countryside Commission. Extensions to DalesRail that autumn included a "long weekend" service and trains from Preston over the freight-only line between Blackburn and Hellifield.

By the end of the year, 5,497 passengers had travelled on DalesRail, helping to generate a remarkable operating surplus of £165, rather than the anticipated loss of £2,000. The most popular of the reopened stations were Kirkby Stephen, the destination for 967 travellers and the departure point for 461, and Garsdale, where 919 alighted from and 557 boarded trains. Dent was also popular as a destination for 747 DalesRailers.

In 1976 services were extended to and from Carlisle and three reopened stations at Armathwaite, Langwathby and Lazonby, with a linking bus service to the Lake District and guided walks organised by the park authority there.

At the end of the 1977 season, the three-year DalesRail experiment was pronounced a success and the park committee resolved to continue it on a regular basis, despite the end of the Countryside Commission's grant. Not only did the scheme enable access to the park by people without cars, but it also offered the chance to manage the number of visitors in particular locations through the guided walk programme, which was enjoyed by some 62 per cent of those who rode on DalesRail Sunday services in 1977.

In 1978, the West Yorkshire Passenger Transport Executive took on the marketing of DalesRail, and went on to organise the chartering of trains from British Rail, taking advantage of its ability to negotiate a better price than the national park authority could.

One of the beauties of the PTE's involvement was that DalesRail passengers were able to start their journeys from any station on the PTE network — at a time when the executive was faced with having to make unpopular service cuts, here was a service which could raise the PTE in the public's estimation.

The reopening of Clitheroe station on the Blackburn-Hellifield link in 1978 brought Lancashire county and Ribble Valley district council (which had funded the Clitheroe scheme at minimum cost, thanks to British Rail flexibility) into the DalesRail steering committee and — with Cumbria, Eden district, the national park authority and the United and Ribble bus companies — there were now eight authorities co-operating in providing the service. "There has still, to my knowledge, never been any other kind of co-operative organisation in public transport like that since," said Colin Speakman.

During its lifetime, DalesRail became something of an institution, particularly among the 6,000 or so ramblers who rode the trains each summer. Indeed, even when the blossoming Dalesman service had effectively rendered DalesRail redundant, its fans — in the shape of the Friends of DalesRail — kept the flag flying by maintaining their own charter operation. For one season, the West Yorkshire DalesRail buffs rode in their own section of a Saturday Dalesman train which also carried regular fare-paying BR passengers. The last DalesRail services were operated by Lancashire County Council on the Blackburn link in 1989. In 1990, the Lancashire DalesRail Sunday service was incorporated into the the BR timetable.

So, by the time the Dalesman service was inaugurated in 1986, DalesRail had already proved that there was indeed a significant weekend market for leisure trips over the S & C. It had also proved that the line had a dedicated clientele who would make a number of repeat trips and back up their loyalty with hard cash, albeit at rates below a standard BR fare. To a limited extent, DalesRail had also indicated that there was at least some market among residents of the Yorkshire Dales who wanted to make shopping or other trips to West Yorkshire. Dalesman would be the acid test of just how elastic the demand for leisure travel might prove; more crucially it would dip a toe into hitherto uncharted depths — the potential Carlisle commuter market.

As described in the last chapter, the Settle-Carlisle Joint Action Committee had set out its stall at the TUCC hearings on the basis of two reports: *Retraining Settle-Carlisle* had been carried out for the JAC by the consultants TEST (Transport and Environmental Studies) and recommended a new local stopping service on the line, alongside an InterCity 125 link between West Yorkshire and Glasgow. The TEST recommendations were expanded in *New Life in the Hills*, compiled by Transport 2000, and it was this document which formed the backbone of the JAC's Reopenings Campaign, launched on March 5, 1986.

New Life in the Hills began by dealing with the failure of the railways ever to adapt to their changing post-war market, and contained some statistical nuggets which certainly provided food for thought. For example, it pointed out, patronage of the stations at both Armathwaite, and Lazonby and Kirkoswald, prior to the withdrawal of local services in 1970 had been comparable with that of both Settle and Appleby. Indeed, Armathwaite — with 11,000 passengers a year — was busier than either Settle or Appleby. On this basis, said *New Life in the Hills*, neither station should have been closed in the first place. Then there was the leisure market that the old stopping service had never sought to exploit. This did not really exist to the same extent in 1970 because railway managers in the 1960s were coping with decline and most did not think of meeting the challenge by seeking new market opportunities and finding people new things to do, using trains to get there. The report pointed out that on just 14 days of DalesRail operation in 1984, Garsdale had handled nearly 3,000 passengers — 900 more than passed through the station on about 300 working days in 1967/68.

Meanwhile, the S & C saga had been enjoying an increasingly high media profile which reached its peak with the TUCC hearings. A bandwagon was clearly rolling and — buoyed by the way the hearings appeared to have gone — local politicians who might have previously harboured doubts were by now moving solidly behind a campaign which was beginning to have the smell of possible success. Thus, in February 1986, Cumbria County Council's Public Transport Committee agreed in principle to lend financial backing to the station reopening proposals of Eden District Council and the town councils at Appleby and Kirkby Stephen. This followed agreement by the latter two each to contribute the product of a penny rate towards local services and the permanent reopening of stations. Eden had first talked to British Rail as early as May 1985 about the idea of chartering a train to run a commuter service, the Kirkby Stephen Flyer, from Kirkby Stephen to Carlisle. BR had quoted a price of around £155,000 to run the service for a year, of which the local authorities anticipated recouping about half.

Around the time of the TUCC hearings came the significant realisation that not only were the JAC and the local authorities batting on the same side but so too, potentially, were Ron Cotton and British Rail. Chapter 5 told how Mr Cotton had engineered a breathing space to work on the Dalesman, or Kirkby Stephen Flyer, idea. Now Cumbria was able to persuade Ron Cotton that a charter train wasn't really good enough as it would deny travellers, and BR, of the benefits of through ticketing.

It would be far better, Cumbria suggested, if the train could be run as regular timetabled service, with the local authorities putting in enough money to make good the likely operating shortfall. And so the basis for an agreement emerged, whereby the local authorities would contribute around £80,000 towards the cost of running a two-car DMU on a daily return journey between Skipton and Carlisle to the end of the timetable year in May. The idea was that this would be a pump-priming exercise by the local authorities and, as the Dalesman's clientele built up over succeeding years, so the local authorities' contribution could be wound down.

So here the various parties stood, on the threshold of a bold initiative: they had got there because, in each pursuing their own ideas, it had emerged that they had their sights set on a common goal. As John Whitelegg, chairman of the JAC put it: "It was a happy coincidence that we found everyone working to the same objective, but historical coincidence is quite a useful weapon. The idea of the Reopenings Campaign was really to be positive and to go on the offensive so we could be seen to be fighting FOR something, rather than just fighting against the closure." Certainly, the JAC's reopenings ideas were conceived wholly in isolation from Ron Cotton and BR. Said Dr Whitelegg: "We were vaguely aware that this Cotton character was a bit of an enigma but some us still felt at the time, myself included, that he wasn't to be trusted at all."

The following weeks saw the various authorities, one by one, putting their money where their mouths were. Eden and Cumbria were first off the mark and, by early June, the JAC was able to tell a campaign meeting at Hawes that most of the necessary funding had been secured, with Cumbria donating £30,000, Eden District and Carlisle City Council £20,000 each, Craven district £10,000, Appleby Town Council £2,500 and Kirkby Stephen Town Council £1,750. But Leeds City Council had turned down a contribution on the grounds that the service would be of little direct benefit to the city. Of more concern was the continued reluctance of North Yorkshire County Council to do anything more for the S & C beyond the token contribution it had made towards the PEIDA study. In an impassioned plea to fellow members of the county's highways committee, Beth Graham, the prominent Alliance member for Ribblesdale and a formidable supporter of the S & C, said: "The railway is more important to the Craven and Cumbria area than the East Coast Main Line is to the rest of North Yorkshire." But her words failed to convince her colleagues to overturn the recommendation of their officers. However, within a few days, the county's passenger transport working party had been effectively shamed by the Alliance's Steve Galloway into making a U-turn after it became clear that the county's cash could be the difference between the service going ahead or not. And although the £7,500 pledged by the working party fell short of the £20,000 asked for, Ron Cotton's reaction on being told the news was: "We can go ahead now."

North Yorkshire had stipulated that the cash should be spent on improvements to stations in the county and this sum exceeded what Ron Cotton had said he would be spending on the provision of essential lighting at the two stations within the county — Horton and Ribblehead. Indeed, research suggests that the budget allocated never was spent up. But it was clear that pledges on paper were, at this stage in the game, far more important to Ron Cotton than cash in the bank to offset directly against the cost of running the new service. Crucially, the Railways Inspectorate had been persuaded that the eight stations at which the Dalesman would call had, in effect, been open to passenger services throughout the preceding 11 years since the inauguration of DalesRail. This avoided the potentially prohibitive expense of upgrading the halts to the standards required of new stations: the only significant additional work that would be required was some form of platform lighting come the onset of darker nights and mornings.

And so, Bastille Day it was. At Carlisle, there was time for a brief press conference before the return journey of the first Dalesman (the train was scheduled to make two return journeys Monday to Friday, and one on Saturdays). Ron Cotton told media representatives the new service represented the fruits of successful and unprecedented co-operation between BR and local authorities. Councillor Vic Davies, Deputy Mayor of Carlisle, waved the green flag at Citadel Station and the Dalesman began its return trip to enjoy a carnival-style reception along the way. At Appleby there was a brass band, bunting and an explosive salvo from detonators on the line.

Even on that first Dalesman, it became clear that the new service had potential — among the 66 passengers who rode into Carlisle were a handful of car-owners in the Appleby area who said they'd be more than happy to let the train go on taking the strain. The first return from Carlisle carried 55 fare-paying passengers — well above the 25 BR needed to break even.

Above — Councillor Vic Davies shows the green flag to the first Dalesman service out of Carlisle, while — below — bunting greeted its arrival at Appleby. Loadings quickly exceeded expectations and, within a year, the trains were carrying 50 to 60 regular passengers.

To coincide with the introduction of the Dalesman, Ron Cotton arranged for a limited number of additional stops to be made by the existing service trains, including Garsdale on the first train out of Leeds, and Kirkby Stephen on the last northbound service. It was a small gesture aimed at providing some increased flexibility to enhance journey opportunities. The fact that it was a long way from perfect was seized upon, perhaps a little unkindly, by Mike Amos, the gifted scribe with the *Northern Echo*, who wrote: "Though British Rail may indeed be getting there, passengers are going to find it rather more difficult coming back. In the new age of the train, a six-mile return journey takes slightly over two and half hours."

Mr Amos was taking the example of day trip opportunities from stations between Horton and Garsdale. "The problem arises because the last northbound stopping train of the day leaves from Skipton at 12.20 pm — just 49 minutes after the first southbound service gets there," he wrote. "Travellers hoping to make rather more than a 49-minute day of it can catch the 4.50 pm back from Skipton. Like every other train for the last 16 years, though, it will speed through stations at Horton-in-Ribblesdale, Ribblehead, Dent and Garsdale.

"Recognising the difficulty, BR has now included the official solution in the timetable. Passengers on the 4.50 pm can watch the station they joined at whizz past and — at no extra charge — get off miles further on at Kirkby Stephen. Then there's just over an hour to wait on a desolate platform before the southbound stopping train arrives to take them back where they've just been.

"And BR goes further. Because there's not exactly much to do at Kirkby Stephen station — a mile and half from the town — they will allow passengers to travel to Appleby. It's 11 miles further, but there's a pub and only 38 minutes to wait before backtracking."

The most extreme case, wrote Mr Amos, was that faced by passengers popping into Settle from Horton, six miles up the dale. "Joining the return at 5.10 pm, they'd be able to alight at Horton just before quarter to eight. The stopping journey takes 12 minutes."

Ron Cotton put on a brave face: "It isn't terribly good, is it? But when you compare it with nothing, it's something." Mr Cotton's problem, he said, was that just one minute added to the evening journey through additional stops would have meant an extra train crew, pushing costs right up.

By the time the autumn timetable revisions came in, bringing addi-

Even while BR was trying to close the line, it was not above using unusual locomotives to boost passenger numbers. Enthusiasts travelled from all over the country to see the last remaining Class 40 locomotive, repainted in its original green livery and given its original number, D200. It worked the Leeds-Carlisle service for several months. It is pictured here rather earlier — in 1983 — at Dent Head. The locomotive was joined by a similarly repainted DMU set, picture — below — at Garsdale.

tional stops, things were already looking up, thanks in part to summer loadings which exceeded all reasonable expectations. On August 12, BR released figures showing that nearly 2,000 people had used the Dalesman in its third week, an average approaching 100 passengers per journey. The most popular service — with standing room only on some trains — was the 12.20 out of Settle. Discerning Dales holidaymakers had quickly realised the opportunity this gave to combine a leisurely start to the day with a return journey over the prime scenic section of the line to Appleby. Clearly, the Dalesman wasn't just siphoning off demand from the existing services, but — by greatly extending journey opportunities — was tapping into a whole new area of demand.

With the reality of the Dalesman came other initiatives. August 4 saw the inauguration by the Yorkshire Dales Society and the Wensleydale and Swaledale Transport Users' Group of a minibus link between Hawes and Garsdale station, funded by Richmondshire District Council, the Dales national park authority and other organisations. By late September, passenger numbers had so exceeded expectations that only part of Richmondshire's £500 subsidy had been used up and the organisers decided to extend the service into October. Innovative BR managers at Carlisle played to the line's new audience by repainting the DMU set, drawn from Cumbrian coast line stock, in green 1950s livery. The DMU was joined for a season by a Class 40 locomotive in similar vintage livery.

Mr Cotton, meanwhile, was "delighted" with the performance of the Dalesman, with only the early train into Carlisle not filled well above the crucial 25-passenger mark. But the arrival of the autumn college term would change this too: previously, young people in the Appleby and Kirkby Stephen areas had enjoyed only limited opportunities for further education. You could go to college in Kendal... or Kendal... and, even then, only if someone gave you a lift. Now the bright lights of Carlisle beckoned, just a short train ride away. Soon, the morning train was carrying as healthy a load as the others and laying the foundations for a classic cry of "hardship" when the TUCCs were called upon again to address the problems that would be caused by the loss of the new services brought in in 1986. Figures compiled by Appleby Grammar School showed a fourfold increase in the number of pupils going on to higher education following the advent of the Dalesman service. There can be few clearer indications of the direct relationship between the availability of transport and opportunities for self-improvement in a

The inauguration of the Garsdale-Hawes minibus link. Cutting the ribbon is Councillor Roger Stott, Chairman of Richmondshire District Council. Among others in the picute are Colin Speakman (in boots) who had earlier played such an important role in establishing DalesRail and — on the right — Frank Cawkill, chairman of the Wensleydale and Swaledale Transport Users' Group who, sadly, did not live to see the salvation of the S & C. He was succeeded in the WSTUG chair by Councillor Stott.

rural area.

And so, in October, Alan Whitehouse reported in the *Yorkshire Post* BR plans to more than double the service to all eight reopened stations. The S & C timetable would be completely revamped, with the Dalesman effectively absorbed to form an integral part of the service, running right through to Leeds to save passengers a change of train at Skipton. The Dalesman was estimated to have carried 20,000 passengers since July to maintain the average of around 100 per train. Travellers were now buying season tickets for commuter and school journeys — even though the line remained under threat of closure. The new service would offer five return trips daily over most of the line through, said Ron Cotton, "better use of our resources". That meant that the two locomotive-hauled train sets would each make an additional journey — three single legs instead of just two — with the former Dalesman DMU providing the additional journey. The plan needed only the endorsement of the Dalesman's local authority backers, but it was not without its critics: James Towler, chairman of the North East Transport Users' Consultative Committee, feared the all-stops plan would render the line unattractive to business travellers. Realistically, however, it has to be acknowledged that most long distance business travellers between, say, Leeds and Glasgow were by this time using the East Coast service via Newcastle and Edinburgh or hadtransferred their allegiance to the air service and been lost to rail altogether.

Ron Cotton's proposals won the necessary local authority backing and Mr Cotton ensured his plans were so firmly in place before his early retirement the following February that, as he put it, "no-one will be able to undo this one". So the knot was tied: the Dalesman experiment had worked and played a crucial role in putting the S & C's passenger figures on a steady upward curve. Ron Cotton's marketing shoes were subsequently filled by men who — although they did not enjoy the same exclusive S & C brief of their predecessor — nonetheless belonged to a new breed of rail manager who actually believed in the railways and wanted to see them both survive and prosper. Eventually, not even a Government with a crushing parliamentary majority would prove equal to untying the knot.

8.
Great expectations

IF YOU go up on the fells today you're sure of a big surprise... for every photographer there ever was, will seem to buzzing about there because, today's the day the steam trains are out on the railway!

Those unprepared for the spectacle may well find it difficult to believe their eyes when they witness the quite enormous number of steam train enthusiasts and amateur photographers who will gather in all weathers to snatch a piece of celluloid posterity, courtesy of the Steam Locomotive Operators Association and the Settle-Carlisle railway.

Here at the very heart of the Pennines — where the rivers Eden, Ure and Clough rise within a few miles of each other and flow respectively north, east and south — the very names evoke the isolation of the place: Mallerstang Common, Dandry Mire, Hellgill, Hangingstone Scar.

The invasion of the camera gang soon shatters the solitude: vaulting gates and leaping ditches, they come by the hundred — thousand even — hell-bent on jostling for the best vantage point. They wait, sometimes for hours, jealously guarding that new camera angle and hoping the beloved iron horse will obligingly belch steam at just the moment to create the classic picture so admired by the connoisseurs.

The moment passed, the few precious frames clicked, the madness for some begins. Some even resort to motorcycles in their endeavours to catch another chance of snapping the object of their admiration further up the line. The maniac road-racing which follows the passage of a steam train through, for example, Aisgill Summit has been widely condemned. Taken at its worst, this increasingly regular pilgrimage of "steam buffs" is an unwelcome intrusion into the lives of the people who farm these lonely hills. The other side of the coin is the extent to which this extraordinary spectacle reflects the strength of the wave of steam-age nostalgia which continues to sweep Britain, and the Settle-Carlisle line in particular.

But the great dilemma lies in finding a means of translating this fanaticism into pounds and pence to run a railway. It was summed up for Stan Abbott the day he took a 280-mile circular steam-hauled excursion, taking in the Settle and Carlisle. Those on board belonged in roughly equal numbers to three categories — members and guests of the Darlington section of the Permanent Way Institution; steam fanatics; and members of the general public interested in taking a ride over the Settle-Carlisle. The Institution had organised the trip to mark its centenary and had had little difficulty filling the other 300 seats with only limited advertising, despite the fact it was running on a week-day.

The steam fanatics were characteristically conspicuous by their notebooks, stopwatches and cameras, taking advantage of every watering halt to rush out and take pictures of the ex-Southern Railways locomotive, Sir Lamiel. "I've travelled the line about five or six times so far this year," said one. "If I'm not on a steam special I'm usually taking pictures of it — I just wish there was some way of converting that photography into cash to keep the trains running." And there lies the catch — British Rail has always seen this ostensibly keep-coming-back-for-more market as a very fickle one: "The trouble is that if the steam enthusiasts had to pay the full economic fare they'd be just as happy to go out and take pictures of the trains instead," said BR's InterCity Services Manager David Ward.

But British Rail's cautious approach to using the line for anything other than its original purpose was not mirrored by the stream of ideas that began to flow from the private sector. Against a background of growing debate on railway privatisation, a number of schemes and ideas were floated which involved almost everything from running *Orient Express*-style luxury trains to developing the entire 72-mile line into a kind of linear museum or tourist attraction, the trains being used principally as a way of getting between the attractions, which, according to taste, might include a restored lime kiln, a navvy museum — the Settle to Carlisle was the last route to be built by pick and shovel — or a travelling exhibition based at Garsdale in the summer.

Towards the end of the S & C saga, the issues of tourism and privatisation became inextricably intertwined, for the official view in Government and BR circles — from the minister of public transport down — appeared to be a vision of the line as a steam-operated relic, opening each Easter, closing each October, distributing ice cream and key fobs, while, out of sight and out of mind, the former commuters scrambled daily aboard minibuses for Carlisle, Settle and elsewhere, defeating the worst of the winter weather.

Train buffs stick their necks out aboard the Cumbrian Mountain Pullman at Newbiggin — "If the steam enthusiasts had to pay the full economic fare they'd be just as happy to go out and take pictures of the trains instead."

The first scheme to come forward was rather more low key, but got off to a bad start when journalists latched on to its proposal for a "theme corridor" and dubbed it a "70-mile Disneyland in the Dales". In fact the idea of Sian Johnson and Associates, a London-based marketing consultancy, was to develop "major high intensity tourist magnets" at only about four lineside sites with the aim of ultimately attracting a million passengers a year on ten or 12 trains a day.

With such traffic levels, the company saw the line as being self-financing and offering a major "leisure investment opportunity". Ms Johnson mentioned ideas such as a "navvy museum" to the work of the great railway builders as typifying the sort of development felt to be in keeping with the line. She drew comparison with other major attractions, such as the Beamish open-air industrial museum in County Durham, with 200,000 visitors a year, and the Blaenau Ffestiniog slate mines. These major magnets would be complemented by "lineside development and tourist services such as shops, pubs, amusements, indoor and evening entertainments, sporting activities, holiday accommodation (for example, time-share cottages)", and accommodation and catering developments "off-line" in nearby towns and villages. Among companies showing interest in the scheme was the hotels and restaurants giant, Imperial Leisure, and clearly a major concern of the national park, as planning authority, was — and would remain — the likely environmental impact of intrusive schemes on this largely unspoilt area. To put the idea into perspective, the number of annual visitors to the then Upper Dales Folk Museum in Hawes (now revamped as the Dales Countryside Museum) was just 20,000 at the time of her report.

Ms Johnson said in December 1985 that the scheme had not been dropped but was merely "on ice" pending the outcome of the closure hearings. Meanwhile her consultancy formed the Settle-Carlisle Railway Company Ltd and an associated marketing company ready to spring into action once the line's fate was known. "We can go with either BR or a private line," she said, reflecting a growing feeling that perhaps the time was right for a stab at railway privatisation. Ms Johnson said there had been "cordial" talks with the national park committee on possible development. Her company also set up a "data base" comprising the country's top 600 tourist attractions and began work on the market research of leisure attractions to help the industry understand why some ventures succeed while others, such as the Britannia British Genius theme park in Derbyshire, are spectacular failures.

This set of proposals appeared to have breached some kind of mental dam surrounding the line and its potential as a tourist magnet. The Johnson proposals were followed by another report, this one less controversial in tone and content, prepared for the Countryside Commission by the Centre for Environmental Interpretation at Manchester Polytechnic. This envisaged a gradual build-up of use of the line through an extended DalesRail-type service, towards 400,000 passengers a year. The research team's suggestions were contained in a report entitled *Interpreting the Heritage of the Settle-Carlisle Railway Line*, "interpretation" being the buzz word to describe the more participative type of educational day out which was (and is) seen as one of the ways leisure time use should be going in the '80s and '90s. The team saw this interpretation as the last piece in the jig-saw which could bring the Settle-Carlisle alive for visitors.

"The conservation and appreciation of our natural and man-made heritage has rightly become big business in Britain, with many millions of people taking leisure trips each year. In 1983 the value and volume of tourism to England increased substantially with 121 million trips and

"We've increased amenities, enhanced the environment and kept the Settle-Carlisle Line running — all in one go." Railnews, June 1989

£7,600m worth of expenditure. There has been a substantial increase in visiting places of interest, particularly where these offer an opportunity to glimpse into the past. The present rate of change in British society is remarkable and as manufacturing employment is replaced by a leisure and service economy this is giving more people the time and the inclination to discover their natural and man-made heritage on leisure trips and visits."

The report identified a number of themes which could be developed for the interest of rail users and others through booklets, self-guided trails and displays. Themes for self-guided trails, combined with displays at the appropriate stations included limestone scenery and quarrying at Horton; the navvy towns at Ribblehead; upland landscape and land-use at Dent; town trails and the development of settlements at Appleby, Kirkby Stephen and Settle; agriculture and land-use in the Eden Valley at Langwathby. The report suggested a more ambitious plan for Garsdale station, where there would be a visitor centre, possibly housed in converted railway carriages which could be used for a travelling exhibition in winter. Like Settle and Appleby, the station should be restored to its original Midland Victorian splendour to "create a feeling of a working museum". The polytechnic group envisaged that such a centre would attract about 30,000 visitors a year. Also suggested in the report were observation cars on trains, with "on-board interpretation", and an annual railway festival.

Even so, it was ill-received in some quarters. The then editor of the *Yorkshire Evening Post*, Malcolm Barker, wrote a scathing review of its proposals, ending with his view that the "wild places" of Garsdale, Ribblehead and the like, should be left to their solitude, unpolluted by the make-believe of tourism and "interpretation".

Although the Manchester scheme, unlike the Sian Johnson one, would clearly be unlikely to raise significant environmental objections, both ideas were variations on the same theme. This theme is the recognition that the Settle-Carlisle line is an important part of Britain's national heritage which should remain, in use, for the enjoyment and education of ourselves and our children.

The lofty ideals became steadily submerged in a collection of increasingly commercialised proposals as the closure saga ran into its final year. The accent was increasingly on involvement by private companies. One scheme mirrored the London Docklands idea for persuading developers to put money into the Docklands Light Railway on the grounds that the railway would make their investment more valuable by adding to its accessibility from the City. A joint report from the Community Programme Division of the Jarvis construction group and the Government's Manpower Services Commission proposed leaving the line in BR hands, but putting cash into "heritage" projects along the way, such as rebuilding Hellifield Station into its former Midland Railway glory, with shops and a quality restaurant — another echo of the past, since Hellifield was a refreshment stop in the days before restaurant cars.

At Settle itself, the heritage project would be a remarkable Hoffman lime kiln, which still today stands disused by the railway tracks between Langcliffe and Stainforth. This aspect of the Jarvis report deserves closer attention as its origins lay in an enterprising local initiative. The Ribblesdale Project was set up in 1986 to look at the possibility of renovating the lime kiln which, until the 1930s, burned lime in a continuous process inside a 700 ft oval tunnel. Although more fuel-efficient than conventional kilns, the Hoffman process was highly labour intensive and the task of removing the fired lime was compared to working at the jaws of hell. The kiln, built in 1873, is still reckoned to be the best preserved example of this highly unusual design and the idea was to make it the centrepiece of a visitor and educational resource centre in the reclaimed

Above: the Hoffman kiln in its heyday, with — inset — John Wakeford and Councillor Beth Graham inside the structure, and — below — a general view of the site.

Langcliffe Quarry which had once provided the raw material for the kiln's industrial process and now served as a North Yorkshire County Council waste disposal site. The project attracted a £5,000 grant from the Gold Fields Trust, a philanthropic body set up by Consolidated Goldfields, whose subsidiary, Amey Roadstone, operates quarries in the Ribblesdale area. Through John Whitelegg, the then chairman of the Settle-Carlisle Joint Action Committee, Lancaster University became involved in the project, with Dr Whitelegg and Dr John Wakeford, of the School of Independent Studies, compiling a feasibility study for an industrial heritage complex in Ribblesdale costing an eventual £1.5m and rivalling established museums like Beamish. Of all the "heritage" developments proposed for the S & C, the Ribblesdale Project remains the most soundly based but, while the long-term goal remains, progress since 1986 has been minimal because of lack of funds and the ending of the Government's Community Programme which would have played an important role in the development.

Further along the line, the Jarvis plan again drew on the Ribblesdale Project proposals, while reverting to more familiar themes, such as a museum at Ribblehead devoted to the lives of the navvies. The report stressed the railway itself as a vital part of the jigsaw, the Yorkshire Dales roads being too narrow to cope with the initial 750,000 visitors per year, rising quickly to one million. The railway would remain in BR hands, with BR operating a form of "park and ride" service from Hellifield, where large car parks would be provided, visitors alighting where fancy dictated. Leaving the line in BR hands would have meant a guaranteed future for the Leeds-Carlisle service and tourism revenue to pay for the repairs needed to the track, signals, bridges and tunnels, which, like Ribblehead Viaduct, had simply been left to rot.

The Jarvis scheme quickly attracted support from the Department of Employment, which saw it as a means of creating much-needed jobs in West Yorkshire, the Dales and the Eden Valley. It earned the tag of the biggest job creation scheme ever and the project was believed to enjoy the personal endorsement of Lord Young, the trade and industry minister. Indeed, Lord Young's intervention — as a minister who had the ear of the Prime Minister — is credited with one of the delays in announcing the line's future. In the event, the Jarvis scheme sank without trace with the announcement by the Transport Minister, David Mitchell, that he was minded to authorise closure of the line. The scuppering of the scheme was, at the time, widely attributed to another man who had the ear of Mrs Thatcher — a senior member of her economic and policy advice team, Greg Bourne. Not long after the Mitchell announcement came changes in the rules governing such job creation schemes that would have far-reaching consequences for a variety of organisations which had become dependent on them as a source of labour for often worthwhile projects. The idea of a vast band of "latterday navvies" using Manpower Services Commission funds to revive the heritage features of the Settle-Carlisle corridor was doomed whether the line remained in BR hands or passed into private ownership.

Indeed, the Jarvis report which might have been the saving the of the S & C may well have unwittingly planted the seed of privatisation allied to tourism in the collective Government mind, for it was less than two months later — as outlined in the next chapter — that David Mitchell's widely predicted reprieve for the line was replaced by an announcement that it would either be taken over by a private buyer or would almost certainly close.

Even so, the Jarvis report aroused a good deal of interest at the time, and was quickly followed by an announcement from the Great Scottish and Western Railway Company that it wanted to launch a second luxury train to operate over the line. The Great Scottish and Western had made its name by assembling a prestige train of vintage and superbly converted BR coaches with five star hotel accommodation standards, stocking them with the finest foods and wines and taking parties of — mostly American — tourists on scenic trips round the Scottish Highlands, using BR tracks, locomotives and crews.

It had proved a successful enterprise. By the time the Settle-Carlisle scheme was floated, the Scottish service had been running for three years, on average 90 per cent full. The Dales service, the company promised, would be advertised around the world attracting up-market visitors to a tour combining the Yorkshire Dales, the Eden Valley and the Lake District. It could be operating by 1990, complementing the Jarvis proposals for a series of high quality tourist attractions over the line. The Great Scottish and Western suggested the train would have a significant effect on the local economy if the Scottish practice of taking travellers off the train once or twice per day to visit local attractions, was followed, and if the train could be supplied with locally produced foods.

Within weeks, the Government decision to try to sell the line, principally as a tourist attraction, had been announced. In August 1988,

Lazard Brothers, the merchant bank appointed by BR to handle the sale, had produced a glossy and expensive looking 45-page brochure, complete with colour photographs, for potential buyers. It was astonishing how attractively the line — said by BR to be run down and obsolete — could be portrayed in what amounted to an overgrown set of estate agent's particulars. It listed the scenic attractions of Dent — "cobbled streets and colour-washed cottages"; Ribblehead — "famous for its 24-arch viaduct", Kirkby Stephen — "an attractive Dales town" and Appleby — "host in June to a famous horse fair", among others. It was a document which appeared to see not only the Settle-Carlisle line as a tourist attraction, but also almost the entire Yorkshire Dales and Eden Valley. It was also a document roundly condemned — by the groups still fighting against the line being anything other than a vital link in the national transport network — as being long on hype and short on the information any serious buyer would need to prepare the business plan which was a condition of sale.

And, at last, even British Rail itself began to get in on the tourism act, firstly by sabotaging any attempts to sell the line as a going concern by the simple expedient of banning private trains south of Hellifield. This would compel prospective new owners to charter BR trains to carry its customers from Leeds — the main traffic centre — to Hellifield where they would have to scramble from a BR train and into a private one before their "heritage" journey could even begin. Secondly, BR issued its own brochure extolling the scenic and tourist attractions along the line. It came in full colour, with a map and brief descriptions of the main centres. It was accompanied by a "discovery guide" which also covered the line from Settle Junction to Carnforth, giving timetables, fare charts and a basic map showing suggestions for walks. In its own small way, this too was a watershed, marking the first time — apart from Ron Cotton's heroic attempts with cheap fares — that BR had set out to do the obvious and really market what, by its own admission, was the most scenic main line in England.

But there was more to come. One of the last-minute bidders for the line was Sea Containers, the company which also owns the Venice-Simplon Orient Express. The bid was presented by Settle and Carlisle Railway Company Ltd, the Sian Johnson company set up specifically to exploit any tourist/heritage opportunities which arose. Ms Johnson would not reveal how the £1m annual deficit — according to BR figures — would be tackled, but informed sources suggested the bid was in-

The S & C saga generated, over six years, a great many reports...These are just some of them.

tended to combine an Orient Express type service over the line — a direct challenge to the scheme outlined by the Great Scottish and Western Railway Company — combined with a completely new role as a strategic freight route, trunk-hauling containers between Glasgow and the South-East and, ultimately, into Europe via the Channel Tunnel.

This idea made use of some fairly basic research carried out by the railway wagon building and leasing firm, Tiphook, which suggested a Continental, or Berne Gauge route, could be set up linking the Channel Tunnel with key industrial centres, employing underused lines across the Home Counties, then curving round to join the Midland Main Line to Sheffield and Leeds, with the Settle-Carlisle carrying it across the border.

But Sea Containers' president, James Sherwood, made it plain that his company had scant interest in actually running the line to serve local passengers. His bid, he told the *Yorkshire Post*, was conditional on £5m being raised to form a trust for the maintenance work. Sea Containers would then build a reception area for visitors and run the trains. But in return, BR would have to agree to run a regular Leeds-Windermere service, where Sealink, another Sea Containers subsidiary, operated three tourist pleasure craft. It was a complex deal and few were surprised when it became one of the first to be rejected, partly because of the threat the container operation would have posed to BR's own Freightliner services.

The English Tourist Board also entered the fray, after a further study by PEIDA updating the consultants' invaluable 1983 groundwork. By this time, the redoubtable Ron Cotton, now retired from British Rail, was a member of the team, adding further credibility to the already strong case for development. The ETB Business Development Plan suggested the line could make a £400,000 profit within five years by combining the existing five-trains-per-day diesel-hauled service with steam-hauled "theme" trains. These would include evening gourmet diners and a variety of excursions.

What most people had forgotten, until it was forcibly pointed out, was that the process had already begun. Even without theme parks, working museums, restored attractions and the like, a growing number of people were using the eight stations re-opened in the Dalesman experiment, to discover the largely unspoiled towns and villages for themselves. A group of traders spread along the length of line formed their own association — the Settle-Carlisle Business Liaison Group — and warned of job losses and millions of pounds lost to the local economy if the closure was allowed to happen. The group went to Downing Street and lobbied Mrs Thatcher. Their complaints epitomise the key to the entire Settle-Carlisle saga.

One of the beauties of the line stems from its conception as a trunk rather than a local route, which means that, by and large, it does not duplicate access to the more developed parts of the Yorkshire Dales National Park. Rather, it provides speedy north-south access to the western part of the park where the number of visitors has not, by and large, begun to cause major problems. It still has the potential to increase significantly the number of visitors to the part of the park most able to accommodate them without increasing (and hopefully decreasing) the number of cars on the narrow Dales roads. The Countryside Commission's DalesRail studies showed how the service could be used to introduce a degree of control to the destination of day-trippers. Clearly, the line could form part of a more fundamental access scheme which would aim to discourage, or actually restrict, access by car to the national park's most heavily visited centres (such policies are already successfully operated in the Peak National Park). It could also help encourage ramblers away from areas where erosion is a problem (the Three Peaks) to less frequented, but arguably even more attractive, areas like the Howgill Fells.

Before the advent of DalesRail, there had been various initiatives to establish rail/bus access to the national park. In 1979 and '80, the park committee backed an experimental Three Peaks bus service from Giggleswick station to Hawes and a Sunday service from Giggleswick to Ribblehead. The response to the latter was disappointing and it was quickly abandoned. A Tuesday and Saturday summer service from Settle to Hawes lasted until 1982. The park committee also assisted BR to the tune of £2,200 between 1978 and 1981 in promoting the Parklink integrated rail/bus service from West Yorkshire. This too was subsequently abandoned. But by using the attractions of the Settle-Carlisle as a marketing device, the line could become the spine of a Dales transport system, building on existing bus and minibus connecting services.

The whole point of fostering the "Disneyland in the Dales" culture in the first place was to encourage the involvement of private companies. When Mr Channon announced his eventual reprieve for the line, he was quite specific that he wanted to see more private involvement to tap its considerable tourist potential. That still has not happened. Sea Containers made owning the line a prerequisite of running a luxury, "Super Pullman"-style tourist service — and had grander ambitions to develop new national and international freight routes rather than promoting the economy of the northern Pennines — so it is perhaps not surprising that this idea never got further than a press release. But the Great Western and Scottish Railway Company did not. Its proposals rested merely on the line remaining open. That has happened, but still the promised luxury train has not.

Similarly, if plans for a series of tourist attractions — the Hoffman Kiln project, for instance, or the navvy museum, were such good ideas five years ago, why are they apparently so unattractive now when the home-based holiday market is supposed to be booming? It may be that, quite simply, the future of the Settle-Carlisle lies, not as part of a sanitised "heritage project" but as a working — and workaday — railway, carrying a healthy mixture of people who actually want to get from A to B, with those who want a pleasant and relaxing day out taking up the next seat. That is precisely the message that the more far-sighted campaigners in the JAC, the Friends and, particularly, the Joint County

The old turntable at Garsdale was part of railway folklore, thanks to the occasion in 1900 when a gust of wind caught a locomotive and left it spinning for one and a half hours at the extraordinary rate of 40 revolutions per minute — a perimeter speed of 70mph. A stockade of sleepers was erected to prevent a repetition of the incident. In 1987 the turntable was again in the headlines as the Yorkshire Dales National Park Authority prevented its removal by giving it listed building status. The park authority's action failed to be upheld by the Department of the Environment and the turntable was subsequently moved to a new home on the Keighley and Worth Valley Railway, amid accusations that the S & C's heritage was being stripped in advance of a decision on the future of the line. The picture shows a Class 47-hauled service train pulling out of Garsdale before the removal of the turntable.

Councils had been hammering in a fight which — including the first "phoney war" from 1981-83 — lasted the best part of a decade.

---

9. From phoney war to final victory

FIVE years into the fight for the line, most campaigners could be forgiven for thinking they were almost home and dry. The Dalesman service, pushed through by Ron Cotton, had been running for a year and was steadily building a regular, daily traffic.

The rest of the service had been redrawn, and, by the simple and obvious expedient of making the rolling stock work one-and-a-half round trips per day, the two trains per day timetable had been extended to three.

This gave an aggregate service of five trains each way, all stopping at the ten stations (eight of them reopened) along the line*. This was the best local service the S & C had ever had in its 110-year history. Even the mighty London Midland and Scottish Railway had never seen fit to provide more than three local trains, in line with the original Midland Railway philosophy that the line was a means to an end — Scotland — rather than a benefit to the places it passed through.

Passenger numbers on these trains were still showing healthy annual increases, despite a couple of indifferent summers weatherwise, and the first suggestions had begun to leak from BR sources both in London and the North that the line was becoming one of Provincial Sector's best performers.

In the mid-1980s it was accepted that rural railways covered between 30 and 40 per cent of their direct costs, the rest coming from the Government grant, used to "buy" loss-making but socially desirable services from BR. But here was a line which, if the leaks could be believed, was coming close to paying all its direct costs — the expense of providing a train, driver and guard and the cost of staffing signal boxes along the route.

But the line's commercial successes were only serving to raise the

---

* *Strictly speaking, the number was nine and half as Ribblehead had — and still has at the time of writing — only one platform.*

stakes. The Settle-Carlisle affair was quickly becoming a highly political football and, with a general election looming, speculation rose that there could be a reprieve before polling day. On April 24, 1987, David Mitchell, the public transport minister, added to the speculation when he made a surprise visit to the line. Boarding the train at Settle, Mr Mitchell was left in no doubt as to the popularity of the new services when it turned out to be standing-room-only for the minister and Cumbria County Council officials. But Mr Mitchell refused to link the fate of the line with election fever, saying he still wanted more evidence before making a decision. "I don't see it as an election issue, but I am seeking to get the work done as qucikly as is consistent with doing so in a thorough and businesslike way," he told Stan Abbott. However, Bill Cameron, chairman of the joint councils steering group, felt sufficiently confident — on the basis of discussions with officials in the Department of Transport — to assert that the minister's mind was made up and that he would announce a reprieve "within the next four weeks".

It was not to be. The twin issues of bus-substitution and privatisation were only just around the corner, and the claim that the Settle to Carlisle line was being used to test the water for a national round of rural railway closures could still not be entirely discounted.

Bill Cameron's four weeks came and went, as did the general election which saw the Government returned with another thumping majority. Any announcement as to the line's fate was further put back while Mr Mitchell studied a proposal from a consortium of civil engineering firms to put up money for essential repairs and there was talk of ownership of the line passing into private hands, with the construction magnate William McAlpine at the forefront of proposals. BR would then pay a rental to run its services on the line. In July, however, Mr Mitchell said he was now anxious to put an end to the uncertainty surrounding the line and wanted only a clearer indication from the local authorities as to how much financial support was likely to be forthcoming for the line in future.

A meeting of the joint local authorities was hastily convened in Carlisle for August 17, at which representatives complained that the minister was holding a pistol to their heads. Nonetheless, a general pledge was forthcoming that the £75,000 annual subsidy for theDalesman service could be increased slightly for two years whereafter the councils' pump-priming role would be complete and support should begin to be wound down.

But as 1987 drew to a close, hopes began again to rise. The line had seen another record year for both passengers and revenue — even without counting in either the money earned by the line when it was used as a diversion for West Coast Main Line trains; or contributory revenue — the money BR earned when someone bought a long distance ticket to travel over the line, say, from Grantham to Carlisle or Stranraer to Leeds. These two sources of income, British Rail steadfastly refused to credit to the line. Also, in November had come news of the Jarvis Community Programme proposals which — as discussed in the last chapter. This envisaged £40m-worth of job creation work over five to six years on projects which would guarantee future traffic levels.

Slowly, word began to circulate once again that David Mitchell could gain a reprieve if the local authorities along the route could come up with more money, this time towards the line's huge repair bill (the construction companies' consortium idea having come to nought). How much more money? According to the Keighley MP, Gary Waller, £500,000 would do nicely. "I think £250,000 would be the absolute minimum at which ministers would begin listening," he told the *Yorkshire Post*.

The councils were due to meet in Carlisle in early February 1988. Mr Mitchell was now promising a decision on the line sometime in the spring. Now, at last, here was the price tag — a tag confirmed by witnesses to a telephone conversation between Mr Mitchell and Bill Cameron.

The joint councils were publicly outraged and privately determined at the turn of events. Outraged, because there was a growing feeling that ratepayers along the Settle-Carlisle corridor were effectively being asked to pay for their trains twice: once as taxpayers via the Government Public Service Obligation grant — which was intended to pay for precisely this kind of rural railway line — and now once again through the rates. The councils had to play a shrewd political game. John Carr, Policy Controller at West Yorkshire Passenger Transport Executive suggested it was only the Department of Employment's intervention which had postponed a closure announcement the previous autumn, pending publication of the Jarvis report which was expected in March. Councillor Cameron said he was convinced the local authorities were being set up as scapegoats who would have to carry the can if the line had to close for want of cash to repair Ribblehead viaduct. Coming up with cash could set a dangerous precedent, he said: "BR could institute closure proceedings in respect of any loss-making line and expect the local authorites to bail them out," he warned. And that, at any rate, was the public stance of the authorities. But — while anxious to protect the interests of local government by not setting a precedent which could be followed in future closure cases — behind the scenes, the councils were determined that the money should somehow be found.

It was. Within two months, a £500,000 package had been put together. The final piece of the jigsaw was a £165,000 grant from North Yorkshire County Council towards the cost of repairing Ribblehead Viaduct. But some tough conditions were attached. BR must agree to keep the line open for 20 years and operate a "satisfactory timetable" during that time. And the annual grant for the Dalesman service would end in two years. The justification for this, said the consortium chairman, Cumbria County Councillor Bill Cameron, was that the group had shown BR how the line could be marketed, given goodwill and a co-operative attitude. Having set BR on the right course, there was no need for further cash support.

In addition, BR now recognised that there was a £1m grant on offer from English Heritage for repairs to the viaduct — this was the largest ever such offer from English Heritage (the Historic Buildings and Monuments Commission) and it had apparently been received amid a deafening silence by British Rail in May 1987, prompting a bitter attack by the Commission's chairman, Lord Montagu. It now emerged that the offer had "gone astray", languishing for six months in the Department of the Environment. Almost imperceptibly, the BR stance had changed from the Settle-Carlisle line being one which no-one used — and for which BR had no further use — to an almost sorrowful shrug of the shoulders and a reminder that BR estimates said the viaduct would cost around £4m to repair. Little by little, it had become the stumbling block. But surely £1.5m was enough to overcome it?

It was not to be. The nods and winks, the unspoken assurances that if £500,000 could be put together, then the line could be saved, proved to be nothing more than a false dawn. When David Mitchell rose to address the House of Commons onMay 16, 1988, he turned the world of the Settle-Carlisle campaigners on its head.

He and his chief, the Transport Secretary, Paul Channon, were "minded to close" the line, he said. But this would not happen immediately. It would remain open until November 1988 while BR tried to find a private buyer to develop its tourist potential — the Disneyland in the Dales option, already rejected by the councils, campaigners and local

I see no trains — David Mitchell pictured at Settle station.

people (and, by implication, the TUCCs) as an unsatisfactory and insecure future.

Mr Mitchell told MPs that only 20 per cent of the line's travellers were regular users. While, perhaps significantly, he did not reveal the percentage of business travellers among passengers using the British

Rail network as a whole, Mr Mitchell said that carrying the other 80 per cent — among whom were the shoppers, hospital visitors and job-seekers as well as the tourists and day-trippers — was not something BR should be involved in. "Although the line makes a loss, I believe it has considerable potential for development as a tourist attraction. This is a specialised activity for which, quite properly, BR is not particularly well qualified. It would be more appropriate to the private sector."

At the same time, Mr Mitchell announced a revised TUCC investigation to examine any fresh evidence of hardship, and British Rail would be asked to update its financial case for closure — a document which had not been made public, and which anti-closure campaigners had hitherto had to take on trust — before the final decision on the line's future was taken.

But the minister was not hopeful about the outcome if a private buyer did not come forward. The revised facts and figures from BR and the two TUCCs were not expected to provide new evidence. The work was clearly being done to ward off any legal challenge which might follow a closure decision. In a brief interview with the *Yorkshire Post,* Mr Mitchell agreed that the line would "almost certainly close" if it could not be sold off. He also agreed that any sell-off would almost certainly mean a summer-only tourist service over the line, leaving local people at the mercy of replacement bus services.

There is little doubt that Mr Mitchell was putting a brave face on a decision which was not his own. He has never spoken about the affair and left the Government three months later, after reportedly refusing a transfer to the Ministry of Agriculture in a Government reshuffle. Certainly some Conservative MPs had believed a solution was in sight. Among them was the Richmond MP Leon Brittan, who served as both Home Secretary and Trade Secretary in Thatcher Governments until he was forced to resign over the Westland Helicopters take-over affair. Mr Brittan (now Sir Leon) had been a late convert to the S & C cause, eventually pledging allegiance as recently as October 1987 when he went to inspect voluntary work at Garsdale Station. Part of the problem had been that the Friends of the S & C had failed to include Mr Brittan on its mailing list, but there were no recriminations when the MP arrived by car and left by helicopter to express support for the line.

"I am extremely unhappy," he was reported as saying after Mr Mitchell's announcement. He went on to speak of "people being let down" and expressed uncertainty about whether a privatised Settle to

Carlisle line could be made to work. Hardly the sentiments of a man who had just heard what he had been expecting.

One other Yorkshire Conservative MP, who even today prefers to remain anonymous — he still has a constituency to mind — summed up the feeling on the day: "This business reeks of intervention by people outside the Department of Transport. I believe David Mitchell has had this decision forced on him. I believe he really wanted to do something far more sensible." Evidence that Mitchell's rescue plan had been hi-jacked quickly mounted. The contents of a letter written by the former Transport Secretary, Nicholas Ridley, were leaked. Mr Ridley had sent the letter to Mr Channon six weeks before the announcement — at about the time Mitchell was cajoling the local authorities into somehow finding the £500,000 said to be needed to tip the scales in favour of a reprieve.

Mr Ridley, notorious until his 1990 resignation as both a hard-liner and close confidant of Mrs Thatcher, said he felt the line should stay open, but only as a tourist attraction. He wrote: "But I feel that in reprieving the line we must establish in people's minds that it is now to be seen as a leisure and heritage-based enterprise and not as a transport matter. For this reason — and in fairness to British Rail themselves — I do not feel that they should be left with the job of running the line."

If Mr Ridley had set out to summarise Mr Mitchell's Commons statement, he could scarcely have done a better job, even after the event, let alone six weeks before it was made. And this from a minister with no brief on transport matters and no official interest in the future of the line.

It was the same Mr Ridley who wrote to a constituent who had objected to the closure of the line to say he thought the line's commuter service — the Dalesman trains — were unnecessary and that minibuses could do the job instead. And that was precisely what was to happen now: the Settle to Carlisle would become a 72-mile theme park with the few odd villagers who actually used the line to get from A to B put on minibuses for a scenic tour of narrow and meandering roads.

It is worth remembering at this point that Mr Ridley was also the man who, as Transport Secretary, revived interest in substituting buses for rural railways. The necessary legislation was contained in his 1985 Transport Act. It might also be argued that Mr Channon, as a minister recently demoted from Trade Secretary to Transport Secretary, would be unlikely to ignore a gentle hint from a colleague widely supposed to have the ear of the Prime Minister.

Another circumstantial, but highly significant, piece of evidence points to a hasty rethink just before Mr Mitchell's announcement. In the run-up to the May Commons statement, Alan Whitehouse wrote to David Mitchell's office at the Department of Transport, asking for as much notice as possible of a decision, to give time for background material to be prepared.

The reply was fairly non-committal, but was followed by an invitation for Alan and his wife to a foursome lunch at the House of Commons with Mr and Mrs Mitchell, with seats in the public gallery afterwards. The business that afternoon should have been transport questions, and in hindsight, it seems highly likely that David Mitchell was to have announced the reprieve that afternoon.

But transport questions were brought forward a week at short notice and the privatisation-or-closure statement given. Instead of transport, the business of the House on the day of the lunch was Welsh questions. It is difficult to imagine why the transport minister should invite a Yorkshire journalist, whom he had met through the latter's interest in a local railway closure attempt, to listen to Peter Walker and Anne Clwyd arguing the toss on subisidies to hill farmers in Dyfed. It would, however, have been a typically kindly gesture on the minister's part to invite someone who had taken a close interest in the affair to be present at the final moment, when the good news could be officially given. The truth may never be known, because David Mitchell has chosen not to break his silence on the affair, departing the Government for life on the back benches and running his family businesses.

There were three immediate consequences of Mr Mitchell's statement. The first was that both Councillor Michael Simmons, chairman of the West Yorkshire Passenger Transport Authority and Councillor Bill Cameron, chairman of the joint local authorities threatened legal action in the event of closure. The second was that the *Metro Pullman*, a forthcoming steam-hauled trip over the S & C, organised by West Yorkshire on behalf of the joint local authorities, was immediately dubbed a wake by cynics. Now it would provide the opportunity to launch the next phase of the fight to prevent closure instead of the celebration that many had been expecting. Mr Mitchell had already been invited and to join the trip to be hauled by the A4 Pacific, *Sir Nigel Gresley*. Bravely, Mr Mitchell kept his appointment. It was a bizarre trip, on which the minister even snipped a tape to open a new visitor centre at Garsdale. But he refused to give anything away as to whether his decision had been hijacked, sticking firmly to the principles of collective Cabinet responsibility. The nearest he came to it was to reiterate in a TV interview that he was "a pro-rail minister". Councillor Simmons chose to infer from the minister's very presence on the trip that Mr Mitchell was going "as far as he can go to indicate his support for the line" and he suggested that he should "do the honourable thing" and tender his resignation.

At a press conference in Carlisle, Mr Mitchell said with a touch of understatement: "You will understand why some of my friends suggested I should chicken out." He continued: "The question is whether the taxpayer should subsidise people travelling simply for the joy of the ride. I want to see a future for this line. But it is not a future that should be subsidised by the taxpayer." There followed a bizarre interlude in which the minister suggested that if anyone knew anybody who might be interested in buying the line, they should put them in touch with his office. Councillor Simmons suggested the failure of the Government to endorse the package which had apparently been hammered out between Mr Mitchell and the local authorities could be laid at the door of No.10. "The story is that a political adviser at No.10 has given this advice to 'she who must be obeyed'," he said, making it clear outside the meeting that he was referring to the premier's economic adviser, Greg Bourne. Councillor Simmons added: "He appears to have persuaded No.10 that this a golden opportunity to bring in privatisation of the rail service." Whether, ultimately, it was Mr Ridley, Mr Bourne or anybody else who had bent the PM's ear was by this time by the by: Mr Mitchell's announcement clearly stood.

But the third consequence of the announcement was a deafening silence from the established railway preservation groups as attempts were made to drum up interest in the S & C's sale. Yet these were the very people held up by Mr Mitchell as an example of what could be done.

The general manager of the Severn Valley Railway — reckoned to be one of the most successful preserved lines — Michael Draper, was blunt: "No-one in their right mind would set out to operate a 72-mile railway. It would need several multi-millionaires to sink their money into it. Even lines the length of the Severn Valley swallow millions almost without trace."

The North Yorkshire Moors Railway is one of the longest preserved lines in the country, with its 18 miles of single track between Grosmont and Pickering. The publicity officer, Murray Brown, agreed with this assessment. "We would not take it on. We have to charge about £6 for an

18-mile ride. If you multiply that up, we would price ourselves out of the market." In what turned out to be a prophetic statement, he added: "The other difficulty is that whoever takes it on will be entirely dependent on the co-operation of British Rail to get into Carlisle and Leeds stations. And private rolling stock needs the equivalent of an MoT certificate which is very expensive."

And to begin with, there was little interest. But then, BR contrived to offer for sale not so much a self-contained railway with tourist potential, as a poisoned chalice. A glossy brochure pointing out the benefits and attractions of a railway line which, five years before, had been classed as worthless and worn out, was produced.

It offered the line as a gift, complete with buildings, track and signals, but very little else. BR grudgingly allowed access to Carlisle Citadel Station, but said that at the southern end of the line, all private trains would have to terminate at Hellifield. The new owner would be allowed to ferry his clientele from Leeds — the main source of traffic — on chartered BR trains which would run non-stop to Hellifield, where passengers would scramble from the BR charter train onto the private train for the ride over the S & C.

It is true that Hellifield was once a major railway junction with grand and extensive buildings which included a huge dining room for use before dining cars became commonplace, surrounded by the exotic wrought ironwork of extensive class canopies. But by 1988 years of neglect and a run-down of the rail services passing through it had left Hellifield a dump. An unstaffed, tumbledown halt with dangerously decayed buildings in the middle of nowhere.

If this were not enough, buyers were warned they would have to find money for locomotives and coaches. BR was also refusing to sell any of the powerful Class 47 diesels needed for hauling the ten and 12-coach summer trains. But worse was to follow.

Under some behind-the-scenes pressure, British Rail withdrew the ban on running into Leeds station, but quickly substituted a scale of charges amounting to the equivalent of £150 per hour for driving private trains from Hellifield to Leeds and back. A confidential document setting out the charges fulfilled Murray Brown's prediction admirably. BR would want five crews available to operate two trains per day into and out of Leeds. The crews would cost the new owners £150,000 per year, even though the longest of the two round trips from Hellifield to Leeds and back would take no more than 116 minutes — including waiting time at Leeds. Typically, BR refused to comment on its own calculations and also refused to say what the crews would spend the rest of their time doing.

It is difficult to understand the precise thinking behind this. The BR proposals were patently absurd on two counts: first, the timetable proposed, of two off-peak services into and out of Leeds, would need no more than two two-man crews per day — or even one, if the principle of flexible rostering of train crews for shifts of up to nine hours was adopted. This was a battle fought and won by the BR Board in 1982 on the grounds that it was vital for productivity. Yet for some unfathomable reason, it was not being applied here.

Second, the BR proposals made it obvious that a lot of men would be sitting around doing very little in between the steady jog down to Leeds and back. It is inconceivable that BR would not make some use of this dead time, if only for working Skipton-Leeds local trains, or the daily freight trips along the Rylstone branch up Wharfedale.

One theory, outlandish at first glance, but believed passionately by some of those involved in the anti-closure campaign, is that British Rail never really wanted to close the line at all. It wanted even less to hand it over to a new owner as some kind of test-bed for privatisation and had therefore to do all it could to make the scheme appear unworkable. Those who believe in an even wider conspiracy theory tie this in with BR's apparent inability to get the original S & C closure notice correctly worded and the equally ludicrous timetable it presented at the public hearings for an alternative Leeds-Carnforth-Carlisle service. Others prefer the cockup theory: that the whole chapter of miscalculations was only too typical of BR's management weakness.

Meanwhile, as the privatisation bids were being evaluated, the anti-closure lobby won its first victory in what had become the second round of the fight to save the line. Originally, the North East and North West TUCCs had not intended to stage fresh public hearings to take evidence from people who had begun using the line since the original hearings in 1985. Instead, objectors were to have been invited to submit written evidence by letter.

In the intervening three years the timetable had grown from two trains per day to five, and eight new stations had re-opened, attracting several dozen regular new daily passengers in addition to the thousands more who had discovered the line as a pleasant way of spending a day out. They quickly made their voices felt, adding more than 10,000 new objections to the 22,265 already under consideration.

Under pressure, most significantly from the local authorities, the TUCCs changed policy and began gearing up for a new set of public hearings, or "joint meetings in public" as they were euphemistically called. These would be held in late September and early October 1988. The TUCCs had also been given the job of investigating whether a replacement minibus service would work and in recognition of the greater workload, were given an extra month to complete their new report. In consequence, the new public transport minister, Michael Portillo, said a final decision on the fate of the line was being deferred until the New Year, without specifying which part of the New Year he meant. The preliminaries to this were a closing date for offers to buy the line of October 31, TUCC reports by the end of November, a hand-over to a new owner in March, and a guarantee that the line would now stay open until the end of the timetable in May 1989 should no buyer be found.

This, then, would leave the Government with a set of three options: if a private buyer came forward, the line could be privatised, hopefully with minibuses replacing the Dalesman service; if no buyer could be found, Mr Channon could reassess the evidence of hardship that closing the line would bring. He could, especially in the light of a new TUCC report, order BR to keep it open; or, thirdly, he could reinforce his previous inclinations with a closure decision.

The rash of new objections was certainly sufficient to make Mr Portillo take notice of his new responsibility. Only a few hours after deferring a final decision on the line, he followed in Mr Mitchell's footsteps and made what was intended to be a secret trip over the line on the 6.34 am from Carlisle to Leeds. Alas, his intentions were leaked and he was met by anti-closure campaigners.

The rest of Summer '88 was quiet politically, but busy for the railway which saw the usual packed ten and 12-coach trains and a string of specials and excursions. But behind the scenes, things were not auguring well for either privatisation or bus substitution.

One notable development was the completion of a test arch-repair on Ribblehead Viaduct. A "typical" arch was chosen for a full repair and the result multiplied up to cover all 24 arches. The results finally demolished the £4m-plus claims made by British Rail, when they reached the conclusion that somewhere between £2m and £2.5m should keep the viaduct in usable condition indefinitely.

This was intriguing news on two counts: firstly because it confirmed a preliminary survey for English Heritage virtually to the last £1, but also because it confirmed a story carried by the *Yorkshire Post* the previous December, which was first confirmed and then quickly denied by BR, that the viaduct, far from being on the verge of collapse, had no fundamental problems.

The story made the point that although BR had predicted the viaducts's demise as long ago as 1981 — when Ribblehead was given a working life of between three and five years — here it was six years on in December 1987 still carrying a daily service of ten trains with no suggestion that it was about to become unusable.

British Rail's response was intriguing. Initially, a press spokeswoman in Manchester was happy to confirm that this was indeed the case. Of the five years' life prediction, she told the *Yorkshire Post*: "That

Ribblehead viaduct is safe, admits BR

EXCLUSIVE
By ALAN WHITEHOUSE, Transport Correspondent

RAIL chiefs have admitted that the Ribblehead Viaduct — centrepiece of the threatened Settle to Carlisle railway — is not collapsing after all. Engineers now say it will be safe for the foreseeable future.

The statement contrasts sharply with official predictions made in 1981 — when British Rail was preparing its closure case for the scenic route. Then, BR engineers were predicting a life of three to five years for the 26-arch viaduct.

Almost seven years later, it is still in daily use by ten trains. A BR spokeswoman said yesterday: "That information is now out of date. When it was quoted, we thought there was a serious structural fault on the viaduct. That has subsequently proved not to be the case.

"We now know that it is the materials that are failing, not the viaduct itself. Some work has been done on it, and more is going on now.

"But there is no possibility of it being declared unsafe for traffic, though our engineers are keeping a close eye on it."

At one point the brick-built viaduct — a listed monument — was cited by BR as the main reason for putting the 72-mile line up for closure.

As recently as last December, a Press release from the British Railways Board, setting out the

Continued on Page 2.

...ROUND: Ribblehead Viaduct — no structural fault, say engineers.

Flashback to the Yorkshire Post's telling revelation on Ribblehead Viaduct

information is now out of date. When it was quoted we thought there was a serious structural fault on the viaduct. That has subsequently proved not to be the case.

"We know know that it is the materials that are failing, not the viaduct itself. Some work has been done and there is more going on now. But there is no possibility of it being declared unsafe for traffic, though our engineers are keeping a close eye on it."

When this appeared in as a front page exclusive, it caused a predictable uproar. Brian Sutcliffe, chairman of the Friends, made the point that a BR report dated as recently as 1986 had cited the viaduct's worsening condition as a significant factor. James Towler pointed out that, as a main plank of BR's closure case was the poor state of the viaduct, much of the closure case was rendered spurious at a stroke.

British Rail quickly backtracked, denying the story to other media organisations which tried to follow it up. But events have proved that here, at last, was the first glimmer of truth from BR about the real state of Ribblehead Viaduct. It was — as Professor MacKay of PEIDA had stated in 1983 — neglect, not old age, which needed putting right.

The initial flurry of interest in privatisation had not brought in many bids with what both BR and its merchant bankers, Lazard Brothers, regarded as adequate financial backing. The list of potential bidders was rapidly chopped to a shortlist of just six serious contenders within a matter of weeks. Five of these based their bids on running passenger services, while the sixth (as discussed previously) proposed to use the line principally for trunking heavy freight — mostly in the form of containers — from Scotland to the South of England. This was quickly rejected by BR as potentially harmful to its own Railfreight business. There is also the strong possibility that the Sea Containers idea was no more than a "stalking horse" instigated by the Government to encourage more serious contenders to come forward.

Another bidder was a group of National Bus Company executives — themselves newly privatised — who planned to join forces with a group of present and former BR managers. This also quickly came to nothing. The bids were whittled down to a shortlist of just three main contenders, two of which subsequently emerged as front runners. One bid came from Tony Thomas, a West Midlands businessman who planned to operate ex-British Rail diesels to a slightly improved timetable. The second came from a group calling itself Cumbrian Railways Ltd, whose leading lights were Michael Heathcote, a Hull businessman, and Kenneth Ryder, a Driffield fish farmer and the proud owner of three former Great Western Railway steam locomotives.

Meanwhile, a new row had broken out between British Rail and the anti-closure campaign over British Rail's final piece of evidence to Mr Channon — its revised financial case for closure, which claimed that even if it was re-equipped with modern trains and signalling, the line would continue to lose somewhere between £330,000 and £1m per year. Even £1m might be considered a small amount, given that BR was currently spending around £500m of public money keeping open other loss-making routes.

But what angered the anti-closure organisations was an apparent determination, even at this 11th hour, to present the line in its worst possible light. BR, they complained, had automatically used the most pessimistic figures possible in its forecasts. The cost of re-equipping the line with new trains was 80 per cent higher than figures BR had previously given for providing rolling stock for a replacement Leeds-

Carnforth-Carlisle service if the Settle route was closed. The cost of operating this replacement service also appeared to have been deliberately understated — the figures were now lower than those supplied by BR two years previously. The full £2.5m repair costs for the Ribblehead Viaduct had been set against the line, ignoring the £1.5m worth of grants on offer.

But even allowing for all this, the Settle to Carlisle was still covering 85 per cent of its costs, something few other lines outside the InterCity network could achieve. Ron Cotton summed it up best when he told journalists some time later: "Without being pro-BR or anti-BR the best way of putting it is to say that the figures are not really fair. They have pitched the costs towards the high end to make a better case for closure." The uncharitable might argue that this was a style of management whose roots could be traced directly back to the first clumsy attempt to get the line closed almost before anyone knew what was happening, after first manipulating the timetables to make sure only a minimal number of people were eligible to object.

The Friends of the Settle-Carlisle Line Association added more fuel to fire by issuing its own report, claiming that BR's own figures could be re-interpreted to show that the line lost only £69,000 per year.

Meanwhile, the writing was on the wall for the substitute buses which Mr Ridley had suggested would be perfectly good enough for anyone wanting to live in the Eden Valley but work, or go to school, in Carlisle. The second TUCC report largely echoed the first, setting out good reasons for retaining the line, and pointing out that hardship would be caused to the people who had begun using the Dalesman service to chase jobs in Carlisle, or to begin courses at the city's further education college. In its conclusions, it stated that the committees "strongly recommend that consent to closure be refused and the lines (Settle-Carlisle plus Blackburn-Hellifield) be developed jointly with local authorities and other interested groups". But it was a separate report by the TUCCs on bus substitution which provided the most entertaining read. It showed that journey times would increase by up to 130 per cent compared with the present rail timetable, with typical increases of between 60 and 90 per cent. Getting from Settle to Garsdale or Appleby, for example, would mean an increased journey time of 87 per cent. Leeds to Appleby would take 60 per cent longer, using a combination of buses and trains. But the trip from Kirkby Stephen to Appleby — adjacent stops on the rail journey — would take 131 per cent longer by bus.

The local authorities' reaction to the privatisation proposals was typically pragmatic. They still believed that the line should stay in BR ownership. However, provided it remained available as part of the national rail network — with good connections at Leeds, Carlisle and, preferably, Preston or Blackburn, through-ticketing, and a level of service at least equal to that offered latterly by BR — the authorities would go along with a new owner.

West Yorkshire Passenger Transport Authority and its executive, Metro, had a particularly keen interest. Metro had led the way in investing in local rail services in the 1980s, reopening stations, buying new trains, improving service frequencies and — above all — vigorously marketing the advantages of local rail travel. When the metropolitan counties, including West Yorkshire, were abolished in 1986, some people suggested that the district councils would become the main players in the public transport game, leaving the PTAs declining in importance. Nowhere has this happened, and certainly not in West Yorkshire where, over one five-year period in the 80s, Metro achieved a doubling of patronage on local rail services.

Metro's activities cost more than £9m per year, and if BR and private operator did silly things with Leeds-Carlisle services it could wreck what West Yorkshire had achieved with its Airedale and Wharfedale services which had to share track over the congested approaches to Leeds.

Metro was therefore to play a critical role in assessing the details of the private operators' proposals once they were disclosed by BR. Some bidders did discuss their plans with Metro, receiving the benefit of professional comment and advice. Others remained aloof, failing to appreciate the complex relationship between BR and the PTEs in metropolitan areas.

The New Year of 1989 came and went with little indication about the fate of the line. It was accompanied by a flurry of reports from various interested parties, including the Joint Councils Steering Group and the English Tourist Board. The ETB report concluded that the line could be operated successfully by a private company, but this would require co-operation from British Rail, the local councils and other public agencies.

The joint councils' report — *The Case for Retention*, or so-called *Red Report* — was a comprehensive restatement of the history of the closure proceedings with a full analysis of the latest developments, including further demolition of BR's financial case and comments on the privatisation option. Argued forcefully in language designed to leave the civil servants at the Department of Transport in no doubt as to the strength of the councils' position, the report started from the point that the line, even on BR figures, was a good financial performer. Its annual patronage was now up to around 450,000, compared with 93,000 in 1983. The train service being operated in 1988 was radically different from the "residual Leeds-Carlisle" timetable imposed by BR as part of its secret closure moves in 1982. BR's financial case for closing the line was inconclusive, and was open to the interpretation that if the line closed, BR might actually lose money instead of saving it. And closing the line would harm tourism and development prospects for the area.

The report also made threatening noises on the legal front, stating that the prcocedure followed by the Secretary of State in commissioning additional reports from the TUCCs was flawed and suggesting that anything other than a reprieve for the line would be "open to challenge in the courts". In its conclusions, it stated: "In view of the radically different train service now operating and almost fivefold increase in patronage, British Rail should have been instructed to withdraw their original proposals. If they still, despite the weight of evidence wished to seek closure, they should have published a fresh proposal based on current service levels and proper evaluation of alternatives to meet the essential travel needs of the corridor." Crucially, it stated — and this may well have touched a raw legal nerve in a way that the Government would only come to acknowledge months later when closure was finally dropped — that: "Further complicating factors are the announcement in May 1988 that the Secretary of State is minded to approve closure, which appears to have prejudged the outcome of the closure proposal, and the request to BR to seek a private buyer for the lines. The closure application should have been determined on its merits before buyers were sought."

But the Government declined to furl its sails and Mr Portillo provoked the anger of all concerned once more by delaying his decision again. Following vigorous submissions by people who stood to lose money through not knowing whether the line would be there or not in the coming summer (this body of opinion was ably represented by the Settle-Carlisle Business Liaison Group), the minister pronounced in February 1989 that the line would now not close before October, rather than May as had been intended by the original timetable. That timetable would have seen a private buyer identified by November 1988, with a hand-over sometime shortly before British Rail's annual timetable change in early May 1989, in good time for the new owner's first summer season.

The delay was infuriating and inexplicable to the campaigners, who were now beginning to weary of the six-year fight for the line. But it was caused because at last it seemed a suitable privatisation candidate might have been found — Cumbrian Railways Ltd, the final name on the shortlist, was now a serious contender for Britain's first railway privatisation attempt.

At the same time, the joint councils' group, scenting a development, proposed a new tripartite scheme for saving the line. The councils, a private buyer and BR would join forces, the private buyer to own the line, operating whatever steam or other tourism-based services he wished, the councils to support a local year-round train service and British Rail to act as a form of glorified haulage contractor, providing rolling stock and crew for the local service, and possibly other trains too. Building on their long established close working relationship with BR, West Yorkshire PTE (Metro) was able to show how services under this compromise arrangement might be interworked with PTE services within the PTE operating area to spread costs and increase revenue. Councillor Simmons wrote to the BR chairman, Sir Robert Reid, setting out the details. Paradoxically, this move very nearly proved the undoing of the close alliance of the local authorities. Throughout the campaign, Cumbria had very clearly been the lead authority, with Councillor Cameron in the chair and Peter Robinson the tireless leader of the officers doing the spadework. Mr Robinson's extended absence from the fray following illness in 1988 had, however, left a vacuum which coincided with the stronger involvement of West Yorkshire PTE, because of the vexed question of access by private trains to Leeds. When Councillor Simmons's letter only arrived with his county council partners in Carlisle and Preston after its contents had been published, a split very nearly ocurred. For his part, Councillor Simmons was still waiting for a reply when the line's reprieve was finally announced.

BR was in no mood to listen to new ideas. Details of a staggered privatisation deal were being worked out which would create a joint company to own and run the line, split 51-49 between BR and Cumbrian Railways. After a bedding-in period — possibly a year — the remainder of the company would be handed over to Cumbrian Railways for a nominal sum.

By October 1988, Cumbrian Railways had submitted a formal 47-page bid for the line. The proposals included a commitment to running a year-round service, with what the company described as a "main line" service between Leeds and Carlisle and a feeder service from Blackburn, meeting the main line at Hellifield. The trains themselves would be a mix of diesel multiple units on the Blackburn service and for local trains over the main line, with locomotive-hauled trains for the longer distances. In summer, these would be steam-hauled between Hellifield and Appleby, necessitating two changes of locomotive over the complete Leeds-Carlisle journey.

Cumbrian Railways also set out its rolling stock needs, which would be bought from BR. Its "shopping list" extended to 35 coaches, including four First Class vehicles and four buffet cars; four type four diesel locomotives, preferably Class 47; two Class 08 shunters and two type two or type three diesel locomotives — probably Class 31 or 37. The bid also called for a range of civil engineering vehicles, including a tunnel inspection coach, two snowploughs and a tamping machine for track maintenance.

The group said it intended retaining double track and semaphore signalling, though it wanted to introduce some form of cab signalling as an additional safeguard.

In all likelihood, it was a firm commitment — repeated at least three times in the course of the 47 pages — to maintain winter services which attracted both BR and the Department of Transport to the Cumbrian Railways bid.

The bid named, among others, Mr Ryder as prospective chief executive and head of the locomotive department, stressing his five years' driving experience with the preserved Mid-Hants Railway and his chairmanship of the Great Western Steam Locomotives Group.

It also named Alan King as prospective chief civil engineer. Mr King was the BR civil engineer who once claimed the Ribblehead Viaduct was in irreversible decline, and who suggested at a press conference that it had a life expectancy of between three and five years, depending on the severity of the winters.

British Rail also gave a distinct impression of clearing the decks, disentangling itself from the affairs of the line in preparation for a hand-over. There was the curious affair of the Warcop branch. The ammunition trains which ran about once per week were axed in March 1989. Two conflicting reasons emerged. British Rail said the Army had told it that the amount of traffic was projected to decline and use of the railway could no longer be justified. Accordingly, Railfreight, working to its commercial remit, discontinued the service, but only after "full consultation". But the Army claimed it had simply been told by BR that the service was to end. "There was no consultation and we were not given any options," declared an Army spokesman. The ammunition trains were to end on March 31, two weeks before the Cumbrian Railways affair reached its crescendo.

But this scheme still depended on the local councils handing over their promised £500,000 grant. As details began to emerge, an angry Councillor Simmons wrote again to the BR chairman, accusing him of using the local authorities as milch cows, and demanding a seat at the negotiations.

The *Yorkshire Post* broke this story on Monday April 10, suggesting that a deal was no further away than the next meeting between BR, Lazard Brothers and Cumbrian Railways, scheduled for the following Friday — then the bottom fell out of Cumbrian Railways' world. On Tuesday April 5, Councillor Simmons released the text of two letters to Sir Robert Reid and Paul Channon in support of his claim that the tripartite survival plan had been hijacked and turned into the Cumbrian Railways bid, minus the local authorities. He launched a strong attack on Cumbrian Railways, saying the local authorities had "grave reservations about both the finance available to Cumbrian Railways and its operational proposals and competence".

The local authorities started making threatening noises about the £500,000 Ribblehead repair grant and it began to appear that yet another deal to save the line was about to come unstitched, with more threats of legal action from Councillor Simmons. To all intents and purposes it was the straw that broke the Department of Transport's back. All thoughts of privatisation were abandoned and a day later, it was all over and Mr Channon had told BR the line must be kept open. The biggest railway closure proposal since the Beeching era had been defeated...

But it was an awkward and messy end to the saga, and one which bears close examination, for there is evidence that the line was intended as a privatisation test-bed until the very last moment. The actual announcement not only caught an increasingly weary campaign off-guard: it also took Cumbrian Railways completely by surprise. On the very morning of Mr Channon's announcement, Mr Ryder said he had been discussing "a point of fine detail" on the take-over with Lazard Brothers, suggesting that Lazards, too,were quite unaware of what was to happen.

Mr Portillo's own actions were also curious. Having delayed an announcement on the future of the line in December, he had then stirred up the hornet's nest yet again in February by promising only that the line would remain open "at least until October". The unanswered question is, why bother? If he knew, or even believed, a reprieve was in the pipeline his announcement was pointless. Equally, if he knew or suspected the line was to be closed, then May — the date of BR's annual timetable change — was the logical time to do it.

In all the excitement, the actual wording of the formal Department of Transport notice, refusing consent for BR to close the line, was largely overlooked. It was a truly amazing document, packed with contradictions, and in the opinion of some, no more than a consent to closure hastily reworded to become a refusal.

The second page refers to the replacement train service between Leeds and Carlisle via Carnforth. It reads: "If he [the secretary of state] were to give closure consent for the Settle-Carlisle line he would not require the [BR] Board to run this alternative service as a means of relieving hardship because it is already possible to make the journey between Leeds and Carlisle via the West Coast Main Line."

In the light of a reprieve, this is a totally meaningless paragraph, since BR only planned to run a Leeds-Carnforth-Carlisle service if the Settle-Carlisle line was closed. But it would make sense if the original decision had been to close the Settle to Carlisle. It seems that BR would not even have been obliged to operate the Carnforth service it had touted as the answer to everyone's problems at the public hearings.

Over the page, the paragraph devoted to hardship yielded more gems. "He [the secretary of state] accepts that closure of the Settle-Carlisle line would cause some hardship to local residents who now rely on it for day-to-day essential transport purposes. He considers that provision of substitute bus services could cater adequately for many such travellers."

Once again, an utterly meaningless statement in the light of a reprieve. Substitute buses would only have been needed if the intention was to close the line. And finally: "He accepts that the hardship case for retaining the line is now marginally stronger than it was but does not believe that hardship in itself would justify retaining the line." Which begs the question: Why keep the line open if, by the accepted yardstick, there is no justification for doing so? And why say as much when the line was to be kept open anyway?

And what is to be made of one of British Rail's own actions, made within four weeks of the final reprieve? An internal memorandum from the InterCity special trains manager instructed staff to impose a 25 per cent surcharge on all excursions over the line. The official justification was the need for additional resources to meet the high demand for excursions over the line. But what an excellent way of cashing in on what might have been the last summer of BR operation over the line. It was an instruction which matched exactly the official BR philosophy that more people travel over the line when it is under immediate threat.

These are questions which are extremely unlikely ever to be answered by those involved. Even now it is by no means clear exactly why the Government finally "caved in". A likely explanation is that the Department of Transport's legal advisers felt that the department's conduct might not stand up to close scrutiny in the surely inevitable judicial review that would follow a closure announcement. The department had, it seemed, been delaying its closure announcement so as to sew up the privatisation deal with Cumbrian Railways — a course of action which lay way outside the legal procedure to be followed when closing a railway, as set down in the relevant Transport Act. So Mr Channon had, it seemed, been exceeding his powers — in legal terms, acting *ultra vires*. Then there was the little problem of the fact that the service that was now proposed for closure was a very different animal to that which had been the subject of the original closure proceedings. At a time when Mr Channon was facing intense pressure over his role in the run-up to the Lockerbie jumbo jet disaster — not to mention the rail distasters at Clapham, Purley and, to a lesser extent, Bellgrove — the very last thing the Government would have wished to contemplate was a messy court action with the vulnerable Mr Channon again under the spotlight.

But why, then, not simply postpone an announcement until the political weather was set more fair? The answer to that question could be found in Cumbrian Railways' date with Lazards and BR the following Friday, April 14. If the *Yorkshire Post* story of April 10 was indeed correct when it was published, then perhaps time had simply run out. If all did indeed hinge on the April 14 meeting — and the various parties were ready to turn up and sign on the dotted line — then there might simply be no scope for further deferral: and, on the other hand, only three days in which to abandon the whole closure plan.

But there still exists no definitive version of events. Edward Album, legal adviser to the Friends, plays down the importance of the threat of a judicial review, preferring to think that the Department of Transport was persuaded by simple power of reason. This viewpoint, however, appears to fly in the face of the evidence of a very sudden and comprehensive U-turn (so sudden that no-one even found time to rewrite the closure announcement). And it completely ignores the fact that the local authorities were making no secret of their resolve to take the issue to court in the event of an unsatisifactory outcome — Mike Woodhall at West Yorkshire PTE enjoyed a brief which all but had him striding into Marsham Street with his finger on the trigger. Bill Cameron, chairman of the joint county councils, remains coy about the final turn of events, but tells of a frantic exchange of communications with Mr Portillo over the weekend preceeding the Channon announcement. Councillor Cameron, whose leadership had held the local authority team together so well over the years, enjoyed a politician's ultimate pleasure: that of graciously accepting the Government's surrender.

When the joint local authorities met in Carlisle just over a week later to toast with him the final success of all those involved in six years of campaigning, it befell John Carr, policy controller at West Yorkshire Passenger Transport Executive, to put what many others had been thinking into words, as he told a crowded council chamber that the consent to closure had been hastily rewritten, probably just hours before the reprieve was announced.

He gave his local government expert opinion on the four sheets of paper which saved the line: "That letter is an amazing concoction. Apart from a couple of paragraphs, it is a letter consenting to closure. It is my belief that the Department of Transport changed its mind and decided it was not worth continuing the fight when the details had leaked out and I believe that is why we got the announcement we did."

And so the likelihood is that a combination of factors had brought about Mr Channon's decision. At the crux of it was the question: are Cumbrian Railways worth embarking on a legal process which could take two years or more to resolve, during which time the line could not be closed? It is now clear that for all their promises, Cumbrian Railways were really only the best of a pretty poor bunch. To have pursued the closure and sell-off policy might well have done no more than kill off the prospect of any subsequent privatisations along S & C lines.

DOUBLE-HEADERS: Above — the ex-Southern Railway Lord Nelson class locomotive Sir Lamiel, improbably teamed with the ex-LMS No. 5407 near Horton-in-Ribblesdale. Below — A pair of low-powered diesels, a Class 25 and a Class 31, head across Smardale Viaduct on a sunny afternoon in November 1983. All are on Cumbrian Mountain Pullman duties.

10. The other pieces in the jigsaw

RAILWAY closures have been a depressing feature of British life since the 1950s. While other European countries have invested heavily in their rail systems, keeping both heavy freight and thousands of cars off the roads, Britain has historically tried to run its railway on a shoestring.

The process began even before the Beeching era, though it must be said that many routes closed in this period would not be considered worth retaining even today. Lord Beeching raised railway closures almost to an art form and his expertise in this field has never quite been forgotten by those in BR who believe everything would be all right if only the dinosaur branch lines could be somehow killed off, leaving them to get on with the real job of running the main lines.

The Settle to Carlisle closure proposal has to be seen in this context: it was never intended as any kind of one-off until much later when the issues of bus substitution and privatisation came to the fore. It was just one (albeit a big one) of a steady trickle of closure proposals — most of them pushed through successfully — which have continued since the Settle-Carlisle affair was started.

It is not widely appreciated that since the first Thatcher Government came to power in 1979, there have been almost three dozen railway closure proposals. In all but two cases, British Rail has been given permission to push through its closure plans.

They have included some substantial stretches of main line — the former Midland Main Line between Sheffield and Leeds, for example. Together with the Settle to Carlisle line, it once formed part of the Midland London-Carlisle artery. A truncated Sheffield-London service is all that remains.

And these officially-notified closures do not take into account the freight lines which BR can close almost overnight without the need for any form of public consultation whatever. Possibly the best example is the Woodhead Line, Britain's first all-electric main line, opened throughout to electric trains in 1954, using a brand new tunnel under the

Pennines. British Rail first stripped the route of all but the basic Sheffield-Manchester service before proposing all but the Manchester suburban electric services for closure on the grounds that the Woodhead Line track capacity was needed for freight traffic. Once passenger services had been withdrawn, such limited protection as the TUCCs might have offerered was lost.

An almost continuous thread can be traced back to the early 1960s, for BR used precisely the same argument in its proposals to axe passenger trains on the former Great Central Railway Manchester-Sheffield-London line between Sheffield and Aylesbury. This deprived the Woodhead Line of one of its reasons for being there, replacing a long-distance inter-city service with what was essentially no more than a trans-Pennine local haul. To long term observers, it came as little surprise when, within five years of the Sheffield-Aylesbury closure, Woodhead itself came under threat.

Luckless passengers were promised a diesel service along the Hope Valley line as a consolation prize, with a journey time that varied between 10 and 15 minutes longer than via the Woodhead Line. BR got its way and in January 1970 the last electrically-hauled passenger train ran between Sheffield and Manchester and the Woodhead route became a freight-only trunk haul line across the Pennines. Then, in 1981, BR was back again, demanding complete closure of the Woodhead line. But, because Woodhead was by now a freight-only line, there were no public safeguards. It was left to the rail unions to sponsor an inquiry into the closure. BR responded by saying it would make no difference. The line would close in July 1981 come what may. It did. The line closed as a through route on schedule, leaving just the stump of the Manchester suburban service to Hadfield, and a freight branch from Sheffield to Deepcar.

As with the Settle-Carlisle closure attempt, there was the usual mix of claims about life-expired equipment — in this case overhead electrification gear rather than a viaduct or tunnel — and the high cost of rectifying the defects. The only alternative to closure was to re-electrify the line from the obsolete 1,500v DC system to the BR standard 25Kv AC. The Woodhead Tunnel was built specifically for electric trains and as such has only one ventilation shaft. It could only be used by five diesel-hauled trains per hour.

But re-electrification was a non-starter, said BR, because of the high cost. The BR estimate was £23m, plus the cost of raising bridges to provide the clearances needed with the higher voltage AC electrical system. Outside estimates were just £8m. These claims were later vindicated when the Greater Manchester Passenger Transport Executive announced a joint project to re-electrify the Manchester-Hadfield line to 25Kv AC to make it compatible with the city's other electrified routes. The cost would be just £680,000. Scaled up, the costs applied to Manchester-Hadfield meant that the entire Woodhead Line could have been electrified at a fraction of the BR estimate of £23m. Except that by now, of course, it no longer existed.

The claims about wide bridge clearances were another obvious nonsense. When the line was electrified, it pioneered main line overhead electrification. Generous clearances between the high voltage wiring were made to prevent even the remotest risk of a flashover as the electric current tried to find the quickest route to earth. The clearances provided were wildly in excess of what was needed for 1,500v and quite adequate even for 25Kv current.

British Rail applied similar costings to the complete new signalling system it alleged was needed. This would cost £20m. Even if the line were re-electrified, many millions more would be needed for new electric locomotives. But would these not be needed anyway? Yes, but ten diesels could do the work of 45 electrics in use at the time, said BR. Today, whenever BR wants to persuade the Government of the benefits of electrifying its main lines — the East Coast Main Line from London to Edinburgh, for example — one of its main arguments is that electric locomotives are more efficient and cost less to run than diesels. Except, apparently, on the Woodhead Line.

But the Settle-Carlisle affair did draw attention to the established BR dodge of claiming a major engineering feature along the line was close to collapse. But even this was far from new and the same basic strategy had been used several times before. For Settle-Carlisle, read Cambrian Coast in North Wales. This, briefly, is how it happened.

Closure scares were nothing new to this spectacular line which runs from the Aberystwyth line near Machynlleth 45 miles round the coast to Pwllheli — the Cambrian Coast Line Action Group was formed in response to the threat to the line. Some of the line's running costs as quoted by BR at the time have a ring of familiarity about them. In 1971, for example, the line's signalling costs were put at £68,000 — by 1973, despite the closure of one signal box, the figure had risen to £112,000. In 1968, BR threatened to close the footpath over the Barmouth viaduct as it was said to need £850-worth of repairs that year and another £3,400 by 1970. After some wrangling Meirionydd County Council leased the footbridge from BR, completed all the necessary repairs for £260 and made a profit on tolls of £216 in the first year.

This bears interesting comparison with the tactics used to justify the Settle-Carlisle closure proposal outlined in Chapter 4, where a two-pronged approach was adopted, with dire warnings about the condition of the Ribblehead Viaduct and its supposedly terminal condition and a general gross inflation of operating costs between 1982 and 1983 — even though BR was operating an identical service of two trains each way per day with largely the same locomotives and rolling stock.

Despite its scepticism, the Cambrian action group remained willing — at least initially — to accept at face value BR's announcement in September 1980 (at a press conference which followed much leaking) that it would have to close the wooden viaduct at Barmouth the following month while a survey was carried out to determine the extent of repairs needed due to worm damage to the wooden piles. By January BR was saying its worst fears had been realised and its initial repair estimate of £2.5m was about right. The engineer in charge was Frank Leeming who, as already stated, was later to find himself playing a not dissimilar role on the Settle-Carlisle. Among options costed was a replacement viaduct, but a £155,000 survey suggested repair might be possible using one of two alternative methods.

The whole debate was taking place in a highly charged political atmosphere in which no secret was made of the fact that BR was using the Barmouth viaduct as a stick with which to beat more money out of the Government. The then BR Chairman, Sir Peter Parker, had told the Cardiff Business Club the previous November that it was impossible to "continue to deliver indefinitely a fixed contract for a declining sum of money", namely to continue running rural railways while the Government kept cutting the Public Service Obligation grant. Sir Peter was even pictured on TV on Barmouth viaduct wielding a piece of worm-ridden timber which had allegedly been taken from it.

The London Midland's divisional passenger manager at Stoke-on-Trent told a public meeting at Barmouth that BR was using the viaduct as an issue so it could achieve a broader agreement with the Government on funding for railways in general and rural ones in particular. "If we can't get a deal for Barmouth viaduct then we can't get a deal for other lines," he said.

On the face of it, then, BR and the action group were on the same side... or were they? There was a very real fear among the action group's members that the Government would simply "call BR's bluff", whereupon BR would either close the line or lose a lot of face. The group's May 1981 bulletin put it this way: "BR — at the highest level — may well be prepared to sacrifice the Cambrian line on the well known and much frequented altar of political expediency; to prove a point to the Government and as a dramatic gesture to 'prove' what they're saying about rural railways."

Then the Cambrian would become just another rural railway closed for want of capital to make repairs, and the sideline of BR's battle with the Government would be irrelevant history for the people affected. But BR's Government-bashing cudgel suddenly began to look a little limp when a BR engineer, Chris Wallis, gave the action group a copy of his report suggesting the viaduct could be satisfactorily repaired for just a tenth of the £2.5m. figure claimed by BR. He had been driven to leak his report by the apparent reluctance of BR to act on it.

Mr Wallis's main finding was that the damage was far less severe than BR had been saying. He claimed that only about ten per cent of the timber piles had been mildly attacked by shipworm — they had all been attacked by gribble worm, which was less serious, causing only surface damage. The rotten timber wielded by Sir Peter had, it seems, come from the remains of the previous viaduct demolished at the start of the century. He also criticised the manner in which previous repairs had been carried out, claiming some were actually more likely to cause further damage. Drawing on his experience in repairing the Loughor viaduct, Mr Wallis proposed what he called a "simple, foolproof and lasting repair".

The immediate effect of this report, apart from the demotion of Mr Wallis, was a halving of BR's original estimate and a new "ultimatum" to the Government. BR said it was doing repairs which would allow the viaduct to re-open, but only for six months, whereupon if the Government did not provide £1.2m. to complete repair work it would have to close again. The Government did not pay up — certainly it was not seen to pay up. But neither did the viaduct close and by the end of 1985 it was again able to take the full weight of loco-hauled trains. Today it is regularly used by Class 37 locomotives hauling MkII coaches — heavier than diesel units — on London-Pwhelli holiday trains. The threat has, apparently, receded completely.

Some piles had been repaired in line with Mr Wallis's suggested method and others had been replaced. BR found the money "from internal sources" — an old favourite — and it is not clear whether the Government made any adjustment in the PSO grant to help BR.

Some remarkable parallels with the Settle-Carlisle affair can be found here. It was the same Chris Wallis who was the first to challenge British Rail's assertions that Ribblehead Viaduct was falling down (he later presented his own evidence at the TUCC hearing in Skipton). He was the first to propose a similar "simple, foolproof and lasting repair" to the viaduct and once again, his opinions were dismissed out of hand at a time when BR had announced its firm intention to close the line.

Equally significantly, when English Heritage asked its own engineers — experts in repairing and conserving old stonework — to examine the viaduct, they concluded repairs would cost no more than £2.5m, compared with the original BR estimate of £4.3m (assuming the viaduct could be saved at all), and offered £1m towards the cost.

And, within a year of the reprieve, it has emerged that Ribblehead Viaduct miraculously no longer has fundamental structural problems. Basic repair work — that is clearing the backlog of deliberate neglect — has proved sufficient to keep it open indefinitely.

The bridge trick was used once more — and again to great effect — when British Rail threatened closure of the Hull-Goole-Doncaster route between Goole and Gilberdyke because of the allegedly poor condition of the Goole swing bridge. The Goole-Gilberdyke line is part of the InterCity route from Hull to King's Cross and is used by about 200,000 passengers a year. Nonetheless BR proposed closing it because some £2.2m. worth of repairs were needed to the bridge. InterCity services would be diverted round two sides of a triangle via Selby. The closure notice brought more than 3,000 objections.

The story was in many ways the same old one we have heard before — the bridge repair bill had steadily mounted over years of neglect. The need for repairs at Goole stemmed from a cause rather different from the ravages of Pennine weather, however. The bridge had been struck by a coaster in December 1973, causing about £1m-worth of damage, but for legal reasons peculiar to the world of marine insurance, BR's claim yielded only £15,016. Since then, up to January 1985, another 22 ships had collided with the bridge's central jetty, 12 of them causing "more than superficial" damage. There was good reason to believe powerful lobbies outside the railways — this time representing shipping rather than road interests — were backing the closure plan to allow access up-river for larger vessels. Humberside County Council chiefs visited the bridge with their engineer and pronounced themselves "appalled" at the way it had been allowed to deteriorate.

But the fact that it would cost BR £1m to demolish the bridge even if it was given permission to close the line helped provide the basis for a solution. The county council offered to put up £400,000 towards the cost of repairs if the line stayed open. The offer was made amid real fear for the future of Hull's InterCity services, because diverting via Selby would have entailed using another problem swing bridge. Months of bartering saw the local authority offer rise to £1.1m or 50 per cent of the repair cost. But BR remained determined to press ahead with closure unless it was given this sum "up front".

Eventually BR appeared to relent and a deal was made under which the county council would give BR £800,000 immediately and the balance would be spread over five years as repairs were carried out. In return BR would guarantee the future of the line for ten years. BR also promised Parliamentary action over the outdated marine insurance laws which contributed to the crisis. Critics of the deal believe it was too open-ended and did not tie BR to specific enough undertakings. Certainly BR had every reason to feel very pleased with their bargaining — if the Clitheroe DalesRail station re-opening, referred to in Chapter 7, had in its small way set the precedent for securing local authority finance for railway schemes, here was a far more significant example. The resolution of the Goole swing bridge saga was believed to be the first occasion on which a local authority had contributed directly to BR's maintenance budget. The Barmouth scare may have cut little ice with the Government, but Goole had quite spectacular results in attracting funds from a different quarter.

Since then, local councils have become fair game for fund raising, with BR using the blanket justification that it is common sense to go to local authorities for money for local railways. But it has since turned to using rather more subtle methods. In 1989, BR threatened to withdraw virtually every last train on the branch line network of East Anglia as a cost-cutting exercise. It would have meant last trains from Norwich leaving at around 7-8 pm instead of 9-10 pm. Norfolk and Suffolk county councils took the hint and came up with the cash for all but two of the threatened services.

They had no reason to doubt BR's word that the trains would be axed.

For that is precisely what happened on Humberside in the same year, when the last train of the day on all three routes out of the city to Beverley, Selby and Doncaster, were withdrawn.

Incoming trains from Manchester, Leeds and Doncaster were either withdrawn or terminated at Selby and Hull Paragon station now closes overnight. At about the same time, Northumberland County Council was persuaded to put up the cash for a new Morpeth-Newcastle service, the first time it had ever agreed to fund a rail service. This was described as "a breakthrough" by the BR staff newspaper, *Rail News*.

So it should perhaps come as little surprise that by the end of the Settle-Carlisle affair, a string of local councils spread along the line had agreed to find a total of £500,000 to fund a mixture of repair work on the Ribblehead Viaduct, revenue support for the Dalesman rail service and a dozen smaller things. They were simply part of a wider, long term campaign to compensate for BR's declining Government grant.

Yet in other ways, the Settle to Carlisle did become a trail-blazer. It could, for example, be counted as the first "intended" victim of British Rail's policy of sectorisation. Towards the end of the closure campaign, it also became a test bed for both bus substitution and privatisation.

Sectorisation can be described as Sir Robert Reid's masterplan. The intention behind it was simple. Few people had ever been able to get to grips with BR's finances because there were few objectives, other than to carry on running roughly the same number of trains over much the same network of tracks as in 1974, when an agreement was struck between BR and the Government of the day on socially-necessary rail services. They were paid for by a special Government grant, the Public Service Obligation, or PSO Grant, which the Government paid to "buy" loss-making, but socially desirable services — to remote communities for example.

But for the rest of BR, there was no real accountability, no "bottom line", in accountancy jargon. Sir Robert set out to change this by creating five sectors, covering InterCity, Provincial, London and South East, Parcels and Freight businesses. Each had a clear set of objectives, which for InterCity, Parcels and Freight, included moving from making a loss to profit.

One side effect of this policy was to make the individual business managers think hard about how to get by with fewer resources. For Railfreight, one answer was to scrap as quickly as possible its remaining old and unbraked wagons, which had the added disadvantage of being too small to allow effective competition against the largest lorries.

Railfreight used the Settle-Carlisle line for shifting unbraked wagons from Scotland to England. The alternative West Coast Main Line was avoided because unbraked freight wagons have to travel slowly and this would make it difficult to avoid delaying the fast, electrically-hauled Glasgow-London expresses. They also require the presence of "catch points" to derail runaway trucks before they cause worse damage. These are incompatible with high speed continuously welded track. As the unbraked wagons disappeared, so did the Freight Sector's reasons for using the Settle-Carlisle.

Following the re-routeing of the Nottingham-Glasgow service via Manchester, InterCity still used the Settle-Carlisle for diversions when the West Coast route was closed for maintenance or repairs, or — as on the very day that BR announced its intention to close the line — the overhead electric wires were brought down either by wind or accident. But InterCity, hard pressed to cut its losses, began looking at ways of carrying out maintenance overnight, by keeping one track open all the time, or by using buses to ferry passengers between, say, Preston and Carlisle.

Even before the closure hearings took place, BR had announced that it no longer intended using the Settle-Carlisle line for diversions. Instead, it proposed to send a Liverpool-Glasgow service via Manchester, Leeds, York and Edinburgh!

This left only the Provincial Sector using the line. Provincial was the largest of the five sectors, with two-thirds of the stations and the worst loss-makers on its books. It found itself running three trains per day over 72 miles of line with only two stations — at Settle and Appleby — to generate traffic. Looking for an excuse to close it must have looked a far less troublesome option than setting out to market the line for what it was — England's finest . And that is what, initially at least, happened.

But not for long. The Settle-carlisle affair was not immune from railway politics. This manifested itself in two ways in the 1980s while the closure campaign was being fought: bus substitution and privatisation.

There is nothing really new about substitute buses. They were first touted as a serious alternative to branch lines as the Beeching plan was being unveiled. Indeed, many closed branch lines actually had substitute bus services launched. But almost without exception, they were dismal failures, attracting on average, only a third of the passengers carried by rail. Considering how lightly-used some branch lines were in the 1960s, this amounted to almost no passengers at all and not surprisingly, these bus substitutes quickly withered and died. However, these buses were designed to, as far as possible, mirror the rail services they replaced: the very rail services which had been shown to be not what the public wanted. In many cases, buses might have served the transport needs of communities quite well had they not pretended to be trains and run to town and village centres, housing estates and so on, rather than the former station sites. Sadly, integrated transport planning — or "horses for courses" — has rarely featured in British transport policy, despite the 1968 Transport Act which established the PTEs and effectively saved the railways around our largest cities, such as Leeds.

The bus substitution idea was revived again in the mid-1970s, but this time on a more ambitious scale. British Rail had begun looking at the long term future of its branch and cross-country lines, with the emphasis on how they could be kept running when the Modernisation Plan first-generation diesel units built from the late 1950s onwards, began to wear out. One solution which ultimately took to the rails was the basic, light weight railbus, combining bus and rail technology to create a cheap and cheerful branch line train. This resulted in the Pacer trains which combined a bus body with a freight wagon chassis and a bus-type diesel engine.

But from those same early discussions also emerged plans for a deal with National Express, the coach arm of the National Bus Company. Put simply, the deal was this: BR would abandon most of its branch lines and cross-country routes, except for the most heavily used ones. The trains would be replaced by National Express coaches, but painted in BR colours. The coach services would call only at the places served by the train and would run to generally similar times. It would be like having a train, but one which used roads as a cheaper alternative to tracks. Again, there seems to have been little thought given to exploiting the flexibility of buses and coaches. On the other hand, where coaches did the job that railways could not for whatever reason — such as the Reading and Woking to Heathrow RailAir links, there was more success. These and the RailLink coach services from Peterborough to King's Lynn and Hunstanton are now an established part of the BR timetable.

In return, National Express would abandon its inter-city, long distance coach services, leaving the "trunk haul" business to British Rail. In the event, no agreement could be reached. British Rail did virtually nothing to modernise its cross-country routes — that had to wait another decade and the emergence of the Provincial Express network — and National Express went on seriously to challenge BR's InterCity operation with its Rapide motorway coach services.

Another decade on, and the 1985 Transport Act, which de-regulated bus services, throwing open all bus routes to total competition, also made reference to substitute buses for trains. This time, some safeguards were built in, requiring a public hearing before a substitute bus service could be axed. At the same time, BR was placed under tremendous pressure to cut its annual Public Service Obligation Grant. Between 1983 and 1986, 25 per cent was chopped from the 1983 figure of around £900m. Between 1986 and 1989, the Government ordered a further 25 per cent cut, meaning that 45 per cent of Provincial's grant — even before allowing for inflation — had been taken away.

It is at this point that the twin strands of bus substitution and privatisation become intertwined. The main obstacle to privatising British Rail would be the loss-making branch lines. If they could be replaced by substitute buses... And, conveniently, here was the Settle to Carlisle line, which the Government wanted to see privatised but which could obviously not make a profit if it had to run through the winters when few people want to travel.

The answer was clear — at least to the then Environment Secretary, Nicholas Ridley. Without even having a ministerial brief for the line he dismissed the newly-launched Dalesman commuter service as unnecessary and said minibuses would do the job instead.

It is a matter of history that the idea backfired. When the North East and North West transport Users' Consultative Committees reported on substitute buses, they found they would more than double rail journey times. But even before the Settle-Carlisle affair was finally settled, this did not prevent the Government from pressuring BR into a national branch line review to select bus-substitution candidates.

A second sacrificial lamb was quickly found in the shape of the Barnetby-Gainsborough line, which carries three Sheffield-Cleethorpes trains, a handful of freight trains and, like the Settle-Carlisle in 1983, has just two stations along its length.

Details of the national review have never been made public, but a BR Board memorandum, leaked to ASLEF, the drivers' union, listed 36 lines with short or medium term civil engineering problems, which ASLEF claimed was the next best thing to a hit list. Within months, BR had announced one of the lines named in it, between Doncaster and Gainsborough, as being up for closure, axing the Doncaster-Lincoln-Sleaford-Peterborough service and thereby severing the direct route north from the sizeable city of Lincoln.

The review took around 18 months to complete — the completion was never formally announced — and failed to identify a single bus-substitution candidate. Perhaps most significantly of all, there was no single common reason for this. The review found that each line was, to a greater or lesser degree, unique and that bus-substitution would not work for a wide variety of reasons.

The two Lincolnshire closure proposals generated such an outcry, particularly from Lincolnshire County Council, which was an early convert to the cause of helping out BR with its PSO Grant problems — it was among the first local authorities to contribute to items such as automatic level crossings, to give branch lines a better chance of financial survival by reducing operating costs — that the Doncaster-Lincoln closure proposal was withdrawn, and the Gainsborough-Barnetby proposal was, in BR's words, "suspended", with the additional guarantee that if it was revived, proceedings would begin from the beginning. BR and the county council began talks on reducing the running costs of both lines and on marketing them better.

But this was only a case of trying to patch up a good relationship that had been very nearly destroyed by BR's ineptitude over the Doncaster-Gainsborough announcement. The manner in which Lincolnshire County Council officers learned of the plans — through a casual aside while engaged on other business with BR — prompted a bitter exchange of correspondence between Dudley Procter, the council's Chief Executive, and the BR chairman, Sir Robert Reid, with Mr Procter asking: "Why have the County Council and the people of Lincolnshire to be treated with such apparent contempt?" BR had told county council officers just weeks earlier that the line was not under threat.

Among those carrying out market research for Linconshire on the Gainsborough-Barnetby line were Ron Cotton, former Settle-Carlisle Project Manger with BR, and Colin Speakman, of DalesRail fame. Interestingly, while regular passengers from the two intermediate stations up for closure were thin on the ground, the research found significant day-trip traffic bound for Cleethorpes from the Sheffield and Retford areas — and scope for growth.

But even this did not prove to be the final chapter of the secondary railway saga. The relative handful of branch and rural cross-country lines left after a combination of the Beeching "rationalisation" and the steady trickle of isolated line closures through the late 1960s and '70s — such as the Bridport line, Dorset's last branch, and the Alston line in the North Pennines — are still under threat.

The first signs emerged just as the completion of the bus substitution review was begin to leak out. They took the form of two simple ultimatums to local authorities in East Anglia and South Wales, which were told that unless they were prepared to subsidise early and late night trains, then these would be chopped.

As already described, in East Anglia, Norfolk and Suffolk County Councils acquiesced. The alternative would have been to see the last train of the day — sometimes the last two — on every line bar one in the two counties axed. Broadly speaking, the Provincial network in East Anglia would shut down every evening at around seven. In South Wales, it was early trains which were targeted. Council leaders here, already annoyed about a string of broken promises from British Rail on new rolling stock and improved timetables for the Valleys Lines, refused to put in any more ratepayers' money. The early trains were promptly withdrawn.

Worse was to follow. BR began what it described as a programme of "controlled cutbacks" to Provincial services mostly in Yorkshire, the North East and on the Provincial cross-country route between East Anglia, the East Midlands and North West. The blame was laid at the door of the new Provincial "flagship" train, the Class 158 Provincial Express, a 90 mph, air-conditioned diesel multiple unit intended to operate over the emerging express network, intended to link towns and cities off the main InterCity network by means of a system of fast and reliable long distance trains. Examples include the Edinburgh-Glasgow-Aberdeen group of routes, Newcastle-Leeds-Liverpool and the North-West to South-East group of services.

The new trains were already a year overdue because of manufacturing problems. Even when they began rolling off the production line, BR engineers found to their dismay that the new supertrains would not trigger electrical track singalling circuits properly. Track circuits constitute the basic safety device which sets signals to danger behind a passing train automatically, which locks points and signals to prevent collisions and which triggers automatic level crossings.

But, in anticipation of the Class 158 entering service, BR had run down its stock of spares for various types of first-generation multiple

"There you go — that should save face all round!"

units, now 30 years old or more and vastly expensive to run and maintain. The result was a chronic shortage of rolling stock. The controlled cutbacks were intended to cope with what BR presented as a temporary difficulty. Lightly-used trains were taken out of the timetable. In a handful of cases, substitute buses were laid on — some so-called "train" services in the North-East, for example, became a standing joke and a quite appalling advertisement for BR.

Then, having failed in its attempt to close the branch lines and substitute buses for the trains, the Government, in the shape of the Department of Transport, came up with a demand for another £77m worth of cuts in Provincial Sector's share of the Public Service Obligation Grant, spread over three years. This was the same PSO grant as was intended to pay for precisely the loss-making trains recently axed in Wales and threatened in East Anglia.

The effects were not long in showing themselves. More early morning and late evening trains were put up for withdrawal on Teesside and Tyneside and in the North West. There was no pretence now that these were temporary measures to ease BR through a passing crisis. The official line had changed to a statement that the services affected were lightly-used, cost anything up to £10 to provide for every £1 collected in fares (compared with an average of £3 for every £1) and were not providing the taxpayer with value for money.

At British Railways Board level, the official attitude at the time of writing was that the PSO reduction target had been agreed with the Government and that BR could deliver it. But comments made by a BR official to a meeting of the North East Transport Users' Conultative Committee shortly before the cuts were announced, were rather more revealing. He said in as many words that BR was facing its biggest problems in 25 years and that the next 18 months would be crucial. At the same meeting, one of his subordinates was equally blunt, warning that the more lightly used Provincial routes could expect no more than a "basic service" for the next five years at least, linking the changes directly to the level of the PSO Grant.

Both the TUCC and passengers on the more lightly-used lines quickly learned what this meant: The Leeds-Lancaster-Morecambe line, intended as the alternative route to Carlisle if the Settle-Carlisle had been closed as intended, lost two of its seven daily trains. The Esk Valley line from Middlesbrough to Whitby was chopped from eight trains per day to four. The Leeds-Goole line was cut back to three trains in one direction and two in the other — a fact quickly seized on by James Towler, by this time a vice-president of the Railway Development Society, who pointed out that the line now enjoyed the worst rail service in Britain.

The Central Wales Line also lost two trains from its already modest timetable and other, lesser examples could be picked out almost anywhere on the Provincial network. The overall aim appeared to be one of paring down each individual line to the point where it could be operated by one diesel multiple unit, saving in both future investment and operating costs.

More ominously, there were ample indications that two different types of Provincial railway were beginning to emerge. On the one hand, was the new Express network, into which money — in the form of new trains, station improvements, resignalling and track improvements — was being poured to create a national system of secondary lines which would be both fast and cheap to operate. On the other were the "has-beens", the lightly-used, deep rural lines which would have to make do and mend with a skeleton service.

Express services are, not surpringly, seen as the jewel in Provincial Sector's crown. Many of them cover their basic operating costs, or come very close to doing so, and current BR strategy is to put more money into improving these routes on the grounds that any extra ticket sales represent a high degree of profit: the basics of infrastructure and marketing are already in place. Each additional train need merely cover its own running costs of fuel, crew, maintenance and depreciation, with minimal terminal costs at the stations it uses.

And, interestingly, BR estimates that almost 80 per cent of passengers feeding in to InterCity services by rail, do so on an Express network service. Talk of railway privatisation was, as we write, steadfastly refusing to go away. Now InterCity services are profitable and therefore privatisable: the real stumbling block is what to do with the secondary services left over.

It is possible to foresee a situation in which InterCity might be bundled — to use City jargon — with Provincial Express, giving potential investors a core long distance railway which is profitable and a secondary system, responsible for feeding in significant numbers of passengers, which at worst broke even and which, at best, turned in a small profit. When the current investment programme is complete, it is quite possible to envisage Provincial Express as a modest money-spinner. The Class 158 trains will be cheap to operate and maintain. Early indications suggest they will be able to work even more intensively than the Sprinter fleet of diesel units. Combine these advantages with a network of routes on which station track layouts and signals have been modernised and simplified, and on which level crossings have been automated, and the investor in a newly privatised railway would find himself in possession of a system capable of running trains more cost-effectively than anywhere else in Europe and quite possibly the world.

This happy picture would be spoiled only by the issue of what would happen to the real loss-makers, the lines, like the Esk Valley, Central Wales and West Country branches which can never be made to pay their way and which would become the unsaleable rump of what was once a nationalised railway system. The skeleton service which many of them have now been forced to operate will look increasingly unattractive as the years roll by and, far from increasing their patronage, railway history teaches us that these lines are far more likely to see it decline.

There is a splendid irony in the fact that, by all natural laws, the Settle-Carlisle line, serving as it does a sparse population spread over largely inhospitable terrain, should be fixed firmly in this group of

Midland Compound No. 1000 and Leander, No. 5690, at Aisgill Summit, February 1983

financially unattractive lines. Instead, it is seeing investment and enhanced services. It could be said that British Rail's hamfisted attempt to run down and close the line was the best thing that could have happened to it. The anger generated forged unlikely alliances, at first uneasy, between a remarkable variety of interests from MPs, to local councils, to business groups, to local residents, walkers, cyclists and railway enthusiasts. With a little help from sympathetic railway personnel of all ranks they shaped a bright new future for the Leeds-Settle-Carlisle line. They are continuing to oversee progress by working together with BR to ensure that their plans are put fully into effect.

A LINE LOOKING FOR A PURPOSE: the crew on the last northbound Nottingham-Glasgow express in May 1982 marked the occasion by displaying this "headboard" from the cab window of the Class 45 locomotive when it stopped at Appleby. The following day the station saw the first Leeds-Carlisle "local" hauled by a Class 31 locomotive.

11.
The way ahead

WHEN the Settle to Carlisle railway celebrated its centenary in 1976, the first clouds were beginning to take shape on the horizon. The West Coast Main Line was newly electrified with state of the art locomotives and signalling, increasing its traffic capacity and making the S & C theoretically redundant.

It had already ceased to be a main route from London to Scotland and its local passenger services were no more than a memory — in any case, the miserable two local stopping trains per day provided in 1970, the year they were axed, were of little use to anyone, and certainly worthless for commuting into either Leeds or Carlisle.

So 15 years on and one marathon closure attempt later, what does the future hold for the Settle to Carlisle?

As the dust begins to settle, it becomes more and more obvious that the real malaise affecting the line was the lack of a clear purpose in life. When it was built, in a fit of pique, all those years ago, it had a simple purpose: to speed Midland Railway Company traffic to Scotland.

Local passenger trains and wayside stations were little more than a sop to local opinion — indeed, in some instances the Midland refused outright to appease local opinion by acceding to demands for a station to be built. Down the years, and especially from the mid-1970s onwards, the Settle to Carlisle steadily lost this main line role and with it, its sense of purpose. It became a line doing no real job, but merely tying up loose ends — the unbraked freight trains which the shiny new West Coast Main Line did not want, the middle-distance passenger trains from Nottingham to Glasgow, via the slow route, for which no-one saw a clear future.

It is to British Rail Provincial Sector's credit that post-reprieve plans for the line revolve almost completely around giving it back a true purpose. Not as an express main line, for those days are gone, probably for ever, but as a combination of cross-country link, commuter line and tourist attraction. With this reshaping of its role has come a re-shaping of the line itself. Some improvements and modernisations have been made. Others, at the time of writing, are waiting in the wings, for cash and resources to become available.

One of the first actions after the reprieve was the holding of a conference in Leeds in July to bring together local authorities, pressure groups and other interested parties in the presence of Michael Portillo, the public transport minister.

The line manager, Roger Cobbe, suggested BR was far from complacent about retaining levels of traffic in the at times fickle leisure market. "We must continue to attract people in volatile markets, like day-trippers. There are so many other things people can do with their leisure time and money."

He said the line could see the introduction of novel types of railcard for local residents, or even for "committed helpers" such as the volunteers who have helped carry out station improvements, as part of "a more sophisticated pricing policy".

With so many positive noises about the S & C emanating from the conference it was — as the chairman, County Councillor Bill Cameron, commented — difficult to find a single person inside or outside BR who would admit to ever having been in favour of closure at all.

Indeed the only real sour grapes appeared to come from private sector representatives whose aspirations towards a leisure-led private railway had been dashed. Fergus Hobbs, Director of L & R Leisure Consultants, spoke of the "quantum jump" in bringing forward money-making ideas which he felt BR would be unable to provide. But the mood of the local authorities — disappointed that not one significant new development to bring new passengers to the line had so far come from the private sector — was summed up by John Carr, of West Yorkshire PTE, who said: "We are not getting a clear indication from the private sector as to what sort of development they are prepared to invest in and how they are prepared to act on a par with us and make the partnership work."

The minister, for his part, denied that the Government had seen the Settle-Carlisle line as an experiment for privatisation — the problems of the line had been "unique" and the Government had had to find solutions to its special problems, he said.

Within six months of the reprieve, BR had to admit that the line had had another record year, with takings up by 13 per cent and passenger number up by seven per cent — representing a significant efficiency gain. Within a year, the timetable was increased again to give a six-train-per-day service and the summer Sunday service (with four daily return workings from Hellifield northwards, thanks to the Lancashire link) was launched a month ahead of normal.

A business plan for the line was revealed by the public transport minister, Michael Portillo. Essentially, this packaged the best of the various ideas for developing traffic over the line, with the ultimate aim of involving the private sector in exploiting the tourist and other potential of the line — one of the conditions laid down when the reprieve was announced.

The first major improvement area has been rolling stock. In October 1990, the first Class 156 SuperSprinters were due to be drafted onto the line, steadily replacing the early MkII and Class 31 or 47 locomotives, which dominated rolling stock policy since the Nottingham-Glasgow service was diverted away. The SuperSprinters themselves will be deployed to quite distinct summer and winter timetables, reflecting the seasonal nature of the Settle and Carlisle's tourist traffic.

Present plans envisage six two-coach trains in traffic through the summer — some doubling up as four-car sets — with fewer in the winter.

But this will create two problems: first, satisfying the enthusiast market, which has become as sentimental about the very mediocre MkII stock as it was about the even more abysmal MkI coaches which it replaced.

Secondly, it will pose the question of what to do with the tidal surges of summer tourist traffic, out from Leeds in the morning, returning from Carlisle in the afternoon. In the high summer peaks, eight and ten-coach trains are regularly needed. How can a two-coach diesel unit cope? The answer lies in a mixture of experimental timetabling, which those responsible for the line hope will spread the tourist surge over a longer period of the day, and the higher density seating in the SuperSprinter fleet.

A revised timetable, tested in the summer of 1990, gave six trains each way instead of five. The thinking here was to provide a better spread of departures from both Leeds and Carlisle. The aim is to offer several alternatives, spreading the load over two or three services instead of just one.

A second plan is to retain and refurbish a set of MkII coaches and a small number of Class 47 diesels — displaced by the Class 158 Express programme — as a "heritage train", offering both enthusiast appeal and high passenger capacity.

Retaining the loco-hauled option would also retain the flexibility for one-offs, such as the freight diesel haulage programme of autumn 1989 and spring 1990, in which the regular Class 47s were augmented by Freight Sector pilot locomotives, including Class 20s and 56s, which are rarely seen on passenger trains, and the unique Leeds-based engineering apprentice training locomotive, Class 25.

These trains, aimed entirely at the enthusiast market, generated worthwhile traffic, some passengers travelling from Scotland and the South West to ride behind a freight sector locomotive. Class 20s proved most popular with one train loading to 1,000 passengers — and this at a time when the line is normally at its quietest.

Indeed, there is a growing feeling that the Class 25 may have been an experiment within an experiment, something to test the reaction not just to an unusual locomotive type appearing on the line, but to the appearance of something that should not be there at all — a preserved locomotive in all but name. The more visionary elements believe the Settle and Carlisle may eventually become a testbed for running preserved diesel locomotives on British Rail tracks, something which, for the moment, BR will not countenance, despite the burgeoning diesel preservation movement.

There have been suggestions that the SuperSprinters will put an end to many of these wide-ranging ideas, but at least for the present, British Rail insists that the door is still open for more special workings — even though no third season has been planned. There is a school of thought that catering for this highly specialised market may be a way of effectively extending the high passenger numbers of the tourist-dominated summer season, so justifying the retention of locomotive-hauled stock.

A final possibility, and one which would achieve one of the business plan aims of involving the private sector, is for steam-hauled "wine and dine" specials over the line, serving gourmet food in plush, restored coaches at a premium price. The evidence from preserved railways is that the market is there. It remains to be exploited on the Settle and Carlisle.

But even if the right mix of trains is arrived at, what sort of railway will they be running over? British Rail made no secret of the immense track, signalling and infrastructure problems facing the line during its closure campaign. Many of these centred on Ribblehead Viaduct, which became seen almost as a microcosm of the line's difficulties, with shattered waterproofing, crumbling stonework and a limited lifespan.

One of the first actions following the reprieve was a two-week shutdown of the centre section of the line — including the Ribblehead Viaduct — to allow repairs to this and two other bridges to be undertaken. As described in Chapter 4, a new waterproof membrane was installed at the very end of one of the driest periods on record, at a time when the whole structure was probably as dry internally as it had been for a decade or more.

This "big bang" technique proved its worth here as elsewhere. A perfectly serviceable railway was handed back to the operators on schedule, with the public transport minister, Michael Portillo, officiating at a ribbon-cutting ceremony at the viaduct.

Two other bridges were repaired at the same time, and all three projects soaked up more than £500,000 of scarce investment funds. It is an indication both of how badly the line had been run down and of BR's commitment to do something about it, that another £500,000 was earmarked for more civil engineering work.

Steady progress was made on clearing the track maintenance backlog, to the point where today, the only significant speed restrictions left are permanent ones, such as the slack over the single track Ribblehead Viaduct section. The restrictions due to rotten sleepers or worn rails which peppered the line at the height of the closure campaign are, happily, a thing of the past.

One undecided question is whether the line will remain double track. One early option which British Rail examined was to turn the Settle and Carlisle into a single-track cross-country branch, with three or five passing places, depending on whether it was to continue being used as a diversion line for West Coast Main Line expresses, during engineering work or after an accident.

This attitude is also being rethought, with latest informed opinion being that it may be just as cheap to keep a double track main line as it it would be to instal the extra points and signals needed to create the passing loops for a single-track scheme. Even the existing single-track across Ribblehead Viaduct might revert to double track, because of the savings this would lead to by closing Blea Moor signal box, one of the most remote on BR and difficult and expensive to staff and maintain.

Another option is to look again at the line speed. It is currently 60 mph, but the idea of having a single, overall maximum speed may be abandoned, in favour of different limits for different types of train. This policy could see a limit of perhaps 75 mph, or higher, for Sprinter and SuperSprinter trains, while heavier, locomotive-hauled trains might be limited to, say, 40 mph. This would bring another, double benefit: anyone using the line for commuting or business journeys would travel more quickly on a Sprinter diesel unit, while the tourists and enthusiasts would be given more time to sample the scenery which makes the line unique.

The overall effect would be to reduce the line's maintenance bills. If InterCity wanted a faster line speed for its heavier trains, diverted from the West Coast Main Line, it would become totally responsible for the additional maintenance costs. Similarly, if Railfreight, BR's freight arm, decided to begin running regular services over the line, it would find itself picking up the bill.

Despite the absurdities of freight trains which travel south before turning north, simply to avoid the line, a return to regular freight traffic over the Settle and Carlisle looks exceedingly unlikely. Railfreight is still under tremendous pressure to save money. One way of doing this is to concentrate traffic on the minimum possible number of routes.

Even the Channel Tunnel offers only limited hopes of generating freight traffic which would need to use the line. When the tunnel is opened, there will be 35 paths for 1,000 tonne freight trains every day. BR believes that the traffic originating in Scotland can be comfortably fitted onto the East and West Coast Main Lines. Since the Tunnel's capacity is strictly limited, there is little chance of unexpectedly large amounts of traffic creating a need for a third freight route to the Scotland.

A second possibility, once widely discussed, was to convert the line as part of a Continental gauge route from the Tunnel mouth to Glasgow, skirting around London via Redhill and Banbury, linking into the Midland Main Line to Sheffield and Leeds. This proposal formed the basis of one of the privatisation bids for the line in the closing stages of the closure affair. The choice of route is critical. Electrified lines are useless because of the restricted clearance between the tracks and the overhead power lines.

Much of the Midland Main Line is still unelectrified. It has also been reduced from four tracks to two along much of its length, leaving ample space for a Continental gauge route alongside. From Leeds, the only unelectrified route north is now via Skipton and Carlisle. It would involve reducing the Settle-Carlisle to single track to achieve the necessary clearance under bridges and through tunnels but, technically at least, it is feasible.

It must be said that these proposals look increasingly like non-starters and, assuming the line remains double-track, signalling will remain largely unchanged for several years yet. Other projects have priority but, when funds allow, a conventional colour-light resignalling scheme is envisaged in preference to the more exotic methods, such as radio signalling which is seen as being better suited to controlling single line railways. There would also be radio reception difficulties with the difficult terrain the Settle-Carlisle traverses.

This resignalling scheme will ultimately close every signal box along the line — including the infamous Blea Moor — leaving the entire route controlled from either Hellifield or Settle Junction, where one signalman would command both the Settle and Carlisle and the Settle Junction-Carnforth route. Final details are still to be worked out, but wide-spaced three-aspect signals look the likeliest option, bringing the added bonus of increased line capacity should the need arise to begin running even more trains.

But the stations themselves had been earmarked at the time of writing as early candidates for attention when the heavier civil engineering work, needed to keep the line in working condition, is complete. The platforms are largely too low and too short, particularly most of those at the eight stations reopened in 1986. This poses a problem for the new Sprinters because of safety requirements which do not permit trains with automatic doors to stop other than at platforms. This means that the Sprinter trains will be limited to a maximum of three cars pending the completion of platform extensions. Then there's the question of Ribblehead station which remains probably unique in the British Isles by only being open to trains in one direction. Reinstatement of a second platform is well up the list of priorities, although this could be influenced by any decision to double the track over the viaduct (an alternative solution being an extension of single-line working to just south of the station).

There are a range of potential roles open for the stations, some of which would also correspond with the aims of the business plan, by throwing open redundant buildings for private sector ventures. To take the most obvious example, even though, strictly speaking, it is not part of the Settle and Carlisle, Hellifield, with its scope for restoration into restaurant, shops, visitor centre and car park, may become an alternative gateway to the line. With tourism being seen increasingly as a major plank of the Dales economy, the local authorities responsible for Hellifield are waking up to its potential and the realisation that relatively little money spent in grants to rebuild and restore it to its Victorian splendour would be repaid many times over in terms of local jobs and money into the local purse. The possibility even exists of a hotel and golf course development and Craven District Council, the lead authority for any development, has pledged £50,000 towards any restoration scheme for the station whose condition, at the time of writing, was increasingly critical. BR, for its part, will spend £50,000 on necessary demolition work should a scheme emerge to save the station which is a listed building. A useful model for any restoration can be found at Tynemouth, on the Tyne and Wear Metro system, where major grants from the European Community and English Heritage have contributed towards the renovation of the fine glazed station building.

Horton-in-Ribblesdale, with its largely intact buildings and signal box is tentatively earmarked for restoration as a heritage station. Ribblehead could become a visitor centre, offering more information about the viaduct, the shanty towns which sprang up during construction work and the Viking remains nearby. Restoration of the Hoffman kiln at Langcliffe and an associated visitor and resource centre could lead eventually to the establishment of a new station there serving Langcliffe and Stainforth.

According to the Business Plan, even the truly remote stations, such as Garsdale (the busiest of the halts reopened in 1986), may attract private development, possibly as a specialist outdoor shop, offering equipment and provisions to walkers and potholers.

More ambitiously, a small and almost forgotten part of the line may yet be converted into the tourist steam railway which some thought suitable for the entire 72 miles of the Settle and Carlisle. One suggestion in Plan is for privatisation of the Appleby-Warcop freight branch, abandoned by BR a few months before the reprieve was announced. The six-mile line could offer connections with main-line Leeds-Carlisle trains over a pleasant, if not dramatic, scenic run. British Rail sources said, at the time of writing, that a deal was near conclusion which could see the introduction of privately operated steam trains as early as 1991.

The map opposite shows some of the "development opportunities" in the Settle-Carlisle corridor.

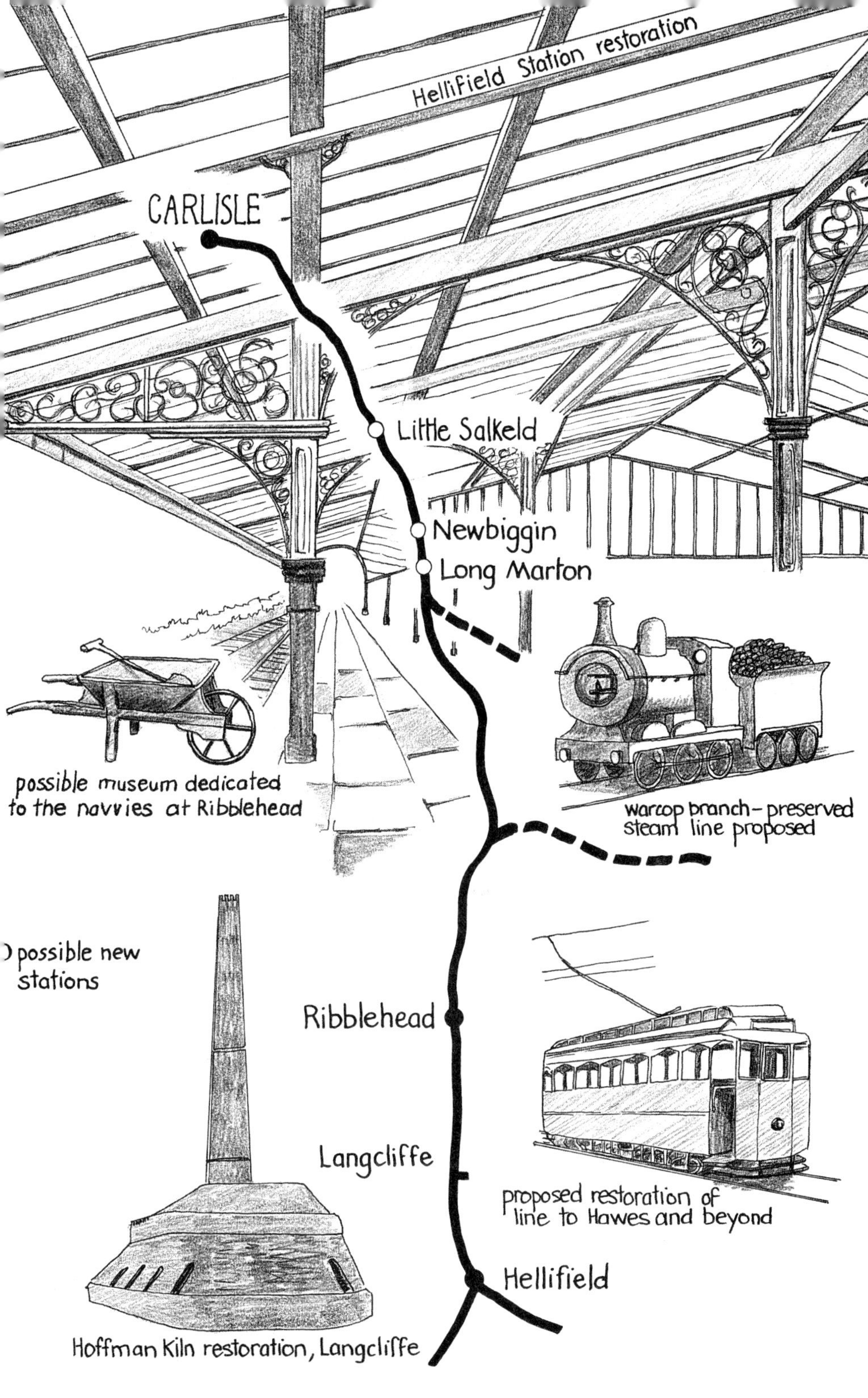

Hellifield Station restoration
CARLISLE
Little Salkeld
Newbiggin
Long Marton
possible museum dedicated to the navvies at Ribblehead
warcop branch – preserved steam line proposed
possible new stations
Ribblehead
Langcliffe
proposed restoration of line to Hawes and beyond
Hellifield
Hoffman Kiln restoration, Langcliffe

A stumbling block on reaching a deal for the branch has been the conflict of interest between Railfreight and its mandate to get the price possible for the line and the Provincial Sector's desire to see an additional attraction for trippers on the S & C by seeing a private operator installed at minimal risk, ideally on easy lease terms.

The Business Plan also mooted the idea of a miniature railway on the trackbed of the old Wensleydale Railway between Garsdale and Hawes. A locally based Wenslyedale Railway Association has been formed and has attracted wide media coverage with more ambitious ideas of restoring a standard gauge railway or tramway with the eventual aim of linking up with the current BR freight terminus at Redmire. A major problem — and one largely glossed over in the Business Plan — is the fact that almost all of the trackbed is now in the hands of around 50 private owners. Notwithstanding that, a survey by BR engineers has put the cost of restoration at between £$^1/_2$m and £1m per mile and the association is proceeding with a more detailed engineering appraisal in the hope of attracting backers to embark on the first stage of restoration.

Following the successful launch in the summer of 1990 of the trust fund which will provide the vehicle for channelling local authority, English Heritage and other monies into the conservation of the line's heritage, autumn 1990 saw the establishment of the Settle-Carlisle Railway Development Company to help foster the kind of business initiatives outlined int he Business Plan. The company aims to bridge the gap between the public and private sectors and — consicous of criticisms from the Business Liaison Group — stresses that it wants particularly to foster local initiatives.

Having knocked the S & C into shape physically, British Rail's Provincial Sector — which has total responsibility for the Settle and Carlisle — has a marketing battle on its hands to keep the passenger numbers rising from the 90,000 people who used it in 1983, the year BR announced the closure attempt, to the 500,000 who made the trip in 1990, onward and upward to the one million mark which everyone now seems to accept as the target figure.

British Rail's own initial contribution was the creation of a "line brand" for the Settle and Carlisle, with a woodcut-type logo showing a section of arches from one of the viaducts. This is now widely used in publicity material and for more practical purposes, such as a new set of signposts pointing out attractions such as Ribblehead Viaduct and Blea Moor Tunnel. Appropriately, Midland Red was chosen for the back-

The last train leaves Garsdale Station for Northallerton in 1954 — now the Wensleydale Railway Association harbours ambitions of Garsdale once again becoming an interchange.

ground colour.

The lifting of the shadow of doubt over the line's future saw the dust blown off one or two ideas that had been lying on various shelves. Among those with potential significance for future traffic levels on the line was the inauguration of the new Settle & Carlisle Way, a 150-mile long distance footpath from Leeds to Carlisle, paralleled between Skipton and Carlisle by a route for cyclists. The route was opened by the entertainer and Ramblers' Association vice president, Mike Harding, and has a significant edge over other so-called challenge walks, like the Pennine Way or the Coast-to-Coast, in that a station is never far away when sprains or blisters strike.*

Finally, what of the commuter? One of the factors which may have tipped the balance in favour of a reprieve was the unlikely emergence

---

** The route is featured is Settle & Carlisle Country, published by Leading Edge Press (see page viii) who are also publishers of the Settle-Carlisle Express, a free distribution newspaper for travellers on the line and one of the first private enterprise intitiatives of the type called for by the minister after the line's reprieve.*

of the Settle and Carlisle as a commuter railway. The experimental Dalesman service, its eight re-opened stations now a permanent feature of the timetable, tapped into a new, lucrative and expanding market of people who want to live in the country while working in the city.

Initially, the market was virtually all one-sided: from the villages of the Eden Valley into Carlisle, for work, school and shops. Kirkby Stephen, at just over an hour's travelling time away from Carlisle, emerged as the outermost point for practical daily travel.

But this is no longer the case. One of the less appreciated features of the improvements package announced by British Rail within weeks of the line's reprieve, was an extension of the early morning Settle-Leeds train back to Horton-in-Ribblesdale by the simple expedient of stopping the early train which starts from Blea Moor after running light from Skipton. This was quickly complemented by a return working in the evenings, making it perfectly possible to live in the heart of the Yorkshire Dales and work in Leeds.

Regular travellers have now seen the clapped-out first-generation diesel multiple units on this service replaced by the SuperSprinters, which cut journey times by means of faster acceleration. They have brought Settle within an hour of Leeds — which is quickly becoming an acceptable commuting time as people travel further in their search for work and as the roads become more congested. Indeed, middle and upper echelon managers relocating to Leeds from London, appear to have thought nothing of commuting in from as far afield as Malton on the Scarborough line, which might even bring stations like Dent and Garsdale within theoretical commuting distance.

As Leeds continues to develop as a major provincial centre of finance, commerce and retailing — indeed, some would say it is destined to become THE Northern centre, outstripping both Manchester and Newcastle in importance — the demand for this type of long-distance commuting seems likely to grow. British Rail, however, did not, at the time of writing, see any significant market beyond Horton-in-Ribblesdale: the advent of Sprinter operation in October 1990 would mark the retiming of the first train from Carlisle to Leeds, to arrive in the city at 09.51 — too late for at least one person known to have moved to Garsdale Station specifically to take advantage daily of the service as previously timetabled. The BR view is that the "old" service was an aberration caused by the fact that loco-hauled trains could not terminate or originate their journeys at any mid-point on the line. The idea of the

The entertainer Mike Harding joins a party of journalists at the inauguration of the Settle-Carlisle Way.

early morning train from Ribblehead and Horton (which runs light from Skipton and reverses at Blea Moor) being retimed to run to Kirkby Stephen or Appleby to begin its return journey to Leeds is dismissed by BR on the grounds of signalling difficulties at Kirkby Stephen and the forecast that revenue would be unlikely to exceed costs.

In drafting the Sprinter timetable, BR has adopted the philosophy of seeking to please most of the people most of the time by scheduling the six through trains at regular intervals through the busier part of the day. Those bemoaning the loss of the early morning train from the remoter Dales, however, suggest that it takes time to build up a firm customer base and point to the early morning train to Carlisle — which has evolved from the Dalesman experiment — to show what can be achieved. Clearly, uncertainty over future service timings would be a significant deterrent to anyone thinking of relocating in the Dales.

So, a forecast of growth in the commuter market, at least as far as Settle and Horton. And at the northern end of the line, Cumbria County Council is planning to investigate the feasibility of reopening those stations in the Eden Valley which remain in reasonable condition, namely Long Marton, Newbiggin and Little Salkeld. But these stations could not be brought back into use for the knock-down price applied to the other eight reopened halts as they would need to comply fully with Railways Inspectorate rules from Day One. On the Blackburn-Hellifield link, a breakthrough in negotiations between BR and Lancashire County Council as this book was being written gave rise to optimism that a full service would be introduced in 1991 or 1992 to link up with the S & C at Hellifield, with the possible reopening of a station at Whalley.

On train services, one much discussed idea is unlikely to be taken any further forward: that of re-creating the Nottingham-Glasgow service as a Provincial Express route. Proponents point out that traffic is growing and the line covers most of its direct costs, making it a promising candidate for conversion to Express status.

Stringing together the Glasgow-Dumfries-Carlisle, Carlisle-Leeds, Leeds-Sheffield (Dearne Valley) and Sheffield-Nottingham services might also provide some economies by making more efficient use of the small number of Sprinter trains with which BR has to cover the entire country. It would also create more journey opportunities, something which BR has been anxious to do as it has steadily redrawn the secondary rail network to create the Express network, linking towns and cities outside London and the South East.

But so far as the Settle and Carlisle is concerned, BR remains to be convinced that there is any point in recreating something it dumped as hopelessly uneconomic only a few years ago. This effectively consigns the Joint Action Committee proposals to create a high speed line, operated by InterCity 125 sets, to the dustbin. A pity, if only because this was an imaginative idea, well researched, which would have made an interesting experiment — though it must be recognised that even a modest HST service operating at higher speeds would destroy high frequency Sprinter paths which have become a proven moneyspinner. It would also have amounted to a joint initiative between the InterCity and Provincial sectors. Each now has its own priorities and it is a matter of history that the High Speed Train sets which might have operated a reborn Leeds/Bradford to Glasgow service have instead gone to other established InterCity routes, notably the Midland Main Line and the Western Region.

In the final analysis, the future of the line rests with British Rail's attitude to it. When the closure proposal was first put, rural railways were seen to have a dismal future. While their future has been thrown into turmoil once again by Government demands for more reductions to the annual PSO Grant upon which they depend, BR's branch lines have at least seen a sea change in the management attitude towards them.

There is evidence, cash shortages aside, that younger BR managers, given more autonomy than before, are beginning to see branch lines as a challenge rather than an encumbrance, that their success will be judged not on the amount of money they save by axing their loss-making routes, but on how successfully they can reverse the trend by marketing their local routes more successfully, reaching people who would not have thought of using their local railway line, or persuading others to ride over it simply for the scenery.

The immediate threat of bus substitution has been beaten off, not just on the Settle-Carlisle, but on perhaps two dozen other lines which are known to have been actively considered for closure during the 1989 branch line review. The latest financial squeeze on the PSO Grant has thrown some of Provincial Sector's plans awry, but at least the talk is no longer of closure.

The road signposted by Ron Cotton, West Yorkshire PTE (Metro), Cumbria and many others is being followed and the rewards are being reaped. Far from falling away as the BR sceptics predicted, passenger numbers on the Settle-Carlisle have continued to grow following the reprieve, aided by some clever marketing ploys like the diesel enthusiasts' trains.

If British Rail's own enthusiasm for running the line can be kept high, then the campaign, at last, will be over.

The end

Afterword

WHEN work began in earnest on this book, the dust had had time to settle on the events surrounding the proposed closure of the S & C and — as the introduction to Chapter 1 suggests — there was a mood of optimism that the challenge of the "shut 'em down" lobby had been beaten off and Britain's rural railways could look forward to a bright future.

Optimism, however, is often ill-placed in the worlds of politics and finance — particularly public sector finance. With the ink barely dry on our initial draft, the pendulum swung wildly back and our original, optimistic, Chapter 10 was rewritten in more sombre terms. We decided, nonetheless, to retain our original version of Chapter 1, as symbolic of all that is good and progressive, as represented by the reprieve for the S & C.

But there remains a grave paradox at the heart of both Government policy and, indeed, the nation's perception of the role of the railways. In an editorial in July 1990, the Mail on Sunday — which perhaps says today what Conservative governments will choose to do tomorrow — called for major investment in the railways on environmental grounds. Yet the likes of the Mail on Sunday are the first to fire the bullets when BR is unable to deliver the goods on quality and safety from dwindling economic resources.

In ten years, we have progressed not one inch since Sir Peter Parker's warnings about the short-term planning and the "crumbling edge of quality" afflicting rural lines in particular. Indeed, we are entitled to ask how far we have come in nearly 150 years. In 1844, Gladstone's Railway Regulation Act gave Victorian governments post-1865 the option to nationalise railway companies. Among considerations which would have to be addressed by governments contemplating such action were whether the companies were pricing ordinary workers out of the opportunity to travel by rail and whether they were putting profits before safety.

In September 1990, an inquest jury returned a verdict of unlawful killing over the Clapham rail crash after hearing how a partially trained and inadequately supervised technician, who had had only one day's rest in weeks, had left an unprotected wire in a signalling circuit. That evening, on national TV, Cecil Parkinson, the transport secretary, said the sky was the limit as far as British Rail spending on safety was concerned. The following morning, when he was questioned more closely in a radio interview, it became clear that BR was unlikely to get a penny more from the Treasury. And this at a time when £300m is being blown on what is said to be the most expensive mile of road in Europe, in London's Docklands.

The Government wants a cheap, preferably privatised, railway. It also wants to mesmerise voters with its green credentials while disclaiming responsibility for declining standards of service and safety on the greenest mode of transport available. It can not have it both ways.

The campaign which saved the S & C has shown that it is only through a long, and at times disheartening, campaign bringing together a wide diversity of groups that this point can be made. The encouraging thing, though, is that the point clearly can be made. We hope, therefore, that this book will give encouragement to groups on lines like the Esk Valley, Pontefract-Goole and Settle Junction-Lancaster who have been quick to realise (particularly in the Esk Valley) that — but for effective opposition — service cuts today can mean closure tomorrow.

Stan Abbott and Alan Whitehouse
September 1990

Appendix 1.

Who's who in the battle for (and against) the S & C

A GREAT many people played a part in the ten-year battle for the line, not all of whom have won a mention in the main narrative of this book. The following pages are intended to plug the more obvious gaps while providing the reader with an easy-to-use summary of the main protagonists. The authors apologise in advance to any deserving cases who may, inadvertently, have been omitted.

ADLEY, Robert, Conservative MP and lifelong railway enthusiast who has championed the railway cause from the back benches of three Thatcher administrations.

ALBUM, Edward, legal adviser to the Friends of the Settle Carlisle Line Association, who used British Rail's own figures to show the line could run at a profit.

ANNISON, Ruth, tireless leader of the Settle-Carlisle Railway Business Liaison Group, formed to put the case of members of the business community along the line who would suffer loss of trade if the line closed.

BOURNE, Greg, policy adviser to Mrs Thatcher believed by some to have scuppered the Mitchell rescue plan for the S & C.

BRIGGS, James Currer, chairman of the old North Eastern TUCC, based in Newcastle, which had a technical responsibility for a few miles of the S & C just north of Garsdale station.

BRITTAN, Rt Hon Sir Leon, MP for Richmond and a late back-bench convert to the S & C cause before his departure for European pastures.

BROOKS-ROONEY, Mike, the brains behind the Jarvis Community Programme Division proposals for a major Docklands-style job creation programme based on the S & C corridor.

BURTON, David, one of two Dales railway enthusiasts who called a public meeting in Settle in response to the growing threat to the line. This resulted in the formation of FOSCLA.

CAMERON, Councillor William, Chairman of Cumbria County Council's Highways and Transport Committee who led the joint local authorities' steering committee to victory.

CARR, John, Policy and Marketing Controller with West Yorkshire Passenger Transport Authority and a key figure among the officers involved in the joint councils' campaign. Was Head of Public Transport Office at West Yorkshire County Council prior to its abolition in 1986.

CASEY, Mike, who — having previously been in charge of selling off British Rail Engineering Ltd — was the second BR man in charge of the potential sale of the S & C.

CAUSEBROOK, Mark, BR Provincial line manger for the S & C, North Trans-Pennine and West Yorkshire who took over Ron Cotton's brief on the latter's retirement.

CAWKILL, Frank (deceased), chairman of the Wensleydale and Swaledale Transport Users' Group who was instrumental in establishing bus links from the new Dalesman service into Upper Wensleydale.

CHANNON, Rt Hon Paul, MP. The troubled Secretary of State for Transport who made the all-important announcement that the line was saved.

CLAYDON, Richard, Cumbria's legal adviser whose input was crucial in the latter part of the campaign.

CLOUT, Councillor John, influential Tory leader of North Yorkshire County Council. A long time in rallying to the cause, but he became a useful player once this had happened.

COBBE, Roger. BR's Settle-Carlisle Manager at the time of writing.

CRYER, Bob, MP. As the Labour member for Keighley, he was a tireless Commons campaigner for the S & C and railways in general, before losing his seat in 1983. He resumed the Parliamentary fight as member for Bradford South where he was elected in 1987. Founder member of the Keighley and Worth Valley preserved line.

CLARKE, Olive, chairman of the North West Transport Users' Consultative Committee, which staged the public hearings into the closure with the Yorkshire TUCC.

COTTON, Ron, British Rail official drafted in to oversee the closure process while also marketing the line in what were envisaged as its twilight months.

CURRY, David, MP for Skipton and Ripon and a keen proponent of privatisation. He asked the Parliamentary question which was expected to reveal that the S & C was about to be privatised and was reportedly as surprised as anyone to be given the opposite answer. Was once heckled by

JAC chairman John Whitelegg at a public meeting after having attacked Dr Whitelegg and his committee from the platform.

DOBBS, Bernard, Lancashire County Council man who did important work on BR's financial case.

FAIRCLOUGH, Tim, civil servant at the Department of Transport dealing with the S & C case.

FAIREST, Professor Paul, chairman of the Friends of Dales Rail, succeeded James Towler as chairman of the North-East TUCC.

FRASER, Tom, MP. Labour Minister of Transport who, in 1964, reprieved the local service on the S & C.

GRAHAM, Councillor Beth, Craven District and North Yorkshire County Councillor who became a leading anti-closure campaigner.

GUNNELL, County Councillor John, leader of West Yorkshire County Council when the joint local authorities campaign was launched.

HAYWOOD, Frank, former secretary of the North-West TUCC, notorious for his hard-line views on the conduct of TUCC hearings. Once said the TUCCs were in danger of being engulfed by "politically motivated fringe groups involved in an environmental crusade".

HARRISON, MIchael QC, British Rail's expensive counsel at the TUCC hearings.

HARTY, Russell (deceased), broadcaster and television personality who became president of FOSCLA.

HILLMAN, Dr Mayer, author with Anne Whalley of an important study of the consequences of rail closures. Presented valuable evidence at the TUCC hearings.

HOLDEN, Paul, formerly leading railwayman (stationmaster) at Appleby. Probably played as prominent a role in the campaign as was consistent with not losing his job with BR. Now based at Settle as S & C manager.

HORTON, Peter, secretary and later chairman of the Joint Action Committee.

JENKINS, County Councillor Wayne, chairman of the Public Transport Committee at West Yorkshire County Council at the time of the launch of the joint county councils' campaign.

JOY, David, noted Dales and railway author and editor of The Dalesman magazine.

KING, Alan, former BR divisional civil engineer who said Ribblehead viaduct needed replacing and who later re-emerged as adviser to a group interested in privatising the line.

KNAPP, Jimmy, leader of the NUR which was the rail union to the fore in opposing closure of the S & C.

LAWRENCE, Peter, prominent member of the Friends. He was a classic "hardship" case when BR first announced its closure plans for the S & C as he would have been unable to commute from Settle to his teacher's job in Keighley.

LEEMING, Frank, the BR bridge engineer whose report on Ribblehead Viaduct became the cornerstone of the "closure by stealth" policy.

LEWIN, David, the first BR officer with responsibility for the potential sale of the S & C.

MacKAY, Donald. His PEIDA consultancy was commissioned by the joint local authorities and coined the term "wanton neglect" to describe British Rail's treatment of its structures, most notably Ribblehead Viaduct.

McVEAN, Peter, important figure at PEIDA consultatns who worked on both the original report for the joint councils and for the later English Tourist Board report.

MARSH, Richard, MP. Labour transport minister who consented to the withdrawal in 1970 of the local service on the S & C.

MARTLEW, Eric, chairman of Cumbria County Council when the joint councils' campaign was launched. Now Labour MP for Carlisle.

MITCHELL, Sir David, MP, junior transport minister during much of the Settle-Carlisle affair. Resigned shortly after the expected reprieve for the line collapsed in favour of a privatisation attempt.

MOORHOUSE, John, secretary first of the Yorkshire TUCC and latterly of the North West TUCC where he replaced the retiring Frank Haywood in a move which undoubtedly brought fresh ideas to that committee.

MORGAN, Keith, Appleby businessman, town mayor and a prominent member of the Friends.

NEWEY, Sidney. Among his final jobs as BR's Provincial Director was in working out the Settle-Carlisle Business Plan.

NEWTON, Gerald, secretary first of the North Eastern TUCC and then of the new TUCC for North-East England following the merger with Yorkshire.

NUTTALL, Graham, co-founder, with David Burton, of FOSCLA, and owner of Ruswarp, the collie dog who allegedly lodged a formal objection to the closure proposal. Found dead in tragic circumstances in 1990.

O'BRIEN, J J, British Rail's London Midland Region general manager when the closure attempt was launched and signatory to a secret memo outlining BR's covert attempt to force a quick closure.

PARKER, Sir Peter, BR chairman when closure attempt began, apparently without his knowledge.

PEAL, Roger, the Department of Transport civil servant who signed the reprieve.

PORTILLO, Michael MP, Sir David Mitchell's successor and the man who — with Paul Channon — finally announced the reprieve.

PRESCOTT, Dave, marketing manager with BR Provincial at York who played an important part in recasting services on the line post-reprieve. Now at BR headquarters in London.

REID, Sir Robert, Sir Peter Parker's successor as BR chairman, and the man compelled to make a go of running the Settle-Carlisle by the Government decision to reprieve it. When he retired in 1990, to be succeeded by his namesake, he suddenly found a voice, which no-one suspected had existed during his term of office, when he spoke up for the railways and demanded more Government investment.

RIDLEY, Rt Hon Nicholas MP, former secretary of state whose portfolios includes transport, environment and trade. He believed Settle-Carlisle local trains could be replaced by minibuses as part of the privatisation attempt.

ROBERTS, John, director of Transport and Environmental Studies, which researched the JAC document, Retraining Settle-Carlisle.

ROBERTS, Jonathan, author of the New Life in the Hills report which encouraged the launch of the Dalesman trains. Also involved, with John Roberts and others, in the Retraining document (see above).

ROBINSON, Peter, Cumbria County Council official who headed the officers' team for the joint local authorities. A key figure in events following the reprieve, including the formation of a development company and the trust fund for channelling public and other funds into the conservation of the line's structures.

RUSWARP, border collie cross dog owned by Graham Nuttall and named after a station on the Whitby branch line, who is said to have registered a formal objection to the closure proposal by appending a paw print.

RYAN, Chris, JAC secretary at the time of reprieve. Presented evidence on diversions at the TUCC hearings.

RYDER, Kenneth, Driffield businessman, owner of several steam locomotives and leading light in the Cumbrian Railways bid to privatise the line.

SCOTT, Eddie, chairman of West Yorkshire PTA's rail working group, an S & C trustee and champion of northern railways.

SEFTON, Peter, Cumbria County Council officer in charge of survey work for evidence to the TUCC hearings.

SHAW, Peter, a key figure in FOSCLA. His painstaking research on a variety of subjects including the diversion of West Coast Main Line trains provided invaluable evidence for the TUCC hearings.

SIMMONS, Michael, chairman of the new West Yorkshire Passenger Authority following the abolition of metropolitan counties. He ensured that the new authority carried on where the old had left off by opposing moves to scrub the Settle-Carlisle campaign from the PTA agenda. Resigned in September 1990 and is now a director of the Yorkshire Rider bus company.

SIMPSON, Phillippa, representative of the Friends on the JAC. Presented a paper on the neglect of long-distance through passenger traffic on the line at the TUCC hearings.

SLYNN, George, chairman of Lancashire's public transport committee and a political stalwart during the campaign.

SMITH, Roger, Manchester businessman whose intervention brought about the reissuing of BR's first closure notice because the original document did not include the DalesRail service.

SPEAKMAN, Colin, a champion of public transport and the man primarily responsible for the introduction of DalesRail. Now director of an Ilkley-based consultancy, Transport for Leisure.

SUTCLIFFE, Brian, chairman of FOSCLA throughout the closure saga. He was the perfect bridge between the organisation and the more politicised wing of the JAC.

THATCHER, Rt Hon Margaret, MP, premier throughout the S & C saga whose office maintained a watching brief during a period beginning with the Jarvis job-creation proposals, running through the Ridley privatisation period and culminating with the Government U-turn.

THOMPSON, Alan, important member of the Cumbria County Council officers' team in the run-up to the TUCC hearings.

TOWLER, James, outspoken chairman, first of the Yorkshire TUCC and, latterly, of the TUCC for North-East England following a reorganisation of boundaries. Has championed the railways' cause with the Railway Development Society since his "sacking" from TUCC duties. Author of The Battle for the Settle & Carlisle, a personal account of the closure saga published in 1990.

WALLIS, Christopher, son of the man who developed the famous Dambusters bouncing bomb. Played a key role in saving the Barmouth viaduct on the Cambrian Coast Line and followed this up with an important submission to the TUCC hearings regarding the condition of Ribblehead viaduct.

WALTON, Peter, railway photographer who has played an important role in station improvements at Kirkby Stephen.

WATSON, John, Tory MP for Skipton and objector No. 1 on the Yorkshire TUCC list. Active campaigner for the line in the Commons.

WATTS, Richard. The Railway Development Society prong of the tripartite JAC. Also very active on rail issues in Lancashire, including user groups.

WHARTON-STREET, David, Provincial Sector manager at BR York who incurred the wrath of James Towler by pursuing BR's request for copies of individual objections to the S & C closure.

WHITAKER, Alan, journalist with the Bradford Telegraph and Argus and author of railway books. With the authors of this book, probably one of the three journalists who have written most prolifically on the S & C.

WHITELAW, Rt Hon William, formerly MP for Penrith and the Borders. His elevation to the House of Lords shortly after the 1983 General Election prompted a by-election at which the fate of the S & C was a prominent issue. The Tories retained the seat with a wafer thin majority.

WHITELEGG, Dr John, first JAC chairman, representing the Transport 2000 wing of that tripartite alliance. An outspoken campaigner who crossed swords on many occasions with "people in high places". Now a leading academic in transport planning with a world-wide reputation. Head of Geography and of the Environmental Epidemiology Unit at Lancaster University.

WILSON, Des, Liberal Party activist now prominent in the Liberal Democrats. Played a key advisory role in formulating the JAC's campaign strategy.

WOODHALL, Mike, West Yorkshire PTA officer who advised Michael Simmons that, if the Government were to approve closure, the joint councils should immediately seek a legal injunction against BR and the DTp on grounds of maladministration.

YOUNG, Lord of Grafham, industry secretary who was reputedly the driving force behind the Jarvis proposals for the country's biggest ever job creation programme based on the S & C corridor.

Appendix 2.

Timetable of main events in the Settle-Carlisle saga

1866

July 16: Midland Railway (Settle-Carlisle) Bill receives Royal Assent.

1869

April 16: Parliament rejects Midland Railway moves to abandon the Settle-Carlisle project.

September 14: First contract let for line's construction.

1870

October 12: First stone laid at site of Ribblehead Viaduct.

1876

May 1: Settle-Carlisle line opens to passenger traffic.

1910

December 24: Twelve killed in accident north of Hawes Junction.

1913

September 2: Another crash, at Aisgill, kills 16.

1920

Peak year for Midland Railway's passenger traffic over the Leeds-Carlisle route, with 374,151 passengers passing through Skipton station and 1,165,350 through Leeds Wellington.

1923

Grouping of Britain's privately owned railways into four new companies sees the Midland Railway merged with its old rival, the London and North Western, to form the London, Midland and Scottish Railway. This event makes the S & C technically redundant for the purpose for which it was built.

1942

February 1: Scotby station closes.

1947

February: Snow closes the line for eight weeks.

Transport Act establishes British Transport Commission, with the formation of British Railways on January 1, 1948.

1952

April 7: Cotehill station closes.

June 2: Ormside station closes.

July 7: Crosby Garrett station closes.

1954

February 1: Ingleton branch closed to passengers between Clapham and Low Gill.

April 26: Passenger services withdrawn on the former NER Wensleydale line between Hawes and Northallerton.

1955

January 21: Robertson Report gives ill-fated promise of massive new investment in the railways.

1956

November 11: Cumwhinton station closed.

1959

March 16: Hawes branch closed.

May 4: Bell Busk station (near Gargrave) closed.

Introduction of Condor night freight trains gives the S & C a new trunk freight role.

1960

January 21: Crash kills five near Settle.

NER line from Kirkby Stephen to Tebay closed.

1962

January 22: Closure of remaining NER lines off the S & C, with the exception of Appleby East-Kirkby Stephen East.

June 18: BR services on the Keighley and Worth Valley line withdrawn.

Passenger services withdrawn between Blackburn and Hellifield.

Transport Act abolishes British Transport Commission and establishes the TUCC procedure for assessing hardship likely to be caused by railway closures.

1963

January: Line closed for five days by snow.

Beeching's The Reshaping of British Railways suggest only Appleby, and possibly Settle, stations running at a profit. Withdrawal of passenger services recommended as a first step to eventual closure.

1964

Goods services withdrawn from stations served only by local trains.

Waverley express goes on to summer-only timetable.

November: New Labour administration refuses consent to withdraw local services.

1966

June 19: Clapham Junction to Low Gill closed as diversionary route.

1968

June 29: Keighley and Worth Valley line reopened as preserved line.

1969

January: Last train runs over the Waverley line between Carlisle and Edinburgh.

December: Plans to close intermediate stations revived.

1970

May 4: Local services withdrawn from all remaining intermediate stations on the S & C except Settle and Appleby, namely — Horton, Ribblehead, Dent, Garsdale, Kirkby Stephen, Long Marton, Newbiggin, Culgaith, Langwathby, Little Salkeld, Lazonby & Kirkoswald and Armathwaite.

October: Settle station closed to goods traffic.

1971

September: Appleby station closed to goods traffic.

1974

Late summer: First ramblers' special calls at stations which had been closed in 1970.

December: Meeting at Settle lays basis for DalesRail service.

1975

May: Yorkshire Dales National Park Authority runs first DalesRail service to the Dales stations closed in 1970, plus Kirkby Stephen and Appleby.

1976

May 1: Centenary of the S & C. Celebrations begin with a marquee banquet at Settle. Intended steam special marked by failure of both locomotives amid classic Pennine downpour.

May: New timetable sees first step towards the end of the former Thames-Clyde Express and other through trains between St Pancras and Glasgow, to be replaced by Nottingham-Glasgow service. New signalling and removal of catch points on the West Coast Main Line brings many unbraked freights (around 13 daily in each direction) onto the S & C.

DalesRail extended to Carlisle, with stops at Armathwaite, Lazonby & Kirkoswald, Langwathby.

1977

May: Remaining St Pancras-Glasgow services withdrawn.

West Yorkshire PTE takes on the marketing of DalesRail.

1978

March 25: Steam returns to the S & C which joins BR's list of approved tour routes.

May 13: The Rt Rev Eric Treacy, the "railway bishop", dies at Appleby station.

1979

May 14: New platform at Shipley enables northbound trains to stop at station without reversal. Facility extended to southbound trains the following year.

1981

Cumbrian MPs and councillors told of concern about structures on the line.

April: Article in Steam World magazine says Ribblehead viaduct needs replacing.

May 13: BR plans to divert the Nottingham-Glasgow service become known.

July: Sir Peter Parker, BR chairman, makes first of many assurances that the S & C is not proposed for closure.

August: Confidential BR document links Ribblehead question with broader issue of whether the line is needed at all. Closure by 1984 predicted.

1982

March: MPs told in a private briefing at Preston that closure of the line is planned but this information not for public release.

May 16: Last Nottingham-Glasgow expresses run on the S & C.

May 17: Inauguration of new Crossflatts station by West Yorkshire PTE marks first reopening between Leeds & Carlisle. To be followed in 1984 by Saltaire, the eight stations reopened under the Dalesman initiative, Cononley and — most recently — Steeton and Silsden in 1990.

June 27: Inaugural meeting at Settle of the Friends of the Settle-Carlisle Line Association.

Serpell Report brings new general threat to the rail network.

1983

March: Railway Development Society launches campaign to save the line.

May 16: Last through freight services diverted from the S & C.

August 18: BR says it intends to close the S & C.

Joint Action Committee brings together the Friends, Transport 2000 and the Railway Development Society in a campaigning umbrella organisation.

November 17: BR announces closure plans. Ron Cotton appointed Settle-Carlisle Project Manager. All West Coast Main Line trains diverted over the S & C because overhead wires are down.

December 15: Closure notices published two days late because of a BR mix-up.

December 17: Joint councils' campaign launched with the running of the Cumbrian Mountain Express, hauled by the Duchess of Hamilton. PEIDA Report commissioned.

1984

February: NUR launches its campaign with a special train carrying JAC members and Labour's deputy leader, Roy Hattersley.

April: First closure notice withdrawn.

May 16: Sian Johnson and Associates plans for the S & C corridor to become a linear theme park, possibly serviced by a privatised railway, attract general derision.

May 17: Second closure notice published. David Mitchell, transport minister, has a good look for himself at Ribblehead Viaduct.

July: Huge demand prompts introduction of an additional York-Carlisle daily return train.

July 26: PEIDA Report reveals the extent of BR's "wanton neglect" of the S & C, but says Ribblehead Viaduct is capable of being repaired.

August: Third closure notice published. JAC forms limited company.

December: S & C revenue is up 80 per cent on 1982 figures.

1985

December: Annual meeting of JAC gives some 18 groups rights to board membership. Plans to launch a station reopening campaign in the spring are announced. BR figures show passenger numbers are 20 per cent up on 1984.

1986

January: Commons Select Committee on Trade and Industry warns of the damage that would be caused to the tourist industry by closure of lines such as the S & C.

March 8: West Yorkshire steam special marks a prelude to the local authorities' case for presentation at the TUCC hearings. Launch of Stan Abbott's To Kill a Railway — exposing the closure by stealth strategy — with support from West Yorkshire County Council.

March 10: Moves to reopen the local rail service gather pace with the launch of Retraining Settle-Carlisle, the first of two key reports by the JAC.

March 24: First North West TUCC hearing opens in Appleby amid unforecast blizzard conditions which leave road transport in chaos.

April 14: First North East TUCC hearing opens at Settle.

July 14: Dalesman service launched, bringing the reopening of eight stations on the S & C which had been closed for all but DalesRail services since 1970.

August 21: Yorkshire Dales National Park chiefs condemn the sale of the S & C's heritage, namely Dent station whose principal buildings have been sold and are to feature in a nationwide advertising campaign by the Woolwich Building Society.

December 2: Parliamentary Select Committee on Transport visits the line.

December 17: TUCC report condemns BR closure case and says the plan would cause extreme hardship both to travellers and people living in remote Pennine areas.

1987

January 12: Friends launch major challenge to BR's financial case for closure.

February 18: Ron Cotton retires from BR, having seen services on the line he was meant to close doubled and revenue quadrupled.

March 31: James Towler "sacked" as chairman of the North-East TUCC.

April 24: David Mitchell, Public Transport Minister, finds standing room only as he takes a ride from Settle. Refuses to link the fate of the line with an imminent general election.

May 11: BR launches the most comprehensive local timetable ever seen on the S & C as the line is set to carry half a million passengers over the year.

May 14: Idea of commercial sponsorship, by leading civil engineering firms, for S & C's structure floated. Government hands pulling the strings are suspected as the privatisation idea emerges again in July.

May: English Heritage offers £1m, its biggest ever grant, towards the cost of repairs to Ribblehead Viaduct. Offer lies unacknowledged in a Department of the Environment in-tray for six months.

July 31: David Mitchell hints that a decision on the S & C's future is imminent. The betting is now on closure, with a stay of execution to allow private bidders to come forward.

August 17: Local authorities, under pressure from Mr Mitchell, agree continued revenue support.

October 8: Colin Moynihan, junior environment minister, becomes the latest member of the Government ranks to visit the S & C.

October: Yorkshire Dales National Park Authority attempts to prevent stripping more of line's heritage as plans to move Garsdale turntable to Keighley become known.

November 3: News breaks of a possible rescue package for the line, based on plans for a huge job-creation programme worked out by the Community Programme Division of the Jarvis construction group.

December: BR admits Ribblehead Viaduct is not falling down, but subsequently denies reports.

1988

January: Landslip closes line at Mallerstang, but major repairs enable relatively swift reopening, prompting speculation that a reprieve is in the offing.

January 20: Gary Waller, MP for Keighley, says £500,000 form the local authorities towards the cost of repairing Ribblehead Viaduct will save the line.

February 4: Local authorities meet in Carlisle and say the Government is setting them up as scapegoats in the event of closure. Moves begin to put together Mr Mitchell's £500,000 package.

April 11: North Yorkshire cash completes the local authorities' £500,000 package and speculation rises that a reprieve is imminent. Only the environment secretary Nicholas Ridley — who wants to see privatisation — appears to stand in the way.

May 16: The anticipated Government reprieve becomes the infamous "minded to authorise closure" announcement by Mr Mitchell as private sector bids are invited. Test repair to Ribblehead Viaduct arch authorised. Threats of legal action by council leaders.

June 6: TUCCs rule out new hearings.

June 18: Mr Mitchell joins Metro Pullman steam special as local authorities and others opposing closure map out strategy for next stage in fight.

July: Michael Portillo replaces David Mitchell and grants a six-month reprieve for the S & C to May 1989.

August 2: BR's S & C sale prospectus published.

August 8: BR sales plans appear to be geared to sabotage potential private operations.

August 11: TUCCs promise new hearings.

August 25: Mr Portillo makes a "secret" trip over the line.

September: BR gives another six months for buyers to come forward. Councils give qualified promise of support for private buyer.

September 23: Fresh TUCC hearings open.

October 18: English Heritage report says repairs to Ribblehead Viaduct will cost £2-2.5m — well below BR estimates.

October 20: New BR figures say the line's losses have eased. But campaigners say the line may be breaking even.

October 24: The right wing Adam Smith Institute accuses BR of a "Machiavellian plot" to sabotage the sale of the line.

October 26: A new English Tourist Board report adds more weight to the case for the line's retention.

November 1: Sea Containers said to be among bidders for the line, with plans for an Orient Express service. Dales businesses warn of the problems closure would cause.

November 28: Research shows minibuses would more than double journey times on the S & C route.

December 5: New TUCC report reinforces first document,.

December 30: Tourism minister John Lee says he would like to see the line saved.

1989

January 16: Business Liaison Group lobbies Downing Street.

January 26: National Council on Inland Transport says loss of contributory revenue if the line closes will cost BR £3.3m a year in lost fares.

February 5: Local authorities propose three-way partnership with BR and private buyer to maintain local services.

March 9: Another stay of execution, this time until October. Local authorities fear their tripartite plan has been hijacked.

March 10: BR announces closure of Warcop branch carrying Ministry of Defence trains.

March 15: BR promises an inquiry into overcrowding on trains over the S & C.

April 5: BR slaps 25 per cent surcharge on weekend charter trains.

April 8-9: A frantic weekend seals the reprieve of the S & C just as a privatisation deal seems set for signing.

April 11: Victory!

Appendix 3.

Transport Users' Consultative Committees

TRANSPORT Users' Consultative Committees were first set up in 1947 and their terms of reference modified in 1962. After more than 40 years, there is a wide body of opinion which maintains it is unjust that British Rail can effectively destroy traffic on a line and then apply for closure later.

Besides the lobby seeking a Parliamentary solution to the problem, there were also important legal attempts in 1985 to clarify the workings of the existing system.

In one, objectors to the withdrawal of services from Tunbridge Wells to Eridge sought a judicial review of the TUCC evidence — only for BR to remove the track before this was complete. A second case stemmed from the London Regional Passengers' Committee's consideration of British Rail plans to close Marylebone station.

Although Mr Justice Kennedy dismissed an application by local authorities for a judicial review in a decision which was subsequently upheld at appeal, he did make a number of observations which were to have at least some bearing on the conduct of the Settle-Carlisle closure hearings. These included imposing some burden on BR to furnish accurate and "honest" financial data.

In the same year, the Association of Metropolitan Authorities arranged for amendments to be tabled in the committee stages of Transport Bill in both Houses of Parliament regarding the widening of TUCC hearings to include matters other than hardship, but these were not accepted by the Government.

David Mitchell, public transport minister, met a joint delegation from the AMA and the Association of County Councils in October 1985 when the apparent shortcomings of the TUCC procedure were put to him. While the Minister did not accept the case for a major change to a procedure which had "stood the test of time", he did promise to consider with his officials a "spring clean".

Since then, there have been two more public transport ministers and the issue has been out of the public gaze. John Carr, who was a key figure in the West Yorkshire County Council approach and is now Policy and Marketing Controller at West Yorkshire PTE, said: "The need for better consumer protection in all forms of public transport remains high. I see the role of the TUCCs coming back on the agenda once the dust settles on the inquests into bus privatisation and the on-off saga of British Rail privatisation."

Index

Refer also to the various appendices.